A History
of Fashion

IN THE 20TH CENTURY

Contributors: Sebastian Fischenich, Claudia Horbas, Alfons Kaiser, Regina Köthe, Judith Meisner, Astrid Roth, Claudine Willemsen, Gundula Wolter, Alexandra Zipperer

© 2000 Könemann Verlagsgesellschaft mbH
Bonner Str. 126, 50968 Cologne, Germany

Editor in chief: Peter Delius
Editing and layout: Barbara Delius
Design: Peter Feierabend
Cover design: Claudio Martinez
Production: Mark Voges
Reproduction: Digiprint, Erfurt

Original title: Geschichte der Mode im 20. Jahrhundert

Copyright © 2000 for this English edition: Könemann Verlagsgesellschaft mbH
Bonner Str. 126, 50968 Cologne, Germany

Translations from German: Neil and Ting Morris, Amanda Riddick and Karen Waloschek
Editing: Lucilla Watson for Book Creation Services Ltd, London
Typesetting: Gene Ferber for Book Creation Services, Ltd, London
Project Co-ordinator: Tamiko Rex
Printing and binding: Druckhaus Locher GmbH, Cologne
Printed in Germany

ISBN 3-8290-2033-3

10 9 8 7 6 5 4 3 2 1

Gertrud Lehnert

A History
of Fashion

IN THE 20TH CENTURY

KÖNEMANN

Contents

Beginnings of haute couture

1900–1918

Clothes and fashion

Fashion is much more than clothes. Humans may simply be the "animals born naked" described by the Scottish writer Thomas Carlyle, but they need clothes to protect themselves from heat and cold, rain, snow and sun. If this were the only reason for wearing clothes, however, we would need only a few items of clothing throughout our whole lives. From the dawn of history clothes have also been used as decoration and as a way of making people different from each other. The prime role of early costumes was to show that an individual belonged to a particular group. Unlike later fashions, costumes remained unchanged over a long period of time. A costume allows the individual very little latitude, identifying that person as a member of a group. It expresses belief in permanence as well as in an archetype.

Up until the 19th century there were regulations dictating who could wear which kind of clothing, an outward sign indicating and emphasizing social differences. Breaching these rules was a punishable offense, but this did not stop it occurring: human vanity is not easily stifled by rules.

Fashion begins when people take pleasure in dressing up, when the desire for novelty relegates functional considerations to a secondary level. Fashion enables the realization of a paradox: it allows people to be unmistakably themselves, yet at the same time enables them to show that they belong to a certain group. Unlike costume, fashion is subject to constant change. It emphasizes individuality and transience, and this is where its great appeal lies.

Fashion as art?

One can explain the development of fashion in social, political, and economic terms, but it is doubtful whether such explanations adequately describe the phenomenon of fashion itself. Such aspects are certainly important, but a significant role is also played by people's wish for beautiful things, in terms of colors, lines, and shapes. Fashion is similar to art in that it follows its own rules of form; like painting and literature, it has always interpreted the human world in its own special way. Fashion is therefore more than simply a product; it has wide-ranging significance beyond mere consumerism. Fashion is poised on the fine line between consumerism and art.

Many fashion designers work closely with artists or indeed consider themselves to be artists. Today's fashion productions – fashion shows and photography – have little to do with practical fashion; they are more like theatrical spectacles, very often presenting works of art which are practically unwearable. Haute couture and fashion productions appear to have become art

1900 Boxer Rebellion in China. World Exhibition and Olympic Games in Paris. First zeppelin flight.

1901 The first Nobel Peace Prize is awarded to Henri Dunant, founder of the Red Cross.

1902 First performance of Strindberg's *A Dream Play.*

1903 First powered flight by the Wright brothers. Physicist Marie Curie is the first woman to receive a Nobel Prize.

1904 Successful wireless broadcast of music in Graz, Austria.

1905 Irish nationalist party Sinn Féin is founded.

1906 Earthquake and fire in San Francisco destroy much of the city.

1907 Boy Scout organization founded. Painters Georges Braque and Pablo Picasso meet and develop Cubism.

1908 The last Chinese emperor (Pu Yi) comes to power, for three years.

The world's first cartoon movie is shown in Paris.

1909 The Model-T Ford is the first car to go into mass production.

The proud owners of a Ford automobile in the early 1900s.

The first color movie is shown in New York.

1910 Japan annexes Korea. Sigmund Freud's *On Psychoanalysis*

is published.

1911 Revolution in China and Mexico. First international Women's Day. Arnold Schoenberg's *Theory of Harmony* is published.

1912 *The Titanic* sinks.

1913 Woodrow Wilson becomes president of the United States.

1914 The heir to the Austro-Hungarian throne is assassinated by a Serb nationalist. World War I begins. Opening of the Panama Canal.

1915 Albert Einstein publishes his theory of relativity.

1916 Battle of Verdun. First Dadaist periodical published.

1917 October Revolution in Russia; the Czar abdicates. The United States enters World War I.

1918 Armistice on the basis of President Wilson's 14-point program. Women's franchise in Germany and England.

An English lady's clothes, c. 1800

The crinoline, originally intended to complement the splendor of European royal courts, dominated women's fashion and made triumphant progress through the second half of the 19th century. At first the crinoline was made up of several layers of petticoats, which gave the skirt the desired volume. When flexible steel was invented, petticoats were replaced with a metal frame which gave the dress a bell shape; at the same time it gave the lady's waist an extremely slender look and caused the skirt to bob about gracefully as she moved. Up to 65 yards of steel were used for each crinoline, and dressmakers would allow up to 8 or 9 yards of material for the skirt that went over it.

It may have been elegant to wear a crinoline, but it was also tiresome and even dangerous. One could only get as close to a lady as the width of her skirt allowed. Women had to go through doors sideways and their enormous hooped dresses started many a fire. Around 1875 the crinoline was replaced by the bustle, a narrower construction consisting of a horsehair cushion worn at the back to puff it out from the rear.

forms that are primarily concerned with creating new ideas about the human body.

Haute couture, prêt-à-porter, and ready-made clothes

Haute couture, the "high art of sewing," came about in the 19th century and for a long time meant almost the same as fashion. Today haute couture is no longer an important economic factor in fashion, but it is still an important advertising medium and the reputations of great fashion houses depend on it. According to a report in French *Vogue* in 1997, haute couture makes up just 6 percent of fashion sales; the rest is made up of licenses and ready-to-wear clothes. In order to be accepted as a couturier, a fashion designer must employ at least 20 dressmakers and show two collections containing at least 75 designs in Paris each year; the designs must be made by hand and to measure.

By the 1960s this elite form of fashion was no longer in demand, and prêt-à-porter came in. The idea and the French term were taken from American "ready-to-wear" clothes, which were already widespread in the United States in the 1940s. Today prêt-à-porter represents the most important economic sector for the large fashion houses. It comprises clothes which are created by fashion designers but produced industrially and sold in large numbers. This means that they are within the reach of many more buyers than are haute couture creations. Many of today's fashion designers, such as Calvin Klein, Donna Karan, and Vivienne Westwood, work only in the field of ready-to-wear.

Prêt-à-porter represents the luxury end of ready-made clothes. This whole sphere spans a broad spectrum in terms of both quality and price, including off-the-rack items in department stores. Ready-made clothes are produced in large quantities and sold at reasonable prices; they are bought by the majority of people, who soon throw them out again in order to make room for new items. The art of their design is not really significant; it is much more important that the clothes are wearable, that they follow fashionable lines, and that they are marketable.

Charles Frederick Worth, 1892

The omnipresence of fashion

Unlike people of past centuries, we can freely choose what we want to wear. We are restricted only by financial considerations. Dress codes operate only on certain occasions and in some quite specific circles, which shows how the spread of off-the-rack clothes made fashion more "democratic." In the Western world fashionable clothes can be bought at all price levels. In fact it would be difficult to avoid fashion today; for example, when one particular color is in fashion, it is almost impossible to find clothes in any other color. Of course we can always wear something from the season before last, just to show that we are not complete fashion victims. Yet every stand against fashion could also be called a fashion statement. There is no longer a single sphere that is totally isolated and unaffected by fashion.

Changing shapes

During the 20th century there was tremendous development in all fields: science and technology, international relations, politics, trade, and social structures changed, as did art in its various forms and trends. Fashion was no exception: indeed, the 20th century was a century of fashion revolution. Styles and shapes of clothes became fundamentally different from those of earlier times. Change is the essence of fashion, and it accelerated considerably during those hundred years, making the 20th century completely different from any period that had gone before.

Skirt lengths are a prime example of these variations. In the entire history of Western fashion before the 20th century, hemlines had always reached at least down to the ankle. During Spain's Golden Age it was said tellingly of Queen Isabella: "A Spanish queen has no legs." For centuries this sentiment was valid for all women, who believed that their legs must remain unseen. Legs were well covered by long, wide, very stiff dresses and endless petticoats, and it was never done for a lady to show an ankle. In the 20th century, however, hemlines constantly moved up and down and, apart from the maxi length of the 1970s, it was not until the 1990s that they were more than calf-length. After the beginning of the 20th century fashion tended to emphasize the body's natural shape, allowing its contours to be seen and giving it freedom of movement. In previous centuries a woman's body had been laced up so that its shape was changed, or hidden beneath masses of material. But are modern fashions more "natural" than those of earlier times? Is it not

Consultation in Worth's studio, 1907
Photograph by Nadar

It was an Englishman rather than a Frenchman who became the fashion leader of the second half of the 19th century: Charles Frederick Worth. He opened his first fashion salon, Worth & Bobergh, on the Rue de la Paix in Paris in 1857, together with the Swedish silk merchant Otto Gustav Bobergh. Worth offered a selection of the best materials and refined styles, from which his customers made their choice while he, or later his sons, stood ready to offer advice.
Worth treated his clients with a mixture of businesslike efficiency and condescension, which as an artist he felt he could get away with. In this way Worth became an institution whose fame spread throughout Europe and beyond. He had many American customers who had heard in New York that his dresses were much more elegant than those available in the United States, as well as being more reasonably priced. Overseas companies bought Worth designs in order to make copies in their own studios.

rather that we have redefined what is natural, and that we have done so according to what is considered to be beautiful and socially desirable in our times? The concept of "naturalness" is a changeable one, and nothing shows this better than fashion.

Fashion and gender

In the 20th century women began wearing men's clothes for the first time. Pants have become standard wear for women, whereas this would have been considered immoral in previous centuries. Today women can wear wide-shouldered jackets, polo-neck sweaters, and flat shoes, and they engage in activities that just a hundred years ago would have been thought suitable for men only. Very few men wear skirts, however, and attempts by avant-garde designers such as Jean Paul Gaultier and Vivienne Westwood to introduce skirts for men will surely not be taken up as everyday wear.

Today many men have long hair, while many women wear their hair short or even have their heads completely shaved. The gulf between the sexes has by no means been bridged, however; indeed, fashion continues to emphasize and reinvent it constantly. What we consider to be feminine or masculine – in the way in which we behave and dress – changes according to fashion, but the fundamental differences remain. Fashion lives from the difference between the sexes, which gives it its excitement and potential for change.

Charles Frederick Worth and the beginning of haute couture

Before the mid-19th century all clothes were made by hand according to individual measurements and wishes – men's clothes by tailors and women's by seamstresses and milliners. Every middle-class woman could sew and could, if necessary, make clothes for herself and her family, or at least keep them in order. Women from poorer families simply had to sew, as they could not afford to buy clothes.

Ready-made clothes first began to appear toward the end of the 18th century, when manufacturers started to make capes, coats, and other garments that did not have to fit the wearer exactly. Wealthier middle-class women could buy clothes that were semi-

Elisabeth de Caraman-Chimay, Countess Greffuhle, in an evening dress from the house of Worth, 1886

Clever use of the mirror allowed French photographer Nadar to capture both the richly decorated train and the front of the dress. It is made of black and silver velvet, with appliquéd ivory-colored lilies and gilt beads embroidered on the train, very much in the style of the period. The large collar could be draped in various ways to give the dress a different appearance. The dress was designed by Jean-Philippe Worth, son of the founder of the fashion dynasty. Madame de Caraman-Chimay, seen wearing the dress, was Marcel Proust's inspiration for the character of the Duchess de Guermantes in his novel *Remembrance of Things Past*, written between 1913 and 1927.

complete, so that they could finish them off and decorate them at home. This saved them the trouble of cutting out material, and they could sew up skirts and blouses in their own individual way.

In the mid-19th century Englishman Charles Frederick Worth fundamentally changed the course of fashion by bringing Parisian haute couture into being. Worth did not sew dresses according to the wishes of his customers, but created individual collections which he presented to society ladies; they chose the material from a series of samples offered by Worth to suit the particular cut of the dress. A distinct individualist, Worth realized his vision of beauty and elegance and succeeded in turning the dressmaker into a creator of fashion, and the craftsman into an artist. Rather than simply sewing dresses, he made fashion; he dressed queens and princesses, actresses and wealthy middle-class women. His taste became the standard for society, and his designs, which were always in keeping with the period, set the tone for haute couture right up to the 1920s. They then continued to have a lasting influence on the creations of later fashion designers.

Fashion for women and clothes for men

What we today call fashion thus really began with Charles Frederick Worth. In those days, however, much more so than today, it was only women from the upper

La Cape Noire (The Black Cape), from *Gazette du Bon Ton*, 1913

Two elegant gentlemen in evening dress enjoy an aperitif at the bar. The man on the right wears a black cape with a broad lapel over his conventional evening suit, complete with dress shirt, tails, top hat, patent-leather shoes, and cane.

Decorating the head and protecting against the cold

THE HAT

Hats have always denoted people's social status, religion, nationality, or political beliefs. Although popular, in the 20th century hats became an important element of fashion – whether cartwheel, toque, top hat, or baseball cap. Hats were never worn again without some sense of fashion.

Father's day, c. 1900

Decoration and symbol

Headgear has always been a symbol by which people could be recognized: the headdress of Egyptian pharaohs had a mystical significance; in Italy hats were worn in the color and with the symbols of the family; the cap of liberty of the French Revolution was a political statement and counterpart to the wig of the aristocrats; and the rank of Catholic dignitaries can still be identified by what they wear on their heads. In the 20th century the hat was worn mainly as a fashion item: women's hats came in many different shapes, colors, and materials, while men's hats tended to retain their classic style and shape.

Important protection

Around 1900 etiquette demanded that a lady never left the house without a hat. Wearing a unique model signaled the wearer's prosperity. The belle époque, a period of glamorous gowns and design, gave women the opportunity to make a grand entrance: hats were large, decorated with feathers, cockades, or birds. By 1908 hats had gigantic, outsize brims trimmed with curled or knotted ostrich feathers, or they were sumptuously decorated with ribbons and flowers. The movie *My Fair Lady* (1964) captured on celluloid the hats of that period: the scene at the Ascot races became a parade of extravagant hats, a picture of reality that is still relevant today.

Then, as now, race meetings and weddings are seen as occasions for showing off magnificent hats.

Haute couture elegance

At the beginning of the 20th century Paul Poiret introduced amazing hat creations to fashion. At his house parties turbans were worn in all shapes and fabrics, trimmed with ornaments that had a slightly Oriental flair. Repeatedly throughout the 20th century, and especially in times of economic hardship, the turban was a popular way of decorating the head, giving the wearer a touch of individuality.

In the 1920s the tightfitting toque, which did not completely cover the short bobbed hair fashionable in that era, took over from large, heavily adorned hats.

Coco Chanel revolutionized the appearance of the elegant lady. The

Hat fashion, 1909

creator of the little black dress believed that a woman's natural figure was more important than her dress or hat. Her designs showed a simple elegance that was rounded off by modest, uncomplicated hats. These added a final touch to the clear lines of her style.

For everyday wear it was the bell-shaped hat known as a cloche that was particularly popular in the 1920s. The cloche was tightfitting and brimless, or sometimes it had just a narrow brim. It was seen everywhere, and countless variations in felt, in velour, and in straw, for example – were produced.

In the 1930s hat designs became more lavish in response to a desire for femininity. Artistic creations such as those of Elsa Schiaparelli had also been developed, so that during World War II women had to improvise to come up with makeshift ways of covering their heads.

New creativity after the war

After World War II the New Look completely altered the fashion world. "What counts in a hat is its profile," said Christian Dior, who early in his career made a living from his hat designs. His hats were like sculptures, such as a little toque worn on one side of the head and trimmed with nothing more than a single feather.

Once again custom dictated that no woman who considered herself well dressed dare go out without a hat. For the last time in the 20th century a strict etiquette was established: as an essential part of a fashionable outfit, the hat had to match the suit or dress perfectly, and even at social gatherings or at the theater these creations were not taken off – though they frequently obstructed the general view. The design possibilities were endless. Tutti-frutti hats were a sensation: artificial cherries, strawberries, and red currants trimmed with latticework tulle looked so real that you could almost smell them. Fashion photography of the time brought couturier designs into the public eye: for example, the hat trimmed with real lilies of the valley introduced by Dior in 1957, or designs by the house of Givenchy with their clear geometric shapes matching the severe lines of the period. Audrey Hepburn, one of the most celebrated followers of Givenchy's designs, paid him this compliment: "In close-up they always made the face look like a beautifully framed picture."

Just before the end of the 1960s, when headscarves and the leather and straw hats of the hippies put an end to hat fashion as such, Jackie Kennedy made the pillbox hat popular. This small, stiff hat perched on top of backcombed hair to add a dash of color to an exquisite outfit.

Short-lived hat fashion

Hats were increasingly becoming items of seasonal fashion. With the arrival of boutiques, a new type of retail outlet developed in the 1960s. This was where young women now shopped for their clothes, including hats and caps. Hats were no longer obligatory, but they were still worn for fun and they served to catch the eye at parties. At the beginning of the

A typical visitor to the Ascot races, 1998

1970s, the 1920s were revisited and men's hats became fashionable for women once again. Christian Dior showed his models wearing bowler hats and stetsons, the traditional hats of the elegant Englishman or sophisticated American. The alternative to the men's hat was the romantic look, with its big soft shapes and flowery decorations in all variations.

Hairstyles were the biggest competition to hats. More and more money was spent on hair care, and Farah Diba, wife of the Shah of Persia and an idol of the time, made the headscarf fashionable.

The classic trilby made by the Italian firm of Borsalino

Men's hats in the 20th century

In terms of fashion even less happened to men's hats than to their suits during the course of the 20th century. The most important change was probably the fact that, like women, men were prepared to break with the convention of wearing hats at all. By the 1970s hairstyles showed an ever-increasing touch of individuality and this had become generally accepted. Whether wearing a cotton sunhat or the ever-popular baseball cap can be viewed as a serious fashion statement is debatable, but such headgear has certainly made its mark.

Hats worn with formal dress retained their 19th-century shape, especially the top hat, which is still worn at weddings with morning coat or tails. In total contrast, the boater became fashionable at the beginning of the 20th century. Men of all age groups and social classes wore this flat, stiff straw hat until the outbreak of World War I, when suits were exchanged for uniforms and hats for helmets.

The homburg or the trilby – the legendary gangster's hat – are still considered to be the correct hats for well-dressed gentlemen. The stiff felt homburg has a round shape and looks very formal with its curled edge. A softer and more casual variation is the hat made by the Italian firm of Borsalino. As portrayed in the Hollywood movies of the 1930s and 1950s, the classic slouch hat went particularly well with the shapeless trench coat. The dark, soft felt hat with dented crown and flexible brim was soon the man's hat to wear with a suit. It dominated until the 1960s and then disappeared from public life.

Sporty hats and caps

The success of youthful sportswear encouraged changes in what had traditionally been classed as sporting hats for men. Here too there were marked differences between what was acceptable for older men and the caps worn by young people, which were always subject to changes in fashion.

Photographic model Anne Sainte Marie wearing a hat designed by Hubert Givenchy, 1951

The peaked cap, worn mainly by workers at the beginning of the 20th century, and its counterpart the tweed cap, which was worn for hunting, riding, and fishing, could also be worn in town if one dressed accordingly.

The American baseball cap became the all-pervasive male head-gear of the mid-1980s. Black youths in emulation of their sporting idols helped promote the cap's popularity. It has become a symbol of sporting spirit, social equality, and urban cool.

Hoods and beanies – a fashionable version of the small, close-fitting hat – have become an integral part of the hip-hop, rap, and techno generation's clothing. The headsock – a fleece or woolen tube pulled tight with a drawstring – became an important accessory during the 1990s.

All these forms of headgear are unisex, and this now applies to fashion hats and caps in general. The classic man's hat has been replaced by the cap. Regardless of their shape or material, hats and caps stand as symbols of their time, reflecting social attitudes.

French singer Polaire with a wasp waist measuring 6 inches, 1890

Beneath the richly decorated bodice, Polaire's waist is laced up with a very tight corset. From her triumphant pose one would never suspect that she was doing herself harm in her search for the refined ideal of beauty. But the wasp waist often left a great price to pay: women fainted as the result of restricted breathing, or they suffered damage to the spine or internal organs.

classes of society who could afford to dress fashionably and wear the creations of the leading fashion designer.

It is striking that since Worth's time "fashion" has been synonymous with women's fashion. After the French Revolution men's clothes were influenced by those of the English gentry, and this style spread throughout Europe; clothes became gradually more plain and functional until, by the beginning of the 19th century, they had become quite uniform.

Until well into the 19th century aristocratic gentlemen had been as colorfully and splendidly dressed as ladies; they wore rich, puffed materials in all sorts of colors, decorated with lace, ruches, and embroidery. Then men began to emphasize their work ethos through severe, functional clothes, leaving women to demonstrate their wealth and idleness through very different clothes. Fashion became the domain, the duty even, of women, and from then on women's "conspicuous consumption" became almost inseparable from the economic success of their husbands.

In the 19th century a middle-class lifestyle was established and manifested itself in men's clothes, which can still be recognized today: the basic wardrobe of a correctly dressed gentleman continues to consist of a gray or black suit, usually with a vest, certainly with a tie and for many years complemented by a hat. For more official occasions he wore a frock coat, which was cut longer than a jacket, with striped pants; and to more prestigious engagements he

generally wore a variation of the frock coat – the morning coat – which can still be seen today at weddings. On very formal occasions a 19th-century gentleman wore black tails, just as he would a century later.

Reform groups

Despite the aesthetic and pragmatic innovations which Charles Frederick Worth brought into the world of fashion, the traditional ideal of beauty still demanded that a woman have a wasp waist. The required S-bend shape could only be guaranteed by wearing a corset. Viewed in profile, an elegant woman at the beginning of the 20th century looked as if her body were split in two: on the upper side her bosom, and on the underside her bottom, divided by a tiny waist with hips and stomach laced away.

Around 1900 vehement protests against this fashion convention were made by various reform groups. The reformers – doctors, educationists, artists, and sociologists – criticized women's fashion of their time for being both unhealthy and unnatural. They said that the corset caused a curved spine, that it made natural movement impossible, and that it created a female shape that was deformed. Many women did undoubtedly suffer injury from whalebone and metal corsets, since breathing was restricted and back muscles were weakened.

In the 1890s styles developed in various European cultural centers as a rejection of the historicism which was seen as being over-ornate and anachronistic. The Arts and

Corset shapes, 1903–04

All corsets that were still available at the beginning of the 20th century served to shape the female torso, but there was a wide range of designs, which were supposed to take individual body shapes and different styles of dress into account. The main material was satin or silk, while the top was often decorated with lace. The so-called "Parisian girdle" (top left) was strengthened with whalebone, while the "Empire" design (center) achieved its curvaceous shape by means of steel rods, which were lighter and more flexible and so were used for more severe corsets. The "health corset" (below right), however, did not have to be quite so tight since it was held up by straps.

Crafts Movement and Art Nouveau came into being, and their design ideas were soon applied to all the fine arts. The new movements tried to break down the barriers between art and craftsmanship. New, organic ornamentation based on natural shapes was applied to textile design, which tended in its basic form toward severe, simple styles. The Belgian architect and designer Henri van de Velde spoke out against fashion, calling it "repeated incitement to replace one's clothes." He considered fashion to be basically immoral and instead promoted timeless clothes which combined beauty and usefulness and were not subject to constant change. He was of the opinion that a really beautiful dress would suit every woman. Esthetic rather than health considerations led him to condemn the corset in 1900: "The corset, at least in the form which dressmakers now demand, does not serve to emphasize a woman's shape or help her move beneath her clothing, but simply to assert the clothes that they have created." Van de Velde did not wish to abolish the corset but to give it a new "logical" and "constructive" form.

As far as artistic reform movements were concerned, clothing was part of their comprehensive esthetic concept of the human environment, both before and after the turn of the century. A new architecture and new ways of furnishing demanded an equally new style of clothing to fit harmoniously into the overall design. Henri van de Velde would have been offended if his wife had worn couture clothes in the interior that he had designed. However, the so-called rational dresses – sacklike and ascetic – that were produced everywhere did not last long. They nevertheless represented an important turning point, since they at least caused public discussion about the relationship between esthetics and comfort in fashion.

These attempts at reform were almost exclusively aimed at women's fashion. It was probably believed that men's clothes had always been comfortable enough and were in no need of reform. This meant that, despite their innovative views, the reformers fell into the trap set by their time – that fashion concerned only women. Gustav Klimt, the Austrian Art Nouveau painter,

proved to be a rare exception in this respect: he designed and wore his own wide smocks, which were nothing like normal menswear of the time.

The fashion department of the Vienna Workshops

The Vienna Workshops (Wiener Werkstätte) were founded in 1903 as a "productive community of Viennese craftworkers." The basic idea was to create a correspondence between all the different areas of human life through new architecture and the design of furniture, wallpaper, porcelain, and all other objects of daily use.

From 1911 the workshops' fashion department, led by Eduard Josef Wimmer-Wisgrill, designed artistic clothes which were also intended to contribute to a complete, harmonious lifestyle. These designs soon gained international recognition. At first they resembled rational dresses in being rather sacklike and shapeless, but they quickly became more elegant as they adapted to general developments in fashion. Nevertheless, decoration always remained more important than the style of the cut, which was not very innovative. Shapes and lines were taken from the decorative arts, which meant that the geometric style of the World War I period was displaced by a more

Reformed Woman, a caricature of German women's fashion, 1904

This caricature shows a loosely cut "rational dress," which hung from the shoulders and ignored elegance in favor of comfort, health, and wearability. This kind of demure, severe "reformed woman" was easily mocked by her contemporaries. She is presented here as the opposite of the ideal woman of the time, without any feminine charm and with an embittered look on her face.

Portrait of Adele Bloch-Bauer II, by Gustav Klimt, 1912. Oil on canvas, 75 x 47 inches. Österreichische Galerie, Vienna.

In this portrait of the wife of a Viennese industrialist, Klimt embedded the subject in a dense framework of ornaments and designs. She wears a straight dress gathered beneath the bosom. The conventionally designed dress with its high collar acquires variation by the shimmering, almost transparent material reaching to the breast. The skirt has graphic designs that clearly show Klimt's proximity to the Vienna Workshops, but he typically added floral patterns to the geometric designs. The long scarf frames the contours of the dress in flowing shapes. Klimt was a careful observer of clothes, and he created many designs for the successful Viennese fashion salon run by his partner, Emilie Flöge, and her sisters. Many of these designs followed the pattern of the "rational dresses" favored by the Flöge sisters.

Paul Poiret, 1924

Le Jaloux (The Jealous Man). Evening dress by Paul Poiret, in a drawing by Georges Lepape, from *Gazette du Bon Ton*, 1912.

Illustrator Georges Lepape had a special talent for placing Poiret's designs in lively scenes, providing the dresses with the fantastic aura of fictional situations.

ornamental, floral style. The clothes of the Vienna Workshops, like all their other products, showed skillful craftsmanship, a high quality of materials, artistic design, and strong functionality. The Vienna Workshops were dissolved in 1932, but their esthetic values continued to have great influence.

Paul Poiret, artist and reformer

The great French couturier of the prewar period shared with various reform groups an aversion to the corset – but not for health reasons. Poiret's aim was to reform fashion from a purely esthetic point of view. His special significance for turn-of-the-century fashion lay in the fact that he created a completely new style. This new line was diametrically opposed to the overblown magnificence of the period, yet it possessed its own splendor.

It was Poiret who finally banished the corset, which until then had been an essential part of any refined lady's underwear. His designs promoted the natural beauty of the female body, though this was still helped by bras and girdles; by today's standards these were like a suit of body armor, but at the time they were seen as liberation from the previous severe corsets.

Poiret served his apprenticeship with Jacques Doucet, where he made a name for himself with his stage costumes for famous actresses such as Réjane and Sarah Bernhardt. Then he moved on to the house of Worth.

In 1903 Poiret opened his first salon on the Rue Auber in Paris, starting with new esthetic designs which for the time were extremely plain and simple but which today would seem rather opulent and almost extravagant. Poiret's fashion flourished between 1908 and 1914, when the outbreak of war interrupted his success. After World War I his designs seemed outdated and no longer in tune with the spirit of the times, though before then they had been seen as avant-garde.

New shapes, new materials, new colors

Poiret's dresses flowed along the wearer's body and allowed her freedom of movement. Their cut was borrowed from the Empire style of the early 19th century: waistless gowns, gathered beneath the bosom, and falling straight to the floor. At a time when the small waist was emphasized, this new style was sensational. Poiret loved tunic dresses, introduced harem pants, designed hobble skirts, used kimono styles for coats and jackets, and wound turbans round the heads of his models, who included his elegant wife Denise. This form of headgear was also totally new, for up until World War I large, richly decorated hats were in fashion. Poiret anticipated many elements of 1920s style with both his dress and headwear designs. Much of Poiret's exclusive couture for the wealthy ladies of high society was democratized during the 1920s.

The Oriental influence on Poiret's designs is as clear as the influence of folklore and historical costumes; he combined them all to create his own new, individual style. He used high-quality, delicate materials – velvet, silk, fine muslins, and netlike textiles; and he reveled in colors – brilliant reds and pinks, greens and yellows, sometimes even intense shades of brown, often making bold combinations of different hues. Poiret's dresses are real explosions of color, at a time when most women usually dressed in subdued shades such as mauve, gray, or blue.

The impression of Oriental splendor and sensuous femininity was complemented in Poiret's designs by his use of colorful embroidery, with sequins and beads, as well as gold and silver thread. His dresses made a great impression when they were worn in the right ambiance, such as the legendary fancy-dress ball known as "The Thousand and Second Night" in 1911.

Poiret's creations made brilliant colors socially acceptable for the first time and since they were of such importance to him Poiret was no longer satisfied with the black-and-white fashion photography of the day. He engaged the artist Paul Iribe, who helped him put together a color fashion album in 1908. Three years later Georges Lepape illustrated the second of these albums. The lines and colors of the graphics, with their Art Nouveau influence, represent much more than simple illustrations of Poiret's dresses; the situations in which the clothes are shown draw the observer into a wonderful, fairy-tale world.

Orientalism in fashion

In the period before World War I, Paul Poiret was not the only fashion designer to find inspiration in a Western interpretation of Oriental styles. The Russian ballet company Ballets Russes had their first season in Paris in 1909, under the direction of Sergei Diaghilev. They presented *Armida and Cleopatra*, *Scheherezade*, Stravinsky's *Firebird*, and Debussy's *L'après-midi d'un faune*, almost all of which were of a romantic or Oriental nature. They were choreographed by Michel Fokine and danced by Vaslav Nijinsky, Anna Pavlova, and Michel Fokine, and Ida Rubinstein, with sets and costumes by Alexandre Benois and Léon Bakst. Parisian audiences were fascinated as much by the "barbaric" colors of the sets and costumes as by the choreography, which they considered to be quite wild, and by Nijinsky's animal power.

The result was an absolute mania for the Oriental, which had a great influence not only

on the theater but also on interior design, painting, architecture, fashion — in fact, all the arts. In this context Orientalism can be seen as an eclectic conglomeration of various influences, including Indian, Egyptian, Byzantine, Arabic, Chinese, and Russian. Intense colors, opulence, and a certain foreignness were all important elements.

Orientalism in all its heterogeneity has its roots in 19th-century exoticism. In the previous century chinoiserie had been in great demand in the European courts, and then as more and more goods were imported from the colonies, designs from the Far East — characterized by clear, reduced lines — became very fashionable.

Vera Fokina and Michel Fokine of the Ballets Russes in *Scheherezade* by Nikolai Rimsky-Korsakov

The figures of the slave and princess from *Scheherezade* wear richly decorated, colorful costumes. During the early 20th century the Ballets Russes were outstanding in the world of dance. The company's repertoire included many Oriental fairy tales. Parisian painters designed sets and costumes in brilliant colors and daring combinations — violet and dark orange, red and bottle green. These shapes and colors inspired fashion designers, especially Paul Poiret, who translated the Oriental style into harem pants and the hobble skirt.

Mariano Fortuny's Delphos dress,
c. 1915

Mariano Fortuny, who has been called the "Leonardo da Vinci of arts and crafts," founded a textile company in Venice. While working there as a pattern designer, he made some amazing technical discoveries. Ancient Greece and the Orient were among the most important sources of inspiration for his dresses. For a long, narrow kind of dress known as the Delphos, he developed a process of extremely fine pleating which cannot be replicated so perfectly even today. The Delphos was a simple pleated sheath which was closed at the neck with colorful glass beads. Its fine silk material hugged the figure and gave a flowing line. Fortuny used this as a prototype for a variety of dresses, but the basic cut remained the same; a caftan was sometimes worn over the dress.

From the middle of the 19th century French painters especially were inspired to produce exotic fantasies of strange, distant lands. Paul Gauguin's South Pacific paintings of the 1890s appealed to a newly acquired public taste for Orientalism.

The terms Orientalism and exoticism may therefore describe very different European phenomena. These ideas were rarely based on any deep knowledge of the Orient.

Mariano Fortuny

Mariano Fortuny is one of the most famous "Orientalists" of the period. Born in Spain, he moved to Venice in 1899. His famous pleated Delphos dress, made of light, brilliantly colored silk, was inspired by the ancient Greek chiton tunic. In recent years imitations of his materials have appeared at all levels of quality, from designs by the

Japanese fashion designer Issey Miyake to simple variations available at reasonable prices in department stores. Fortuny created heavy brocade and velvet robes in the style of Italian Renaissance portraits, as well as various Oriental shapes and styles. He developed his own materials and had them produced in his studio.

In his novel *Remembrance of Things Past* Marcel Proust described the suggestive magic of Fortuny's gowns: "Imitations of ancient costumes and yet completely individual, they flooded Venice from the Orient, and these turban-wearing figures evoke the secret colors of the city more than any relic from the shrine of San Marco."

Fashion lines before the Great War

The eccentric creations of designers such as Poiret and Fortuny had little in common with the fashions that most women of the time wore, just as today's haute couture is far removed from off-the-rack clothing. The exquisite designs of the couturiers were reserved for a privileged class of women. Nevertheless, they had more influence on general fashion styles than haute couture does today. Poiret's silhouettes were taken up in the world of refined fashion, though in a somewhat restrained form.

By 1907 skirts had become narrower and shorter, and ended above the ankle. The overall style was straighter, more functional, and more severe than it had been at the turn of the century. Dresses were mostly two-piece and high-necked; a lower neckline was only allowed in the evening. Hats were still large and often decorated with feathers. Tunics and suits were popular, as were dress and jacket combinations, and jackets were cut in a similar way to men's. The riding outfit that had appeared in the 19th century was the forerunner of the tailored suit, but this was reserved for sporting occasions.

Futurism

Futurism was the most important avant-garde movement of the prewar period, and among other things it stirred up enthusiasm for the war. The movement's aim was to discard all tradition as outdated and bourgeois. It celebrated the modern: all forms of progress, technology, and speed were guiding principles which informed the literature and plastic arts of the Futurists. Life and art were supposed to come together and adapt to the tempo of the new age.

From this perspective some Futurists involved themselves in fashion. In his manifesto of 1914, Giacomo Balla demanded that somber, oppressive, and cumbersome men's clothes be replaced by dynamic, colorful, asymmetrical, and varied clothing, and he presented some colorful designs. His belief that people's clothes influenced their nature and behavior soon led him to reformulate his manifesto in a tone that glorified war: futuristic clothing was no longer supposed to make men livelier and more dynamic but rather to make them more aggressive and warlike. This new form of clothing did not, however, become established, either then or later.

Pause for war

World War I interrupted all kinds of artistic endeavor, including fashion. Many writers, painters, and fashion designers were called up for military service or enlisted voluntarily.

Those who were able to continue with their work found that things were greatly affected by the tense situation, as well as by a shortage of materials, at least as far as everyday clothing was concerned.

The situation was different for haute couture, however; couturiers took little notice of the altered circumstances and went on trying to create fashion independently of politics and the changed economic climate.

Menswear scarcely changed, and most men wore uniform, whether voluntarily or not. Womenswear, however, soon became more severe and functional. Slimmer silhouettes and shorter skirts came in. Military uniforms also influenced the cut of women's coats and jackets. Hats became smaller and plainer, hairstyles simpler.

Then the so-called war crinoline was introduced and lasted for a few years. This consisted of a wide, calf-length skirt, which allowed the wearer to move easily, worn over several large starched petticoats. To an extent this style anticipated the New Look of the 1940s. In wartime women felt more feminine and ladylike in a wide skirt, even though by then the tighter skirts allowed their legs and lace-up boots to be seen.

Toward the end of the war dresses became straighter and looser again, sometimes with flap pockets, in a style which was revived in the 1980s. This tendency toward the straight and plain would develop into a characteristic style in the 1920s. The war crinoline lived on in the form of the "robe de style," an evening dress for which French designer Jeanne Lanvin became famous in the 1920s.

Futuristic suit by Giacomo Balla, c. 1923

From 1912 onward Giacomo Balla, a protagonist of Italian Futurism, wore vests and suits that he designed himself. Among his aims was to introduce artistic methods of expression into daily life; he believed that in this way the two areas would become combined. He developed elements of menswear in many sketches and color drawings, which he started to translate into reality in the 1920s. Colors and shapes were not chosen at random: Balla suggested that a man's body and his clothes could be brought together through geometric structures and organic colors. He described a brilliant red, for example, as "muscular." Phosphorescent colors and lightbulbs were supposed to correspond to the body's energy; on a jacket, differently shaped sleeves were supposed to lend optical dynamism.

American fashion, 1918

During World War I clothes in Europe assumed lines similar to those of the omnipresent uniforms. This transformation took place in the United States too, where a functional, severe style was reproduced in high-quality, stiff cotton.

Charleston girls,
garçonnes, and divas

The roaring twenties

1920–1929

Postwar Europe

After the experiences of World War I, life could not simply return to the way it had been before. Too much had changed – economically, socially, and psychologically. The new division of Europe, the destruction of large parts of industry, the disappearance of important economic markets, and (for the defeated nations) reparation payments – all had grave consequences for the countries of Europe.

At the beginning of the 1920s European production had fallen to approximately two thirds of its prewar level. Inflation caused social restructuring: the middle classes became poorer, while mass unemployment affected everyone, but especially the lower middle class and working people. Throughout the 1920s unemployment ran at a level of at least 7 percent in Germany and 10 percent in England.

New political groups and parties were able to profit from these social problems, as well as from an increasingly radical nationalism. Benito Mussolini came to power in Italy in 1922, and by 1921 Adolf Hitler was leader of the National Socialist German Workers' Party, which had as its aim a totalitarian nationalist state. At the end of the 1920s a world economic crisis spread from the United States to Europe and fanned the flames of social and political unrest which had existed for the whole decade and which had hindered democratization, especially in Germany.

At the same time, however, huge wealth was being accumulated. Enormous financial empires were being built, and the media acquired a high standing in the new economic structure. People wanted to enjoy themselves again, and the entertainment industry boomed once more. Before long this had its effect on the world of fashion. Like the cultural world as a whole, the clothing industry discovered the potential of the broad mass of people as consumers and began to direct its production toward them. More members of the broad social classes dressed fashionably than had been the case before the war, and they also spent more time – and more money – in bars, music halls, theaters, cabarets, and movie theaters.

Variety shows became all the rage, and Berlin was especially noted for them. Movies also had a significant cultural influence in the 1920s. Committed partly to expressionist, partly to objective esthetics, movies were the perfect expression of the new awareness of life: pulsating city life with all its opportunities and vices, sexuality ranging from the boudoir to the brothel and shown more openly than ever before, a never-ending balancing act between decency and dissolution, poverty and riches, normality and madness.

1920 In India Gandhi calls for nonviolent resistance to British colonial rule. The League of Nations meets for the first time in Paris. Mary Wigman opens a dancing school in Dresden and founds expressive dance. The Salzburg Festival is held for the first time. The Washington agreement makes the use of poisonous gas in war illegal under international law.

1921 Division of Ireland. The Communist Party is founded in China. The National Socialist German Workers' Party (NSDAP) is formed in Germany for the first time. Insulin is isolated for the first time. Albert Einstein is awarded the Nobel Prize for Physics.

1922 Mussolini's "March on Rome" establishes fascism in Italy. James Joyce's *Ulysses* is published in Paris. Gandhi is sentenced to six years in prison.

1923 End of the Ottoman Empire and foundation of the liberal Republic of Turkey under Kemal Atatürk. Hitler's putsch in Munich. The USSR is founded. Rainer Maria Rilke completes the *Duino Elegies*. First attempts at talkies in the United States. Mount Etna erupts on the island of Sicily.

1924 Death of Lenin; Stalin wins the battle for political leadership in the USSR. The first 35mm camera is brought out by Leica. First performance of George Gershwin's concert work *Rhapsody in Blue*.

1925 Virginia Woolf's *Mrs. Dalloway* is published. Premiere of Charlie Chaplin's *The Gold Rush*. André Breton publishes the first Surrealist Manifesto. Hitler's *Mein Kampf* is published. Louis Armstrong, the "King of Jazz", forms his Hot Five combo. Premiere of Sergei Eisenstein's movie *Battleship Potemkin*.

1926 Germany joins the League of Nations. First recordings by Louis Armstrong. The Charleston spreads to Europe. Walt Disney shows his first Mickey Mouse movies. Fritz Lang's movie *Metropolis* comes out. The General Strike by English workers ends unsuccessfully for them.

Mahatma Gandhi at his spinning wheel, 1925

1927 Charles Lindbergh makes the first solo nonstop flight across the Atlantic. The first talkie, *The Jazz Singer*, comes out in the United States. Marcel Proust's novel *In Search of Lost Time* is published posthumously. The Fascist Labor Law is carried through in Italy.

1928 Fifteen nations sign the Kellogg-Briand Pact in Paris, condemning wars of aggression. Discovery of penicillin. First television set comes out in the United States. Compulsory collectivization of farms in the USSR. An uprising against the military dictatorship in Spain is suppressed.

1929 October 29, Black Friday on the New York stock exchange; losses set off the world economic crisis. The Graf Zeppelin airship flies around the world. First Academy Awards (Oscars) presented.

This climate created new ways of looking at things. American movie actress Louise Brooks represented the female image of the times, swinging from innocence to depravity and captivating both men and women. In literature and painting the Realist movement presented contemporary reality coolly and analytically. Culture became much more international in the 1920s; the modern age really began in cities such as Paris, Berlin, and New York, giving rise to the concept of the roaring twenties.

Music was revolutionized by jazz, which when it first came from the United States was mocked by conservative Europeans. It soon cast its spell over young people, however, and came to personify a new intense lifestyle. In 1925 the American singer and dancer Josephine Baker enchanted the whole of Europe with her Revue Nègre. The most popular dance was the Charleston, which became an international craze with its twisting, toe-in steps. For this dance women wore short dresses with fringed edging and long, swinging necklaces.

Architecture, painting, fashion, and music had been freed of all flourishes and fitted clearly and dynamically into the tempo of the new age. People felt that they were beginning a new life, free of prewar stuffiness, released from the constraints of the corset, and liberated from sexual restrictions. The decade was dominated by people's desire to enjoy themselves and live life to the full, but they were unaware that they were on the edge of a precipice.

In Russia the revolution of 1917 had ushered in Communism, however, and there was no question of the 1920s being "roaring" in that part of the world. The Soviet Union experienced many sweeping social reforms, and they had their effect on fashion. Fashion

Josephine Baker, c 1925

In the 1920s Josephine Baker captivated the whole of Europe with her completely new, rather absurd dancing style to the accompaniment of jazz music. Dressed only in a costume of feathers or bananas, she introduced many of the Charleston-style movements.

Japanese dancer Mucheo Ilo practicing the Charleston with New York society ladies, 1926

The mid-1920s became a high time for jazz and the Charleston, which captured a whole generation of dancers. The dance was named after the town in South Carolina, where it started off as a fast form of the foxtrot. It quickly conquered the cities of the world. According to a saying of the time, there were two kinds of women: one kind danced the Charleston, and the other did not. Those who did wore relatively short, simple dresses, which soon came to be called Charlestons; dancers often wore a long, narrow silk scarf and garish jewelry, which made their fast, jerky movements on the dance floor seem even more hectic.

was seen as an element of a bourgeois way of life that should be banished and replaced by functional, beautiful, and rational clothing similar to peasant costume. These attempts did not have any lasting effect, however.

Fashion and the modern arts

In the 1920s fashion took a decisive step in the direction of the modern arts. The clear lines and functionalism typical of the architecture, design, and painting of the age were also reflected in fashion of that period. What is now classed as modern design has its roots in that time.

The function of objects was no longer coyly hidden but openly portrayed, and this became the decisive factor of formal design. The Bauhaus set the standard for clear design without frills; Constructivism experimented with abstract shapes and bright colors and sought out new ways of perception. Realist painting also devoted itself to an unsentimental analysis of the contemporary world of everyday life.

Just as the architecture of the Bauhaus remains to this day an unrivaled example of design and construction, the fashion of the 1920s fundamentally changed all subsequent fashions. Straight, clear lines, definite design, and functionality combined with esthetic individuality all ensure that in countless variations it retains its relevance to up-to-date everyday wear and is constantly revived, as has recently been shown by the creations of John Galliano for Christian Dior. Reminders of the sumptuous fashions that existed at the beginning of the 20th century, which were orientated toward décor and glamour, on the other hand, are to be seen only at haute couture fashion shows. But these garments are not designed to be wearable clothes, but to embody artistic playfulness or promotional ideas which have little influence on the fashions available in shops. The influence of 1920s fashion, however, can be detected in many of today's everyday fashions, either directly or indirectly.

New self-confidence, new fashion

Women now had both feet firmly on the ground and confidently strode through the city streets. They could drive an automobile and they wore clothes which enabled them to move about more freely and to cope with the dynamics and challenges of modern life, so that they could work and participate in sports. They had hairstyles that were easy to look after and hats which did not require a balancing act to wear, but which actually fulfilled a function and protected their heads. During the war many women had been forced to be more independent. Since their husbands were fighting at the front, necessity had often demanded that they take on a job, and in that way they had gained more self-confidence. Women were no longer just seen as the pretty companions of men in public, but quite naturally and as a matter of course as independent personalities.

This trend continued throughout the 1920s. New areas of work opened up for women.

Winter clothes by Augustabernard and Jacques Doucet, from *Art Goût Beauté*, 1926

In her 1926 winter collection the young Augustabernard and her colleague Jacques Doucet presented afternoon garments for the elegant Parisian. Totally in the style of the time, and including the required automobile, the images were presented at the Place Vendôme, the traditional home of exquisite fashion houses. While a rose-patterned overcoat complements the rose-colored, three-piece crepe de Chine ensemble, a brown muslin cape keeps the wearer of the Doucet dress warm.

Art - Goût - Beauté

In addition to the traditional, typically female occupations such as governess, home help, or seamstress, there was now office work, which soon became an all-female occupation and enabled thousands of modern young women to lead an independent life. In the mid-1920s, for example, a third of the working population in Germany were women. Nevertheless, women rarely held highly qualified or particularly well paid jobs, though an increasing number had a degree.

For their many and diverse activities women needed a new type of clothing that would allow them to move about freely and express their newly gained self-confidence and awareness of their body. Accordingly, in the 1920s the ideals of the beauty of the human form changed completely. Suddenly women were no longer supposed to be curvaceous, but tall and slim. Narrow hips and little bosom, a small head and long legs were desirable, which gave the impression to some contemporary observers that women were becoming more manly.

Fashion for all

In some respects the new fashion took up trends of the prewar period, but it was made more generally available. New production and manufacturing techniques meant that it was brought to a wider section of the population. The comfortable but extremely lavish garments of rich, elegant ladies during Poiret's time were now developing into more modern clothing for active, modern women.

It was not difficult to mass-produce these new simple lines, and as a result most women were able to afford relatively fashionable clothes. These fashionable lines had become more democratic. Women of all classes wore short, straight dresses, shoes with straps, and cloche hats. It required a very close look to reveal that one dress had been mass-produced in cheap fabric whereas another one was of exquisite fabric and had been skillfully made, despite its seemingly simple design.

The distinguishing features of social discrimination had not disappeared; they had only been shifted. A greater knowledge of society and fashion and a more highly trained eye were needed to recognize these features. The silhouette as a whole no longer

betrayed a person's social background, but the fabric, colors, details of the cut and finish of the garments, and most importantly the way they were worn and the accessories they were worn with, provided the clues to social class.

An all too manly femininity

Many men saw the "new women" as professional and sexual competitors. The self-confidence and physical awareness that were displayed in such a fashion-conscious way went against the image of the modest woman of past decades; the new image seemed indelicate, even shameless. This resulted in many of the reservations and negative comments which were widely expressed in articles and reports of the time, describing the new fashion as manly because it was equated with a particular attitude of mind. Consequently only those who wanted to meet such women supported the new fashion.

This was not only an expression of a new self-awareness; the new fashion itself promoted self-awareness by giving women a totally different image of their bodies. Thus Eduard Jacob wrote in 1929 about women's new hair length: "Women not only wear boys' heads on their shoulders today, they even have the Eton crop, that ugly short schoolboy haircut. Women who have only just discarded the insignia of female slavery have voluntarily taken on a symbol of

Garçonnes Bibi, Olga Day, and Michèle Verly during filming of *La Symphonie Pathétique*, Paris 1928

The garçonne trend was shown in the now largely forgotten movie *La Symphonie Pathétique*, which presented all the different types of 1920s women. The young women in the movie led independent, exciting lives, took driving automobiles for granted, and in fashion terms had distanced themselves from the old image of women. The woman with the Eton crop and cigarette holder is the prototype of the garçonne; she wears a dinner jacket and bowtie with her knee-length skirt, while her companion with a wavy pageboy hairstyle wears a loose day dress.

Turban, from *Gazette du Bon Ton*, 1912

Silk was artistically wound into a turban and offered endless possibilities for individual creation. Paul Poiret introduced the large heron feather fastened at the front with an ornate clasp, which bobbed majestically up and down. Turbans were also decorated with smaller feathers or jewelry.

COCO CHANEL

(1883–1971)

As mistress of the simple, elegant cut Coco Chanel first caused a sensation with the invention of the "little black dress" and made sure that women's clothes were freed from the unnecessary burden of decoration and discomfort. Even though she never created fashions for broad sections of the population – her designs were too expensive for that – she was justified in claiming to have dressed every woman with good taste. Today Karl Lagerfeld represents the house of Chanel, which now as ever creates classic and elegant fashions.

The little black dress, from American *Vogue*, 1926

Modest beginnings

Coco Chanel was born in 1883 in the French provinces, the daughter of a casual worker and pedlar, and was brought up in a nunnery after her mother's early death. She learned to sew when she was still very young. She gained her first social contacts through her lover Etienne de Balsan, and in 1910 she opened her first shop in Paris with financial help from the Englishman Boy Capel, de Balsan's successor in matters of the heart.

In the days when hats were gigantic and overloaded with all sorts of trumpery such as birds, feathers, flowers, tulle, and embroidery, Coco Chanel first earned her living with simple, almost undecorated designs. Actresses and society ladies wore her hats and were photographed in them, which made the designs very popular.

Chanel's success with hats soon extended to her dress designs. She had always made simple, unassuming clothes for herself and now she was frequently asked who dressed her. Her reply – that it was she herself – brought a large number of clients for her creations. During World War I she opened boutiques in Deauville and Biarritz, both places favored by the rich, and so created a firm base for her subsequent career as an influential designer.

Simplicity and comfort as a recipe for success

Unlike her contemporary Paul Poiret, Coco Chanel did not borrow from the past or the exotic when creating her designs. She was inspired mainly by menswear. During her affair with Etienne de Balsan she had often worn his clothes on the estate because she could move about in them much more freely. As a sporty young woman she was keen on riding and wanted a more comfortable outfit than a stiff riding costume, which consisted of a full, long skirt and a dark, tightly waisted and high-necked jacket worn with a white blouse with a jabot or a neckband. Instead Coco often wore tightfitting riding breeches and a shirt – an outfit that was never worn by women before World War I. The ability to move about freely soon became one of her maxims for modern women's clothes. Chanel's dislike of too much splendor and decoration in ladies' clothes might also have been partly due to her humble origins, which had never allowed her to be extravagant. " I should have hated it," Mademoiselle Chanel once recounted, "but I just can't dress differently."

The fabrics that dreams are made of

The new simple patterns required new fabrics. Gabrielle Chanel bought the remaining stock of beige jersey from the French firm of Rodier, a material which up to then had been used only for sportswear, working clothes, and underwear. Chanel used it to make her chemise dresses and jackets which, contrary to all expectations, were amazingly popular with clients. The fabric which at last made it possible for women to move about freely had arrived, starting its triumphant progress through 20th-century fashion.

At first Chanel favored plain skirts, sweaters, and jackets, decorated only with a scarf or a little jewelry and often combined with a modest white blouse with a schoolgirl collar. She promoted shirt-dresses with a sash instead of a belt around the hips, which made them seem simple but at the same time elegant.

At the beginning of the 1920s Chanel started designing costume jewelry. She made long chains and large earrings in suitable materials very popular, and they are still a hallmark of her house today.

Left: Coco Chanel in 1932

Right: Costume jewelry à la Chanel, a piece made of semiprecious stones designed by Christian Bérard. (Private collection)

They could be worn with real jewelry, and it is the contrast between this ostentatious decoration and the plain dresses and sweaters which has always made Coco Chanel's fashion particularly attractive.

In the 1930s her dresses had a more flowing silhouette. She often used frills and bows and her designs were more in line with Hollywood's fashionable styles. But she never broke with her belief that clothes should above all be functional.

From the little black dress to the classic Chanel suit

The "little black dress" which Coco Chanel created in the mid-1920s is still alive today, having been reinterpreted in many different ways by various couturiers. Its opponents described it as a boring uniform; the fashion magazine *Vogue* once compared it to a Ford – just as practical, beautifully shaped and simple, omnipresent, versatile and easily adjusted to individual requirements as the successful American car.

No greater praise could have been bestowed on Chanel, because she wanted to design clothes for all women, not just for the privileged, and so did not object to being copied. However, only a few

Claudia Schiffer wearing an outfit by Karl Lagerfeld for Chanel, 1995

people could actually afford to buy fashions with the Chanel label: from the very beginning Mademoiselle had stipulated such high prices for her clothes that her own creations remained the prerogative of the very rich. As a clever businesswoman she had quickly realized that exclusivity inevitably raises market value.

In the 1950s and 1960s the Chanel suit, now regarded as the symbol of Coco Chanel's fashion, was introduced. It is a simple suit made from colorful tweed or

bouclé, with a collarless cardigan-jacket trimmed with plaited braiding and fastened with a gilt chain or gilt buttons. With it went a knee-length flared skirt with four panels. Chanel designed this suit with the idea of its being suitable attire for all occasions and so paved the way for contemporary designers such as Jil Sander and Donna Karan, who base their collections for the modern working woman on this very concept.

As design director of the house of Chanel, Karl Lagerfeld has meanwhile brought the rather outmoded suits up to date. He shortened the skirts, slit them, used brighter colors and more eye-catching accessories, made the jackets tighter and combined them with crop tops and bustiers.

A trendsetter who transcended fashion

Coco Chanel claimed to have pioneered the short haircut and was one of the first women to allow her face to be suntanned. Up until then a lady had to have white skin, as a suntan was considered to be a sign of the lower classes, who had to work outdoors. With Chanel, however, a tanned complexion became the epitome of health, sportiness, and leisure in the 1920s, a must for every modern woman for whom Chanel designed clothes and for whom she served as a model – a sporty and independent woman who never married a single one of her lovers.

A few drops of Chanel No. 5

The first perfume by Chanel, the famous Chanel No. 5, was launched in 1920. This classic became even more famous in the 1950s with Marilyn Monroe's well-known reply to a journalist's question about what she wore at night: "Why, Chanel No. 5, of course." Chanel perfumes secured the survival of the fashion house during World War II and enabled Mademoiselle to regain her success as a fashion designer after the war.

The big comeback

During the war Coco Chanel had closed her house and only opened it again at the start of the 1950s. Her first postwar collection in 1954 was not a great success. Parisian newspapers described it as a dull revamp of 1930s fashion. On the other hand, America had now discovered the advantages of Chanel's simple, functional, and sporty clothes and so nothing stood in the way of the great lady's comeback. Within a few years she was once again classed as one of the most important designers in Europe.

Averse to experimenting and in the face of the luxurious glamor of the New Look, Chanel stuck to her proven principle that a woman had to exist in everyday life rather than in a fantasy world. She denigrated the new star Christian Dior as a homosexual who dressed women like transvestites and

A Chanel suit from the early 1960s

who did not have a clue what "real" women wanted – which was certainly not true of all women because many worshiped Dior and his creations of unapproachable femininity in grand, magical gowns.

In the last few years before her death in 1971, Mademoiselle Chanel lived in the Ritz hotel in Paris, very close to 21 Rue Cambon where she had opened her salon 60 years before and which to this day is the headquarters of the house of Chanel.

Since 1983 Karl Lagerfeld has been design director of the house. Having retained those ever-recognizable classic elements, he has given Chanel a completely new and more youthful image.

male slavery with their shorn hair. The hairstyle of today's woman proves that she has cast off the yoke of womanhood in order to carry the yoke of manhood." Though seemingly written in the interests of women, this shows quite clearly men's fear of losing their exclusive masculinity – which is denigrated here to encourage women to stop enjoying it and return instead to their traditional femininity.

Androgyny

Men's fears were caused by a greater freedom in matters of sexuality: sexuality was, so to speak, in the air, and homosexuality and androgyny in particular were the "in" subjects of the 1920s. To a certain extent fashion brought sexuality to light, because it questioned the role of the sexes, by showing women dressed in seemingly masculine clothes, taking on men's occupations and making men look more feminine.

The sexology of the time certainly attributed homosexuality to an altered gender identity: the tendency was that gay men were considered to be more like women and lesbian women more like men. The first genuine gay and lesbian subculture developed in 1920s Berlin, which is one reason for its reputation as the capital of the decade. For the first time there were clubs and restaurants where homosexual men and women could meet, get to know somebody, or simply be among like-minded people. On such occasions many women wore men's clothes and had men's hairstyles for preference. They used the insignia of the opposite sex in order to appear "different" and to add spice to the game of erotic attraction.

Severe elegance

Many other women also contributed to a new fashionable appearance by wearing severe suits and short dresses. Everything had to be simple and practical, giving women freedom of movement and yet still giving them an elegant appearance. Sportiness was in, and tennis outfits and hiking clothes became part of everyday fashion. Even if one was not sporty, one at least wanted to look it, which meant that new materials such as knitted fabrics were now very much in demand.

Dresses took on a straight, squarish silhouette, hiding female curves. These designs only appeared to be worn without a corset. To conform to the current ideals of a boyish figure – in total contrast with the accentuated bust of a decade earlier – a little help was often needed in the form of supporting underwear or a cut that flattered the figure. So the corset had not disappeared at all, only its shape and material had changed. Instead of whalebone and metal strengthening, elastic was used.

It did not escape contemporary observers that the new line was shown to its best advantage when worn by slim young women. Broad hips and a large bust can be hidden, but the 1920s fashion tended rather to accentuate them. Although a skirt might loosely swirl around ample hips, if there was no slender counterweight to offset it the whole figure could look boxlike. The new fashion seemed almost childish. The denial

Fashion for winter sports, 1924

The freer lifestyle that women enjoyed in the 1920s was reflected by many sporting activities such as gymnastics, swimming and tennis in the summer, and skiing in the winter. The skier shown here is wearing a knee-length overcoat and a knitted hat with matching gloves and scarf. Under the coat she is wearing knickerbockers in the same color as the coat and knee-length socks. Sportswear for men was similar. But they preferred Norwegian jumpers and anoraks.

of bust, waist, hips, and bottom, all of which had up till then identified an adult woman, suggested a physically undeveloped, childlike being. The new erotic signals still had to be learned.

Hemlines rose to the knee in the course of the 1920s. In between they also dropped to the ankle again, but only briefly. After that dresses could never trail on the ground again. Coco Chanel once said contemptuously that a knee was only a joint and not beautiful at all, but she could not halt the trend toward the short skirt, even though in the 1920s the hem still only swirled around the knee. For the first time women's legs were erotic – at the expense of bust and hips.

This changed preference explains the overwhelming success of Marlene Dietrich and her beautiful legs in the 1920s and 1930s, as well as the inconceivable notion of having her legs insured! Stockings with a seam gave the impression of even longer and slimmer legs and added an extra touch of glamor.

In the 1920s one-piece dresses, which initially were relatively shapeless, were particularly popular. Later they became tighter-fitting and more clinging. "Snakiness" was in demand, according to the fashion magazines. The flowing gowns of French designer Madeleine Vionnet are an example of this.

During the course of the decade the waist fell lower and lower until it dropped to the hips and continued into a bias-cut flared skirt which dipped at the front and back. Lavish sleeves offset the simple basic silhouette of the dress.

Often a number of garments were worn one on top of the other; for example, a transparent tunic over a shorter dress or an embroidered dress with an irregular hemline over an underdress of one color. This style was not only very elegant, but by veiling and unveiling the body it made it both mysterious and seductive.

Suits had a severe cut and were often noticeably influenced by men's suits. A two-piece suit offered its wearer endless possibilities for variation.

Sport, especially tennis and driving, had a great influence on fashion. Many of the most influential designers of the time began their careers with designs for sportswear, the

Evening dresses for dancing the Charleston, c. 1926

Accessories give a characteristic touch to these long, off-the-shoulder dresses which these girls are wearing for an evening at a variety show. The fluffy feather boa and long strings of pearls were innovations introduced by Coco Chanel. The tall, slim garçonne has a tightly cropped hairstyle. Pale foundation, cherry-red lips, and darkly outlined eyes give her that perfect look.

principles of which they then adopted for fashion in general. As a result it became fashionable in the 1920s for women to wear long pleated skirts with a long pullover on top – a combination that is still often worn today.

In the 1920s hardly any women wore pants in public. But in private pants made their mark as an elegant and comfortable part of pajama suits made of rich fabrics. They were widely worn for sporting activities.

Eveningwear

Evening dresses had the same fashion silhouette as daywear: mostly one-piece and cut straight, they were also often short. Sometimes the skirt was longer at the back, and skirts which were made of sheer fabrics tended to have an uneven hemline with flared dips. Evening dresses had to have a décolletage, either at the front or at the back. The only difference between eveningwear and daywear was the amount of bare skin that was revealed and the different

Eveningwear by Drecoll (left) and Martial et Armand (right), from Art Goût Beauté, 1928

Oxford bags, c. 1925
The undergraduates of the exclusive English university brought these unusual men's pants into fashion at the beginning of the 1920s, and they soon caught on in Europe and the United States. They were cut very wide; the hem at the ankle initially measured about 24 inches and later increased to 60 inches. Oxford bags were totally contrary to the traditional concept of pants worn at the time. This fashionable innovation was often made fun of and caricatured, and it was soon dropped.

fabrics on show. The silhouette basically remained the same.

Despite predominantly clear, straight lines, the sheer and lavishly textured fabrics, gold and silver embroidery, sequins, feathers, and fringes made evening gowns often look like fairy dresses.

Accessories

An eye-catching fan, preferably one made of large ostrich feathers, made an evening garment complete. Fans, those eminently feminine accessories, had been essential items in the elegant lady's wardrobe in the 18th century and again in the 19th. A fan could always be used to great effect, accentuating femininity, and allowing a lady to occupy her hands gracefully, as well as drawing an observer's attention to the elegance of her movements. The language of the fan certainly facilitated communication of a non-verbal nature because the face could be hidden or partly hidden behind it, giving the user an opportunity seemingly to withdraw from the observer's glances.

In the 1920s the fan was no longer as indispensable as it had been two decades earlier, but many women exploited the dramatic potential of a fan made from large white or black ostrich feathers or silk sparkling with gold and sequins to set the scene for their grand entrance. After the 1920s the fan went totally out of fashion.

Up to the end of World War I women had long, wavy hair, artistically pinned up high on the head. The hairstyle of the 1920s, by contrast, was the revolutionary bob, with straight, chin-length hair and often short, straight bangs. The garçonne, as that type of

woman was then described, either had a bob or the even shorter Eton crop. The term garçonne (the female form of garçon, French for "boy") was used to indicate a mannish kind of woman.

Small hats complemented this look. Shaped like bells or pots, they no longer perched on top of the hair – whatever could they have been pinned to, anyway? – but were now pulled down low over the forehead.

In the evening women wore aigrette plumes, feathers, or diamonds in their hair, or turbans of rich fabrics draped around the head. Hats, however, had almost totally disappeared from the elegant lady's eveningwear.

At the turn of the century makeup, apart perhaps from a little color delicately applied, had still been associated with women of a doubtful reputation. Now, however, it became quite acceptable to wear makeup; being fully made up, especially in the evening, was no longer disreputable. The later the hour, the more vamplike women looked. As compensation for the simple hairstyles, lips and eyes were accentuated. The famous heart-shaped, cherry-red mouth came into fashion. Regardless of the natural shape of their mouth, many fashionable women simply created it with lipstick. Eyes were outlined and brows were plucked so that the face often looked like a mask.

Trends in men's fashion

Generally, men's fashion retained its classical line in the 1920s too. Although there was a tendency for slightly more colorful suit fabrics than in previous years – dyed threads were used in tweed and other woven fabrics – the extremes recommended by Futurists such as Giacomo Balla continued to be avoided.

Some dynamism was added to men's fashions by tighter cuts and slightly altered proportions, whereas the period before World War I had accentuated a more static line. On the whole, however, men's clothes generally remained dark and correct. The colored tuxedo and dark trousers were still an exception, even though they were occasionally seen.

The suit known as a stresemann, with a single-breasted black jacket, gray vest, light-colored tie and striped pants, is a formal lounge suit which is still worn at weddings today. It takes its name from the German imperial chancellor who favored that type of suit. Jacket and pants were the preferred form of menswear during the 1920s, especially suits with a jacket teamed with trousers of a different but matching fabric. It can be argued that this is the original man's suit; the trend for making jacket and trousers of the same fabric only came around the beginning of the 20th century. Matching suits used to be considered lower-class and were only worn, if at all, on informal occasions.

In the early 1920s jackets seemed rather stocky, because they were relatively high-waisted; later the waist dropped, resulting in a rather more elegant look. Usually the chest was stiffened to make the male silhouette appear more muscular, and a suit jacket had only two buttons.

Within the decade the shape of the jacket took on a more informal look – only slightly waisted and with less padding, resulting in suppler lines. Toward the end of the decade shoulders were again accentuated, and before long the hard outlines based on military uniforms had returned.

The pants known as Oxford bags, worn with a colored, slimline jacket, were brought into fashion by Oxford undergraduates around 1922. Oxford bags could be taken as a kind of protest against traditional male pants, which tapered toward the ankle. They were worn by fashion-conscious young men in Europe and did not have a very

respectable image, which made them all the more fashionable and provocative. Oxford bags constitute one of the first examples of an unusual fashion element in 20th-century menswear.

For leisure, on the beach or in the country, it was normal to wear a pullover under a jacket, or white pants and a pullover which was inspired by tennis wear – always with a shirt and collar, of course. For everyday wear – and at all formal occasions – a gentleman would always wear a hat in public. It would also be incorrect to wear a coat without gloves.

Overcoats were similar to jackets, with a tight, sporty cut and lapels which – depending on the fashion – were narrower, wider, dipping lower or going up to the neck. The ulster and paletot were the most common. Overcoats for men were often lined with fur or trimmed with a fur collar, though this was more for fashion than warmth.

The tuxedo – and tails on very formal occasions – were the norm for eveningwear.

Three fashionably dressed gentlemen at the races, England, 1926

Knickerbockers were very fashionable. Worn with a long jacket for playing golf, they were combined with knee-length socks and Fair Isle pullovers in the country and for other sports.

Clothes for an autumn walk, from *Der Modediktator*, 1929

This outfit shows details of men's fashion around 1929: a long, single-breasted, slightly waisted jacket with broad, curving lapels; white shirt and striped tie. The suit trousers have narrow turnups, and are worn with light-colored socks and red-brown two-tone shoes. Coordinating accessories were just as important for the well-dressed man as they were for women. He never went out without a hat, and the gloves and handkerchief in the breast pocket were also indispensable. The finishing touch was added by the elegant cigarette holder. A man's coat could be in a matching color or it could be in classic subdued colors, as shown by the man in the background, who is wearing a light ulster coat.

Advertising poster for Jeanne Lanvin, drawing by Paul Iribe, 1927

The fashion house of Lanvin was represented in advertising by its characteristic coordination of matching dresses for mother and daughter. In contrast to the clear shapes of the 1920s, Lanvin preferred a more romantic style that was in some ways reminiscent of the Rococo. Paul Iribe's artistic drawings emphasize the generous pleats of the dresses and bring out the high-class material and transparency of the veil on the mother's dress.

Dandies and tramps

Side by side with the traditional lines was an ever greater variety of fashion styles brought by increasing international links. Most men wore conventional suits which were virtually identical, but even at that time there were some men who showed a greater interest in fashion and were keen on perfection in every detail of their dress. The mannered dandy, represented in the 19th century by the likes of George Bryan Brummell, known as Beau Brummell, Charles Baudelaire, and Oscar Wilde, had become fashionable again. Baron von Eelking, the editor of the fashion magazine *Der Modediktator* (*The Fashion Dictator*), which appeared in Germany between 1927 and 1931, embodied this type of blasé gentleman by dressing in the finest designs and richest fabrics. An American version of the dandy, in life as well as in fiction, was F. Scott Fitzgerald. In his novel *The Great Gatsby* (1925) he describes the excesses, the pleasures, and the dark side associated with this way of life.

Black jazz musicians had their own specific style and widened the male image of fashion: baggy long pants and very loose jackets expressed nonconformist views and for a time drew attention to these exotic-looking males.

The tramp, epitomized by Charlie Chaplin, was obviously not an official fashion model, but he served to point up the contrast between the correct gentleman and the social outcast who lived in poor circumstances.

Generally, these trends continued to be restricted to certain sections of the population. Although they had little influence on the everyday dress of men in the street, in the office, or at an evening reception, they altered the male image and introduced diversity of expression within fashion.

New fashion houses

The lavishly designed fashion magazines of the 1920s show us clearly who the couturiers were who set the style in Paris and everywhere else. From among the great masters of fashion design who had laid the foundations of their success within the first two decades of the 20th century, the houses of Worth and Poiret especially continued to feature in the 1920s. As ever, their names stood for the height of elegance and quality.

There were also a number of new names that were proof of the French capital's continuing creativity in fashion.

The name ever associated with the 1920s is Coco Chanel, whose real name incidentally was Gabrielle Chanel. With her, fashion

Beachwear by Jean Patou, from *Art Goût Beauté*, 1927

Patou designed fashions and sportswear for the active woman from the end of the 1920s. He was a trendsetter in this sector of the fashion industry. The short beach dresses of various materials with matching light coats became a lasting part of summer leisurewear throughout the 1920s.

became really fashionable. The simplicity of Chanel's designs caused a sensation in the days when most women were still highly dressed up and severely laced up. Chanel's trump cards were her "little black dress," which at first sight was a plain, short black dress but which was always elegant, and the Chanel suit.

The clothes that Coco Chanel promoted were decisive in establishing an image of women in society which is now taken for granted. She wanted to help women to become emancipated by designing clothes which were comfortable, informal, and suitable for all occasions. She produced garments for modern, independent women like herself.

Jean Patou was always rather in the shadow of Coco Chanel. Patou was a clever businessman and designer with a feel for the spirit of his age. He created mainly sportswear and sporty fashion for modern people. He designed clothes for the 1920s tennis star Suzanne Lenglen and this inspired him to bring out sporty women's daywear. He became famous for his tuxedo outfits, as well as for bathing suits and leisurewear. In the mid-1920s Patou launched his first perfume by the name of Amour-Amour, and his Joy, launched in 1929, is still available today. Patou not only had the materials that he wanted to use for his collections specially made according to his instructions; he also had yarns produced in the colors that he selected or specially created. He had very good business contacts in North America, and his collections were bought up by fashion houses there. American women were very keen on his creations, just as they were on Chanel's practical lines.

In the mid-1920s Patou became the first fashion designer to engage professional models. He chose American models because he felt that their look – tall, slim, and sporty – was much better suited to the image of the modern woman at whom his fashion was aimed than that of the daintier Frenchwomen. Besides, the first model agencies were already in existence in the United States, whereas they did not come into being in Europe until many years later. Patou was also one of the first designers to turn fashion shows into popular social

events and deliberately to use the press to promote his own name. He even went so far as to put his own initials on his designs and was able to convince his customers that they were wearing and showing a sign of distinction. This promotional innovation was soon copied by others and gradually led to the situation today where one can scarcely buy clothes that do not quite clearly display a trademark, whether this is an exclusive name or not.

Jeanne Lanvin's early work included hats, as well as dresses for girls and young women that allowed for plenty of movement. Up until the early 1920s children's dresses had been very similar to those of adults. Jeanne Lanvin introduced fashionable clothes that were more suited to children, and the adult fashions that followed were also geared toward the new youthful styles.

Today we can scarcely differentiate between clothing styles for children and adults, but it is undoubtedly young fashion which sets the trend; the fact is that, whatever our age, we all dress like young people. Since Jeanne Lanvin it has seemed quite natural to choose clothes to suit a particular type of person rather than according to someone's age.

Jeanne Lanvin was particularly successful with her matching dresses for mothers and daughters. She also had success with her robes de style, which were usually worn in the evening. Unlike many of her contemporaries, Lanvin loved romantic decoration and embroidery, which she often employed in her designs.

Fashion designers such as Augustabernard, Louiseboulanger, and Madeleine Vionnet were also representative of 1920s fashion. Madeleine Vionnet had opened her first fashion salon in Paris in 1912, and her bias-cut technique was imitated by many other designers. While Christoph Drecoll appealed to the city-dwellers' sophisticated style with his extravagant creations, Maggy Rouff showed a simpler form of elegance more in keeping with Chanel. Englishman James Redfern was one of the few foreigners who managed to establish himself in France with his sporty collections. Like Jean Patou, he also succeeded in spreading his business activities to the United States.

The entrepreneurial spirit and increasing internationalism of fashion in the period

Madeleine Vionnet designing a dress on her miniature wooden doll, toward the end of the 1920s

Madeleine Vionnet was described as the queen of haute couture, and she led the way in a new artistic form of creation. She worked with material such as crepe romaine, crepe de Chine, silk muslin, and chameuse to create a new style of bias-cut dress. The free style in which she designed her dresses also played an important part in the success of her fashion house. Ever mindful of the spatial effect of a dress, she preferred to make her first designs in three dimensions rather than on paper. Her wonderful draping came from her practical work with the material, which she shaped and modeled on a simple wooden doll. She went on working on a miniature design until she felt that it was just right. Then she passed the design on to an assistant, who reproduced it in full size.

Design for simultaneous clothes and furnishings, by Sonia Delaunay, 1924

Dress for female motorists, Ljubov Popova, a collage for a cover of the magazine *Leto*, 1924

From 1921 onward the Constructivist painter and stage designer Ljubov Popova dedicated herself to industrial esthetics and created designs for the First State Textile Print Factory in Moscow. Her dresses and suits were generally intended for a particular purpose, such as work or sport. Popova employed the technique of collage, which she had seen used by the Cubists at the Paris Academy. She put together a montage of various pictorial elements in order to emphasize the function of the design. For motoring she designed a robust yet cool dress, presenting a topical image of a modern woman. The opposed stripes in contrasting colors of black, red, and white emphasize the severe style of the summer dress, which is somewhat lightened by the black belt.

between the two world wars produced a wealth of important fashion houses. Most of these have since been forgotten, but some have survived to this day.

Once again, Futurism

"Fashion is an art, like architecture or music. A creatively inspired and attractively worn

dress has the same value as a fresco by Michelangelo or a Madonna by Titian." This emphatic endorsement was made by the Futurist Volt in 1920. He was taking up where his enthusiastic colleagues had left off immediately before World War I, showing that their provocative work had by no means lost its effect. Clothes were supposed to be an art form, made up of new shapes and colors.

This art form was no longer geared toward the human body, but toward the movement and speed of modern city life. It was no longer limited to traditional materials, but adopted paper, rubber, glass, fish skin, packaging materials, and even live animals. This remained simply a concept to the Futurists, however. The new materials were used much later by other fashion designers such as Elsa Schiaparelli. And it was left to other, practically minded avant-garde artists such as Sonia Delaunay to combine art and life by incorporating the Futurist designs into clothes.

Sonia Delaunay

Russian-born artist Sonia Delaunay played an important role in the history of fashion. She developed simultaneous painting with her husband Robert before World War I. Futurism attempted to express a linear successiveness, while simultaneity represented a contemporaneous approach. Geometric, often circular structures and brilliant, undiminished colors were used to create this effect.

Sonia Delaunay used her artistic skills to practical effect when she created "simultaneous" clothes for herself and her husband. According to the French poet Apollinaire, Robert Delaunay was dressed as follows one evening: "Red coat with blue collar, red socks, black and yellow shoes, black trousers, green jacket, sky-blue vest, tiny red tie."

After losing everything in the revolution of 1917, Sonia Delaunay began to design and sell textiles, porcelain, furnishings, and other beautiful and useful items. In this way art and life were indeed brought together, which had been one of the aims of the avant-garde movements in the early years of the 20th century but which had rarely been fulfilled.

Many of Delaunay's dresses were printed or embroidered with poems written by contemporary poets from among her circle of friends. Poetry and fashion penetrate each other in a fascinating way in these garments. In her dress designs Sonia Delaunay used the styles that she found and combined them with certain patterns. The basic geometric shapes of her paintings, which she appliquéd to materials, complemented the angular silhouette of 1920s dresses perfectly. In the 1930s Sonia Delaunay returned mainly to painting. The more flowing, complicated and tightfitting silhouette no longer allowed her to express her modern ideas through the clothes of the day.

Russian rational dress

After the Revolution, fashion in Russia was seen as a bourgeois phenomenon to be resisted. Fashion was put in the same context as art and was to contribute to the building of a democratic society. The creations of the Constructivist Vladimir Tatlin should be viewed in this context; they were aimed mainly at functionality, as shown by his "module coat," which had exchangeable parts.

The designs of Varvara Stepanova and Ljubov Popova were also based on the notion that the design of clothes should be fully based on their purpose. They designed three kinds of clothes: for work in general, for quite specific jobs, and for sporting activities. The designs of Nadeschka Lamanova and Alexandra Exter were colorful and showed interesting shapes. Lamanova used elements of traditional Russian clothes in a way in which they could be mass-produced. Exter believed that an object's shape should be determined by the material from which it is made and that an item of clothing should not be cut but properly constructed. She designed simple, functional clothes, some of which followed many Western fashion trends, while others stood in opposition to these.

Alexandra Exter also designed theater costumes, which Elena Rakitina calls "masks which turn the actors into colorful, dynamic sculptures." Historical accuracy and opulent materials were ignored, since it was color, rhythm, and shape that mattered the most in these clothes.

The *Triadic Ballet*

Alexandra Exter's theatrical costumes typify the unusual association between fashion and the stage in the 1920s. They influenced each other and were both shaped by trends in the fine arts. Constructivism had its effect on the angular shape of dresses and geometrical patterns of textiles. Experiments could be taken further in the theater, where wearability was less important than new shapes.

The costumes created by the artist and Bauhaus teacher Oskar Schlemmer for his *Triadic Ballet* in 1922 are among the most famous examples: the dancers became geometric shapes. Bulging material and padded sleeves and pant legs made them look clumsy; the wire costumes lent the dancers an ethereal yet technological appearance. Movements were governed by the costumes, and the result was the creation of a new esthetic.

Figurines from *Triadic Ballet* in the Berlin revue *Wieder Metropol*, 1922

The fantastic figures which appeared in Oskar Schlemmer's dance theater were like caricatures of real people. There were problems of movement, balance, and construction with each of the figurines. The costume of the "abstract" (far left), for example, consists of a leg covered with white felt and a black leg that does not stand out against the background. The bell-shaped sleeve and the club in place of a left hand mean that the dancer must feel completely new and communicate the illusion of a nonhuman being to the audience. Schlemmer tackled the fundamentals of clothes in a playful way.

Discreet elegance

Fashion in times of crisis

1930-1945

Change of scene

"The curtain fell and a new play began. Women's dresses and women's hair both got longer again. You who have just witnessed this fashion happening will not see its like every year." This is how Eduard Wimmer-Wisgrill, head of the Vienna Workshops' fashion department, described in 1932 the changes that made 1930s fashion different from that of the 1920s. In reality these changes may have been slightly less dramatic and sudden than Wimmer-Wisgrill described in his theatrical analogy. The fashion revolution that had come about in the 1920s was partly reversed in the following decade and partly taken in a new direction. In the history of fashion such a clearly discernible turning point between two decades is rare.

The boyishness and sportiness of the 1920s gave way to a more traditional, more elegant femininity. The angular shapes of the 1920s turned imperceptibly into flowing lines; short, straight hair became wavy and long enough to be put up; the waist was more emphasized; hats became more imaginative; in short, the whole silhouette changed, becoming less severe and less defined.

Generally there was now a stronger orientation toward traditional values than there had been before World War I. This change can be attributed to the global economic crisis, which reached its climax in 1932, with about 30 million people unemployed around the world. Large sections of the European population readily accepted Nationalist and Fascist propaganda because of its promise of a way out of the prevailing misery. A woman's role formed an important element in these ideologies: she was supposed to be thoroughly feminine in a very old-fashioned sense, bearing children, devoting herself to housework, and seeing to her husband's needs; she should attend certain social functions and be a welcome sight for all the men present, but without competing with them – that was a big step backward as far as emancipation was concerned. Women were only expected to work outside the house again when there was an increasing need for workers in the armaments industry during war.

In a time of political differences between European nations, clothes became a way of strengthening national identities. At the beginning of the 1930s fashion still spread out into the world from Paris, but increasingly there were signs that the Italian and German fashion industries were gaining momentum; at the same time they were harking back to a traditional look.

In Germany traditional costumes were becoming more popular than newly fashionable clothes because they were functional and were without "decadent" decoration. During the 1930s many women

---

1930 Theodor Adorno and Max Horkheimer found the Sociology School of Critical Theory (the Frankfurt School). First soccer World Cup in Uruguay.

1931 Proclamation of the Spanish Republic. Surrealist Salvador Dalí paints *The Persistence of Memory*. Fritz Lang's first talkie, *M*, is shown.

1932 Climax of the world economic crisis. Military coup in Japan. First international film festival in Venice. International exhibition of architecture at the Museum of Modern Art in New York. First Tarzan movie, starring Johnny Weissmuller, is released.

1933 Hitler becomes Reich chancellor. German opposition parties banned after the Reichstag building is burned out. Start of anti-Semitic legislation in Germany. Autobahns built in Germany and expressways in the United States. Books burned in Berlin.

1934 USSR joins the League of Nations. Murder of political opponents in Germany and the USSR. Henry Miller's *Tropic of Cancer* is published in the United States.

1935 Prototype of the Volkswagen Beetle is built. First regular television broadcasts made in Berlin. Alban Berg's violin concerto has its first performance shortly after his death.

1936 Start of the Spanish Civil War. Olympic Games in Berlin. First helicopter. Abolition of compulsory veils for women in Persia. Swing Time sweeps Fred Astaire and Ginger Rogers to fame.

1937 Events in the Spanish Civil War cause Pablo Picasso to paint *Guernica*. First performance of Carl Orff's *Carmina Burana*. The Golden Gate Bridge is opened in San Francisco.

1938 Austria is annexed by Germany. Discovery that the uranium

German javelin thrower, 1934

atom can be split. Production of nylon made possible. The 40-hour week is introduced in the United States.

1939 Germany invades Poland: start of World War II. Franco seizes power in Spain. Nonaggression pact between Germany and the USSR. Pius XII elected pope.

1940 Blitzkrieg tactics used by Germany. Premiere of Chaplin's *The Great Dictator*.

1941 Germany attacks Russia. Japanese attack on Pearl Harbor. Konrad Zuse builds the first program-controlled electromechanical digital computer.

1942 Battle of Stalingrad, turning point of the war. The movie *Casablanca*, starring Humphrey Bogart, is made.

1944 The Allies land in Normandy.

1945 Unconditional surrender of Germany. Americans drop atomic bombs on Hiroshima and Nagasaki. Liberation of prisoners at Auschwitz concentration camp. Founding of the United Nations Organization, which replaces the League of Nations.

dressed in typically "German" clothes, but there were plenty of others who still saw Paris as the capital of fashion and so followed Parisian styles. Many French fashion houses stayed open during the German occupation between 1940 and 1944, despite a shortage of materials.

Fashion and the movies

Since the 1920s the feature film has been an important medium of communication for fashion. Movies were revolutionized by the introduction of talkies toward the end of the 1920s. Realistic dialog meant that plots could be handled in a much more sophisticated way, and movies could present characters who appeared much more natural and led audiences into fictional worlds which seemed more realistic than had been possible in silent movies. Comedies were very popular because they provided a diversion from people's everyday misery and could also be used to put across ideological notions.

Silent movie actresses of the 1920s often wore the same clothes on screen as they did in everyday life, but in the 1930s movie costumes were developed which formed part of the cinematic story: costumes made actresses part of an ensemble made up of interiors, clothes, and body language, all the elements of which mutually interacted. Clothes provided a foil for the behavior and emotions of the character played by an actress; they could produce contradictions and point toward future events in the plot; in this way clothes could carry a great deal of meaning.

Actresses of the 1930s presented a different image from the over-made-up stars of the 1920s, who concentrated on strong gestures. The androgynous type of the previous decade was no longer popular. Toward the end of the 1930s and during the war Zarah Leander became the archetypal femme fatale. With her red hair and smoky voice, curvaceous figure and body-hugging dresses, she was a forerunner of the favorite type of the postwar period.

The actresses who dominated the international movie scene were considerably more fashionable than their European counterparts. Greta Garbo, mysterious and unapproachable; Marlene Dietrich, who took her role as a vamp in *The Blue Angel* (1930)

with her when she emigrated to the United States and perfected it in movies such as *Blonde Venus* (1932) and *The Garden of Allah* (1936); Joan Crawford, Tallulah Bankhead, Ginger Rogers, and Jean Harlow; all these stars became ideal images of femininity.

The movie world did not only show fashion; it also created it. Elsa Schiaparelli was one of the first to recognize the importance of the relatively new medium as a fashion show for the broad masses. She realized that today's movie costumes are tomorrow's fashion. Designers such as Gilbert Adrian and Travis Banton created the costumes for famous Hollywood movies. Adrian's creations were later turned into clothes that could be worn by the general public, and this allowed the marketing potential of a movie to be fully exploited.

Lisa Fonssagrives on the Eiffel Tower, 1939

This spectacular photograph of model Lisa Fonssagrives high over the roofs of Paris was taken in 1939 by Erwin Blumenfeld for his collection entitled Eiffel Tower. The surah-silk dress by Lucien Lelong, with its long, wide skirt and low-cut bodice with broad straps, anticipates the silhouette of the 1940s. In Blumenfeld's photograph the geometric pattern of the material is reflected by the iron girders of the tower.

Fred MacMurray, 1936

Hollywood actor Fred MacMurray, best known for his part in the American television series *My Three Sons*, in which he was perfectly dressed in the style of the times. The double-breasted jacket of the pinstripe wool suit is dominated by the wide lapels, which almost cover the whole chest. It is complemented by the narrow shirt collar and the dark, tightly knotted tie.

Beautiful, androgynous Katharine Hepburn was filmed wearing men's suits, and in *Sylvia Scarlett* (1936) she played a woman who disguised herself as a man. She and Spencer Tracy – her husband in real life – became a dream couple in the world of American movies; they theatrically portrayed the difficulties of modern marriage in a time of growing emancipation and increasing numbers of working women. Katharine Hepburn is always dressed in perfect, figure-hugging outfits of a working woman, while Tracy's wide suits, often worn without a tie, show that he is successful however less career-oriented.

Sporty jackets belonged to the outfit of the 1930s gentleman; they often had strong patterns and were worn with a cravat. Cary Grant in a sporty jacket or a correct town suit and tie became one of the most important male fashion models of the 1930s. Fred Astaire wore evening dress with a white tie for dancing and a polo shirt with

wide trousers for rehearsing, and thus became a model for the casually elegant kind of man. As reported by Richard Martin, when Clark Gable took off his shirt in *It Happened One Night* (1934) and revealed that he was not wearing an undershirt, the sales of undershirts dropped dramatically.

Changing shapes

Shapes started to change around 1929, and the changes went on developing throughout the following decade. The female figure remained very slim but took on new contours and became reminiscent of Greek statues. Having moved back to its natural position, the waist was narrow and was often emphasized by a thin belt, especially for everyday wear. Belts were made of leather or of the same fabric as the dress. Skirts fit tightly over slim hips and then often widened into a bell shape. Godets were important for this style: their triangular shape was used to increase fullness in the skirt. Skirts covered the knees or went down to the calf. This length had been introduced by Jean Patou, and it allowed designers to make particularly elegant skirts. Tops were comparatively narrow and clung to the body, and sleeves were also narrow. Unlike in the 1920s, the bosom was also slightly emphasized, though still in keeping with the overall slim figure. In order to achieve the required new shape, women once again wore corsets, though these were now much more elastic since both materials and production techniques had improved.

What was known as the princess line showed off the new ideal figure particularly well. The princess line took the form of a one-piece, narrow, calf-length dress with vertical seams, high at the neck and decorated with a bow or a small collar, which gave it a slightly old-fashioned, conservative look. In the evening the same style was worn full-length with a plunging neckline; sometimes incorporating a small train, which gave the wearer a more majestic appearance.

The fabric was generally cut on the bias, using the technique which Madeleine Vionnet had brought to haute couture and made popular; only she gave dresses such a soft, flowing line. The fabrics that were used for the style had to have the appropriate characteristics: crepe de

Chine and silk jersey, for example, as well as the new artificial fibers that were gradually appearing. In 1934 the first stretch latex materials came out, and though they cannot be compared to the stretch materials of the late 1990s, they opened up new possibilities and even allowed designers to make clothes without fastenings.

In the 1930s skirt and blouse became a standard combination for daywear, especially for women who worked in an office. Sometimes a bolero was added, and Elsa Schiaparelli made this an indispensable part of her collections. Suits could also be worn with a bolero jacket. The suit jacket was usually longer and fitted at the waist, with austere lapels and worn with a belt. The skirt was narrow and calf-length, pleated or widening to a bell shape. During the day and especially the morning these outfits could be worn on almost any occasion, like men's suits, and skirts sewn in panels had a particularly elegant line. In the afternoon a dress was considered more appropriate, and this was certainly the case in the evening, though Elsa Schiaparelli designed jackets specially for eveningwear and started to change people's conceptions.

By the end of the decade the style of everyday wear was altogether more severe and functional. This was partly due to a shortage of material caused by the war, but also to the influence of military uniforms, which were now widely seen throughout Europe and North America.

Eveningwear was even more extravagant than in the 1920s, however, with long, wide skirts, narrow waists, and tightfitting tops. In many respects these flowing robes were forerunners of the New Look launched by Christian Dior ten years later.

Fashion, design, and lifestyle

Changes in fashion cannot always be explained by social or political events, but it is striking that it was at a time of economic hardship that the angular shapes and geometric patterns of the late 1920s began to look outdated. People were seeking new styles and these began to replace the functional austerity of the 1920s with a bit of glamor that offered some harmless decoration to traditional clothes.

This trend was also noticeable in other areas of design. In interior design, for example, the softly flowing lines of Pierre Chareau and Maurice Dufrène replaced the straight lines of glass and metal furniture that had been so fashionable. Automobiles became more streamlined, perfectly complementing the clothes worn by the gentlemen and ladies who drove them. Those who could afford it used their automobile to show off their fashionable clothes at all the smartest places. For overseas travel, ocean liners offered incomparable luxury and comfort. Air travel became a symbol of casual cosmopolitanism. Duke Ellington and Benny Goodman made their jazz style popular, and in the mid-1930s swing was being

played and danced all over the United States and Europe. People wanted to look smart – casual, cool, and elegant. Discreet makeup became a matter of course for all women. Everyone agreed that beauty and elegance required some amount of assistance, but women tried to look as naturally beautiful as possible. Looking back, the style of the 1920s appears over-elaborate and unnatural compared with that of the 1930s.

Taste now acquired a new definition. It was made up of the unity and refined simplicity of the total look, as well as the affluence of decoration. A woman no longer wore

Bas-Relief, a dress by Madeleine Vionnet, 1931

Inspired by the shapes of classical antiquity, Madeleine Vionnet wrapped her models in flowing materials. The bodice is only lightly gathered, while the full skirt swirls artistically around the model's legs. In order to achieve the desired effect, Vionnet had her fabrics produced to a width of 2 yards. The two flowing ends of the scarf underline the ancient theme. This is reinforced by the model's pose in this photograph by renowned *Vogue* photographer George Hoyningen-Huene. The stark contrast sculpturally emphasizes the interplay between body and fabric.

different kinds of jewels, for example, but limited herself to one kind. New methods were found to dye furs, and they became highly fashionable; in the mid-1930s the most popular fur was silver fox. Fabrics were printed with flowers rather than severe geometric patterns, and monochrome materials in subdued colors enjoyed great popularity. People experimented with new stretch fabrics and PVC, and artificial silk or rayon was used. Imagination was needed in the field of artificial fibers, especially in the hard economic climate of wartime.

Fashion designers of the 1930s

Many of the renowned French fashion houses closed only for the duration of the war, however once it was over things were never the same again. Nevertheless, during the 1930s, some great designers were able to lay the foundations for their worldwide reputation.

One of the most famous was Marcel Rochas, who was a master of dramatic effects. He brought out the first pantsuits for women, though he otherwise concentrated more on a fanciful, lavish style which in many respects went against the linear style of the 1930s.

In 1937 Cristobal Balenciaga moved from Spain to open his fashion house in Paris. Despite the seclusion that he preferred, Balenciaga acquired great fame worldwide, and he is often rightly called the architect of fashion. He created wonderful gowns, which Ingrid Loschek described as combining "simplicity and drama."

Sir Norman Hartnell dressed the ladies of the British royal family; his designs are discreetly classical and feminine at the same time. Mainbocher was well trained for design by working as an artist for *Harper's Bazaar* and as fashion editor of *Vogue*. As one of the first Americans to find his feet on the Paris fashion scene, he was very successful. An inquisitive press surrounded the American, and he was soon able to establish a reputation as the dressmaker with the highest prices who worked with exquisite fabrics. He experimented with the artistic aspects of fashion and created perfect, suitable clothes for elegant women such as his compatriot Wallis Simpson. Her tall, slim figure made her the perfect model for his designs, and she wore a Mainbocher gown for her marriage in 1937 to the former Edward VIII. In 1939 Mainbocher went to live in New York, and he continued to run his business there until 1971.

There had already been a noticeable trend toward female fashion designers in the 1920s. This trend became predominant in the 1930s, and the female designers were a match for their male colleagues in every respect. As capable businesswomen who were particularly assured at creating up-to-date designs, they were able to make their mark on the international scene. The trend stopped after the war, however, and women designers did not play a significant part in fashion again until the 1960s.

Nina Ricci's fashion empire

The Italian Nina Ricci founded her fashion house in 1932, and today it is still one of the biggest names in Paris fashion. As well as haute couture, the company today creates ready-to-wear fashions for women and, since 1986, for men. It also produces leather goods, select accessories, perfumes, and cosmetics. The fragrance L'Air du Temps was launched in 1948 and has become a classic. Nina Ricci was born in Turin in 1883 and learned dressmaking by working her way up from the bottom. She lived in Monte Carlo and Paris and worked for several fashion houses before finally opening her own house in 1932 with her son Robert. She was soon successful with her extremely feminine, youthful, elegant, perfectly cut creations, and seven years later she had 450 people working for her. She got by without any need for daring provocation or experimentation; she simply met the need for discreet elegance and soundness of style. Nina Ricci died in Paris in 1970. The business was continued by Robert, and after his death in 1988 his son-in-law Gilles Fuchs became president. Gerard Pipart has been responsible for haute couture at Nina Ricci since 1964, while Myriam Schaefer designs the ready-to-wear lines today.

Madeleine Vionnet

Madeleine Vionnet, who came from a modest background, learned her trade in Paris and London. After working for the famous fashion houses of Callot Soeurs and Jacques Doucet, she was able to open her first salon in 1912, which she ran with breaks until 1940. The famous silhouette which she developed in the 1920s had its greatest triumphs in the 1930s. The fashion of the 1930s, which she greatly helped to shape, showed off her cutting and draping techniques to their best advantage.

Vionnet tried out all her designs in simple cloth on a small wooden doll and then transferred them to a live model. She never conceived her dresses as two-dimensional drawings, but always as a physical structure. She followed the silhouette of ancient Greek

statues and paintings on Greek vases, and in turn this had a great influence on the creations of her contemporaries. Rather than being sewn, her dresses were draped around the body. The arrangement of the folds could be simple and straight, or it could be extraordinarily rich and turbulent. Many of Vionnet's dresses were draped according to a cleverly devised scheme which made a lively dress and allowed them to assume an ever-variable shape.

Beachwear by Jean Patou, from *Art Goût Beauté*, 1931

This image of three women in beach clothes appeared on the cover of the August 1931 edition of the Paris magazine *Art Goût Beauté*. This monthly publication, as its title suggests, was committed to feminine elegance and showed in colored lithographs the most beautiful designs by the great couturiers. These particular clothes really were intended for wearing on the beach rather than for afternoon tea, and they show the long figure that was characteristic of the beginning of the decade. The sleeveless, low-cut tops contrast in color with the long, wide pants. The tops were often tight and could also be worn with a jacket. The outfit was worn with a cap or with a very wide-brimmed sunhat.

Spectators at the races, 1930s

Even those spectators who watched the horseracing from the roof of their automobile paid attention to style. Sweaters for women had come in and were worn with short skirts. But it was still the done thing for both men and women to wear a hat outdoors.

Red evening dress by Coco Chanel, from *Vogue*, 1934

This narrow spotted dress swirls around the model like a light, flowing veil. It shows the soft style that Chanel developed in the 1930s, in tune with the general trend in fashion. The floor-length princess-line dress is made of colorful silk chiffon, and the white spots suggest summery freshness. The model is sitting on the tubular steel Wassily chair designed by Bauhaus student and architect Marcel Breuer in 1925.

Madeleine Vionnet's dresses demanded a slim, firm figure. The figure also had to hold its shape during movement, but never with the help of a corset. Although Poiret claimed to have freed women from corsets, Vionnet was among the first to reject the corset at the beginning of the 20th century. She then caused a scandal with her loose robes that inclined toward a dishabille look. She always emphasized the dialog between the dress and the figure. "When a woman smiles," she is supposed to have said, "her dress must smile with her." Vionnet constantly strove to achieve a timeless beauty, and in this way she consciously placed herself beyond the confines of fashion.

In the mid-1930s Vionnet, sensing the spirit of the times, changed her style and turned more toward the romantic. She designed dresses with wide skirts made of tulle and gauze. These were robes de style similar to those created by Jeanne Lanvin in the 1920s. They were loosely inspired by the fashion of the mid-19th century, with its long, wide skirts supported by crinolines, but were much easier to move in being more suited to modern life.

Madame Grès

Alix Barton, or Madame Grès as she called herself after World War II, had the same love of sculpture as Madeleine Vionnet. Originally she wanted to become a sculptress, but her middle-class family were opposed to the idea and she turned to fashion. In 1931 she opened a couture house called Alix in Paris. After the war her salon was called Grès – the pseudonym of her husband, a painter.

Like Madeleine Vionnet she was inspired by ancient Greek robes, and like Coco Chanel she designed her dresses directly on human models. Her dresses had a timeless elegance; they were made of soft, flowing fabrics such as silk jersey, silk crepe, or muslin, in subdued colors, cut on the bias or pleated, and often artistically draped. Grès saw her work as a form of art that was concerned not so much with making women's lives more comfortable as with bringing out the beauty of their bodies. Her style remained fundamentally the same over the years.

Madame Grès died in an old people's home in 1993, at the age of 90. She had had to sell her business and her name in the 1980s.

Coco Chanel

Having been a revolutionary designer who caused a great sensation in the 1920s, Coco Chanel remained faithful to her stated aim of ensuring that clothes were of service to their wearer and adapted them to women's modern lifestyle. Nevertheless, she changed her style considerably in the 1930s. She eschewed the functional, angular style of the times and stayed true to her principles regarding the fashion requirements of modern life by moving toward a more romantic, flowing style for eveningwear.

In the 1920s Chanel's greatest rival had been Jean Patou, and in the 1930s she witnessed the rise of another competitor, Elsa Schiaparelli.

Design for a hat by Elsa Schiaparelli, 1937

This strange design, based on the shape of a shoe, is typical of Elsa Schiaparelli's designs from the Surrealist period. The hat was actually quite becoming, and Salvador Dalí's wife, Gala, was photographed wearing it. In addition to this design, Schiaparelli created numerous fantastic hats by bending, knotting, and folding bags and tubes of fabric. These avant-garde creations were worn by fashion enthusiasts but were never commercially produced.

Fashion and Surrealism: Elsa Schiaparelli

Elsa Schiaparelli is one of the most ambivalent characters in the history of fashion. For her, fashion was art, inseparably linked with developments in contemporary fine art, and especially painting. She worked with painters such as Salvador Dalí. Surrealism was one of her most important sources of inspiration; she transformed it into fabric and wool and used it to create unique designs.

Unlike Madame Grès or Madeleine Vionnet, Schiaparelli's aim was not to mold the human body to an ideal of antique beauty. When she attached scraps of fabric to a garment or printed a giant lobster on a dress, or when she designed a hat in the shape of a shoe or added drawers to a dress in the style of Dalí, she was using surprise effects similar to those used in avant-garde art. Schiaparelli's and Chanel's views could not have been more different. Chanel worked for modern, independent women; she created clothes which were simple, functional, beautiful, up to date, and which represented the advances modern women had made. Schiaparelli, on the other hand, was more for color and decoration, for fantasy and playfulness, characteristics which are traditionally associated with women's fashion and which she developed to match the spirit of the age.

Elsa Schiaparelli was born into an upper-middle-class family in Rome in 1890. After marrying, she took up fashion design. When the marriage ended, Schiaparelli was left without means in New York with her daughter. She had no alternative but to look after herself, and this she did by using her good name, good contacts, and good taste. She was fostered by Paul Poiret, and after moving to Paris in 1929 she was greatly influenced by the Surrealist circle. Her clothes were widely admired, and her first resounding success came with the design of a sweater with a trompe-l'oeil effect: the black sweater was knitted with a white bow which gave a three-dimensional appearance. Like Chanel and Patou, Schiaparelli also produced sportswear, which followed the trend of the last years of the 1920s. From there she moved on to haute couture. Her first evening dress came out in 1930. It was combined with a short tuxedo-style jacket, which was a totally new idea at the time. This was soon followed by her first evening pants. In 1931 she was able to expand the fashion house that she had founded six years earlier, and despite the economic crisis business continued to flourish. The outbreak of war then caused Schiaparelli to emigrate to the United States.

Salvador Dalí and Jean Cocteau created fabrics and designs for Schiaparelli. She used new materials – synthetics, rayon, cellophane, which looked like glass, and rough silk – to underpin the surreal, often surprising effect of many of her creations. She was able to realize what the Futurists had wished for a generation earlier – to make clothes out of every imaginable material and so destroy the conventional perception of clothing.

Schiaparelli showed herself to be a forerunner of 1980s punk by creating an evening dress that was printed to make it

Desk Suit by Elsa Schiaparelli, 1936/37

Collaboration with Surrealist painter Salvador Dalí inspired Elsa Schiaparelli to design this suit. The pockets in the top had rings which made them look like drawers. Schiaparelli's personal style can often be seen in details such as buttons, which she used to great effect to round off a simple, fashionable garment.

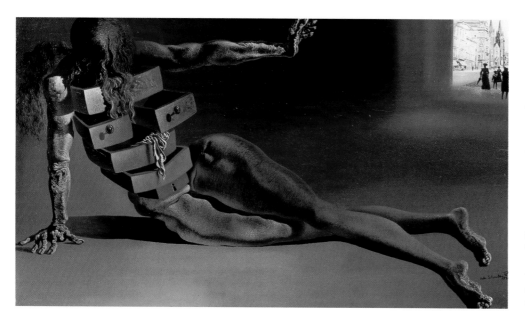

***Anthropomorphic Cabinet with Drawers* by Salvador Dalí,** 1936, oil on panel, 10 x 17 inches, North Rhine-Westfalia Art Collection, Düsseldorf

Salvador Dalí wanted his picture of a woman with a torso of drawers to be seen as a kind of allegory of psychoanalysis, a symbolic representation of the inner being coming out. He often concerned himself with the alienation of living beings or created objects out of an unusual combination of familiar things. His Aphrodisiac Jacket of 1936 was hung with drinking glasses, and in the same year he created a telephone in which the receiver took the form of a lobster – a design which he transferred to fabric for Elsa Schiaparelli. They shared an interest in the analysis of everyday perception.

German spring coat, 1944

This young woman is wearing a tightfitting coat with full-length, narrow-cut sleeves which underline the austere, yet elegant line. As ever, gloves and hat were an essential part of the complete wardrobe. It was fashionable at the time to wear one side of the wide-brimmed hat turned up. The photograph is in the style of a movie poster, and like the coat this at least gave an appearance of peacetime normality.

look as if was torn to pieces. Her masks and her famous hat objects were extremely provocative in the 1930s. The theatricality and wit of her creations were taken up decades later by Karl Lagerfeld, who managed to combine the opposing styles of the two great rivals, Chanel and Schiaparelli. Schiaparelli also created theatrical effects with strong colors, which she used in unusual combinations. A very intense pink, known as shocking pink, became her trademark. Shocking was also the name of her first perfume, for which Surrealist painter Leonor Fini designed a special glass bottle: it took the form of a dressmaker's dummy with

proportionally the same vital statistics as famous Hollywood actress Mae West. Jean Paul Gaultier took up this idea decades later when he launched a ladies' perfume in a bottle shaped as a female torso.

All of her collections had an imaginative theme. One of the most famous was the Circus collection, for which she had her boleros – in themselves a trademark of her fashion and which were taken up by others – decorated by the renowned embroidery house of Lesage with circus horses, elephants, and trapeze artists. There was an Astrology collection, a Music collection, and a Commedia dell'arte collection.

When Schiaparelli returned to Paris after World War II, she found her salon unscathed and continued to run it until 1954. Her greatest time was over, however. Like Poiret a generation earlier, she had lost her feel for the spirit of the times and her fashion seemed slightly outdated.

The international scene

American designers gradually began to free themselves from the predominance of French fashion. Among those to cause a sensation were Valentina, Elizabeth Hawes, and Muriel King. Hollywood costume designers Gilbert Adrian and Travis Banton were admired all over the world for their creations. Nevertheless, it was not until the 1970s that American fashion firmly established itself in the European market.

Group of English cyclists, 1942

These women were no doubt happy to be able to present such a cheerful image of keeping up standards during wartime. The bicycle had become a rare luxury item, and it was almost impossible to buy fashionable clothes. Fabrics had been rationed since 1941, when detailed instructions were given as to how to use limited materials and how to alter old garments. Designers such as Norman Hartnell, who designed clothes for the firm of Berkertex Utility, helped make modest yet elegant clothes possible, even under these conditions. The slender silhouette, with an emphasized waist and a reduced skirt length, is typical. The sporty combination of skirt and blouse was sensible for cyclists and probably offered the only opportunity for variation.

In Britain there was a long tradition of men's tailors on the one hand and royal dressmakers on the other. It was often difficult for the latter to show genuine originality, but Norman Hartnell was an exception to this rule. His creations for the ladies of the royal household were certainly able to compete with those of contemporary French couturiers. Digby Morton and Hardy Amies combined the British tradition of country life with romantic dresses, and they gained fame that spread far beyond the shores of the British Isles.

Parisian couture had also become more international: Captain Molyneux, an Irishman, and the American Mainbocher lived and worked in Paris.

Wartime improvisation

By the end of the 1930s the dominant ornamental style had become simpler and developed a more angular line. This became the style that dominated throughout the war years, not least for purely practical reasons.

Skirts had got shorter and now mostly just covered the knees. They were also narrower and tighter, sometimes pleated, and looked altogether more severe. The effect was heightened by the accompanying jackets and coats, which often had belts and padded shoulders, and with the addition of epaulettes even espoused a military style. Robust, warm fabrics such as tweed were very popular. Dresses were also shorter, tighter, and plainer.

This led to hats becoming ever more imaginative, as the increasing shortage of fabric forced women who wanted to dress up to improvise. They made their own fashionable hats, as well as other items of clothing, out of all sorts of materials that had never been used before.

French writer and feminist Simone de Beauvoir remembered this period of restriction in her book *The Prime of Life*: "It took a real effort not to go completely to the dogs. A coupon was needed for shoe repairs. I made do with the wooden clogs that had just come on the market. Power cuts meant that hairdressers worked irregular hours, and a shampoo and set became an enormous affair. That's why turbans came into fashion; they replaced hats and hairdos."

Haute couture stagnated. Many couture houses closed at the outbreak of war, and many designers went abroad. Some went on working in Europe, but their only clients were people with political influence. Designers could no longer develop any trendsetting ideas, so they made do with variations on existing themes. As president of the Chambre Syndicale de la Haute Couture, Lucien Lelong succeeded in ensuring that there was some fabric left to work with and managed to foil the German plan to move the whole of haute couture to Berlin and Vienna. In Berlin the fashion salons had been brought together to work for export, and Viennese fashion also became more important.

For ordinary people the most important thing was to get tips on how to alter and improve existing clothes. This was what mattered most to fashion-conscious women without a great deal of money.

Hat made of newspaper, 1941
Stocking service in an English shoe store, 1940

The dearth of nylon stockings led people to apply colored cream to the legs and add a "seam" with an eyebrow pencil.

From the evening gown
to jeans

The New Look
in full swing

1946–1959

Théâtre de la mode

After the war fashion did not change very much. Partly due to a shortage of fabrics, dresses and suits continued to be slim, severe, boxy, and with pronounced shoulders, although first attempts had been made by haute couture to create a slightly softer silhouette, with full-skirted and long evening dresses in particular. These dresses were given a touch of traditional elegance and were supposed to make people forget about simple designs and fabric rationing.

Both the predominant style and a tendency for change were mirrored in an exhibition which caused a real sensation in Europe and America shortly after the war – the Théâtre de la mode. After the end of the German occupation of Paris and while war was still raging in the rest of Europe, it was decided to show the French and the whole world that the capital of France remained a creative, innovative, and pioneering force in the development of fashion and art. A fashion show in miniature was created. Wire-frame dolls just 24 inches tall – wire was the only available material which was both light and capable of producing a transparent effect – with heads modeled in clay and sporting elegant hairstyles were dressed by the leading fashion houses.

The dolls' dresses were as meticulously made as lifesize couture designs; their shoes were made by specialist shoemakers,

their purses could be opened and closed and were filled with everything that women might really carry. Hats were milliners' creations, and later real jewelry was added to the outfits. The stage sets for the dolls were created by painters and stage designers such as Christian Bérard and Jean Cocteau, and they were colorful designs in the style of the time. The sets consisted of a theater complete with a stage, an auditorium, and boxes with elegant spectators and actresses; there were even street scenes, apartment interiors, and imaginary harbors.

The exhibition opened in Paris in March 1945 and was a great success, despite the generally prevailing poverty. After the liberation, coal and food, and, of course, clothes, were rationed more than ever. But it was for that very reason that the imaginative fashion theater held such incredible attraction. It offered a glimpse into another, more beautiful and glamorous world and gave people hope for the future. More than 100,000 visitors saw the fantastic fashion show, before it toured Europe after the war. In 1946 the dolls were dressed in new fashionable clothes and were then sent off to New York and San Francisco so that they could prove to the American people that Paris still led the way in fashion.

For a long time it was thought that the dolls had been lost, but in 1980 they were

1946 The CARE cooperative starts sending aid parcels to countries suffering the aftermath of war. First electrical digital calculator in operation in the United States. The first Cannes Film Festival takes place.

1947 India gains independence from Britain. Resolution of the Marshall Plan for the economic recovery of Europe. *The Plague* by Albert Camus is published. Maria Callas starts her career as an opera singer.

1948 Soviet blockade of Berlin (until 1949); the city is supplied by the Western powers' airlift. The Warsaw Conference leads to the formation of the Eastern bloc. Founding of the state of Israel, followed by Israeli war of independence against Arab states. George Balanchine founds the New York City Ballet.

1949 The Communist People's Army under Mao Zedong conquers the whole of China. Proclamation of the People's Republic of China.

George Orwell's *1984*, a novel about a future totalitarian state, is published. Founding of NATO.

1950 Korean War (lasting until 1953). First World Congress of Sociology in Zurich. Jackson Pollock paints *Autumn Rhythm* in the Abstract Expressionist style.

1951 Marlon Brando rises to stardom with *A Streetcar Named Desire*. Communist World Youth Festival in East Berlin.

1952 Hussein becomes king of Jordan. First performance of Samuel Beckett's *Waiting for Godot*.

1953 Suppression of a people's uprising in Berlin on June 17. Mount Everest is climbed for the first time. Marilyn Monroe becomes a star with *Gentlemen Prefer Blondes*. The coronation of Queen Elizabeth II is followed all over the world thanks to modern broadcasting technology. Death of Stalin.

Rock idol Elvis Presley, 1956

1954 Start of the Algerian war of independence. Federico Fellini makes the movie *La Strada*. Gamal Abdel Nasser becomes prime minister of Egypt.

1955 James Dean becomes a cult

hero following *East of Eden*. Vladimir Nabokov's novel *Lolita* is published. The death of James Dean in an automobile accident.

1956 Egypt nationalizes the Suez Canal, resulting in war with Israel, France, and Great Britain.

1957 The first artificial satellite (the Soviet Union's Sputnik) orbits the Earth. Jack Kerouac's *On the Road* is published and becomes a cult novel of the beatniks. Premiere of Leonard Bernstein's musical *West Side Story*. Beginnings of the Civil Rights Movement in the United States.

1958 First assembly of the European Parliament. Hendrik Verwoerd, prime minister of the Union of South Africa, pursues a policy of racial segregation (apartheid).

1959 The Cuban Revolution places Fidel Castro in power. The Chinese army marches into Tibet.

rediscovered and shown again in a grand retrospective exhibition in Paris and New York.

A newcomer creates the New Look

It happened in 1947: Christian Dior, who had been relatively unknown up until then, revolutionized European fashion. The American press immediately christened the designs of his first haute couture collection "the New Look." This truly feminine, lavish, and extremely luxurious fashion accentuated women's curves; it was an overnight success and was soon copied everywhere.

The new line was very different from the severity of prewar and wartime fashion. Full, calf-length skirts, wasp waists, tight tops, padded hips, and a gently sloping shoulder line were characteristic of the new femininity that was reminiscent of 19th-century role models: delicate women who did not have to work (or at least did not look as if they did), who spent their days at leisure making themselves look beautiful, and who indulged themselves and lived a life of luxury. According to sociologist Thorstein Veblen, these women made a point of spending money in order to show off their husbands' wealth.

It is no accident that this reminder of outdated gender images resurfaced in the postwar period. People craved a new reality that was in total contrast to the one they themselves experienced. The ruins of war were removed, a new prosperity was being created, and everyone was only too keen to forget the misery, death, and destruction of the preceding years. Dior's fashionable luxury stood for everything that was new, for

the other life that people wanted to be part of. This meant a revival of traditional, bourgeois values and gender images which suddenly seemed to promise security after all the destruction.

The most noticeable feature of the new fashion was a completely changed line. Women's shoulders became narrow and looked natural again, as shoulder pads were avoided. Compared to prewar fashion, the new style suggested gentleness and femininity: tightly fitting bodices, minuscule waists, with skirts that were ankle-length or calf-length and very full. Another line which accentuated the figure – helped once again by padding and corsets – had a very slim cut.

Théâtre de la mode, 1945. Musée des Arts Décoratifs, Paris

The Théâtre de la mode ("theater of fashion") was an advertising promotion organized by the Chambre Syndicale de la Couture in Paris to draw attention to continuing high standards in the art of French haute couture. The various sets were like a miniature world in which mannequin dolls, dressed in the latest fashions, met up in the streets and in imaginary boutiques.

PIERRE BALMAIN

Pierre Balmain's Robes Blanches collection, 1946. Drawing by René Gruau

This design by Pierre Balmain is part of a set of 20 fashion sketches which were published for a special fashion show on behalf of the Paris seamstresses' organization, the Maison de la Midinette. On the initiative of French poet Paul Eluard, the heads of the most famous fashion houses – Lelong, Patou, Fath, and Balenciaga among them – collaborated on this event by each designing an evening dress all in white. On December 10, 1945 the robes blanches (white dresses) were modeled in the hall of the Théâtre des Champs-Élysées, and the mannequins followed a choreography by Christian Bérard and Boris Kochno. Balmain's design, with its floor-length skirt and strapless bodice with heart-shaped décolletage trimmed with flowers, is one of the most girlish creations in the collection, which was otherwise characterized by ladylike elegance.

Fashion lines by Christian Dior,
1954–56. Left to right: Ligne Muguet ("lily of the valley line"), Y-line, A-line, and Ligne Flèche ("arrow line")

In the mid-1950s Christian Dior's famous and much-noted lines appeared, among them the Ligne Muguet (1954), with a tight waist and a pleated skirt, the slender Y-line, and the A-line, in which the skirt flared from the waist to form two sides of a triangular A. The shape of both designs followed the outline of the relevant letter. In the Ligne Flèche (1956), the waist was concealed by the open top, which just covered the waistband.

Schumann, a summer dress by Christian Dior made of cotton tulle with pale satin and silk flowers, 1950

The new dresses required vast quantities of fabric, and the quality of the fabrics became more splendid than it had been for years. For this reason the New Look initially met with a great deal of criticism: surely nobody could afford such luxury so soon after the war, and it was more important to make sure that everyone was well fed before bothering with such dresses for the privileged few. But such criticism had no effect, because women were simply intoxicated by this beautiful new fashion.

In fact affordable fabrics that were eminently suitable for these elegant new dresses soon became available. A number of synthetic fabrics had come onto the market; they had the sheen and feel of silk or taffeta but were much cheaper and more hard-wearing than traditional fine textiles.

Eveningwear became important again, and it gave the opportunity for living out fashionable dreams of luxurious femininity. Glamorous gowns with immensely full skirts and low-cut bodices, often strapless and relying on a boned understructure, were made of the most luxurious fabrics, such as taffeta with gold embroidery. For the less well off there were even off-the-rack versions of this design, in synthetic fabrics and printed rather than embroidered materials.

A new type of dress came in: the cocktail dress, more dressy than the afternoon dress, but less formal than an evening gown because it was never floor-length and generally less ornate. Cocktail dresses could be worn at various functions, and under

certain circumstances even in the early evening. Although many dress codes were still welcomed by fashion enthusiasts, they were no longer adhered to as strictly as before because after the war manners had generally become more relaxed. As time went on there was less differentiation between various social events and the form of dress that was required.

Everything that went along with dresses was also given a new look. Curls were no longer worn high on the head, and hairstyles generally became shorter and gently waved. The improvised femininity of the war years was replaced by a well-thought-out elegance. Dior demanded a look that was perfect from head to toe: gloves went with every outfit and so did hats, matching shoes, and purses. Small, understated hats were varied with large, flat, eye-catching headgear. Shoes became narrower, looked more rounded and had high, but relatively thick heels. Evening shoes were cut away more. Peep toes were considered the height of chic, especially when a varnished red toe peeped out. As the 1950s progressed, toes and heels became more and more pointed, culminating in pointed pumps with stiletto heels in the 1960s.

Everyday fashion

The silhouette of the New Look was also reflected in everyday wear. Suits continued to be most women's basic fashion requirement. Skirts were usually tight and calf-length, jackets were hip-length and fitted with relatively high, accentuated revers; sometimes jackets buttoned asymmetrically. Some designs had wide, bell-shaped backs and little collars. The proven combination of skirt and blouse or skirt and twinset – the timeless sweater and matching cardigan, usually in the same color and machine-knitted with fine yarns – were also part of women's standard clothing. For winter they were made of the finest woolen fabrics in muted colors, and in summer colorful cotton fabrics, silk, or the new synthetic fibers were used. The silhouette was the same as that of the suit: calf-length and pencil-slim, or full and swirling skirts which were either gathered or pleated. The tightfitting tops which clearly defined the bust demanded good bras. Sleeves, long or three-quarter length, were usually fitted.

In the summer many dresses were sleeveless with a low-cut neckline. The décolleté was in again. But strapless dresses were only allowed for eveningwear or the cocktail hour; during the day a lady kept her shoulders covered. High-necked, sleeveless dresses were an elegant innovation.

Toward the end of the decade skirts were less full but stiffer, and at times the waist was higher again but not as tight as dresses with full, spreading skirts. High-waisted dresses had an altogether narrower cut. Only in evening dresses could the waist billow like a balloon and fall from under the bust into a wide, full skirt. At the end of the 1950s and start of the 1960s petticoats became popular among young girls. Their stiff material made the girls' skirts stick out almost horizontally.

It is impossible to draw comparisons between the leisurewear of that time and the end of the 20th century. Despite having broken free from many prewar conventions, certain set rules were still upheld and these did not permit a totally individual choice of clothing. Tight, calf-length pants were very popular with young women. They looked sporty and were worn with a bodice, blouse, or sweater. Bathing costumes still had a relatively low-cut leg and often a little short skirt. The bikini, however, which had been launched in 1946, did not become widely acceptable until the 1960s. For the night (and also for pajama parties) the baby-doll came in. This short nightdress with puffed sleeves and matching panties could only be worn by young women.

The characteristic image of the 1950s is that of the elegant, fashion-conscious, young but adult woman. Fashion photography of the time shows scarcely any of the scenes favored by photographers of the 1920s and 1930s. The fifties woman is presented as self-confident and independent; she is shown on her own as a perfect work of art with cool, unapproachable elegance. The statuesque tranquillity of totally stylized beauty represents the image of the time. Photographs by Irving Penn of his wife Lisa de Fonssagrives, or Richard Avedon's shots of top model Dovima, are perfect examples. They have joined the annals of fashion photography and are highly important in the history of photography in general.

Men's fashion

Immediately after the war most men wore old uniforms that had been

City suit, 1950s

This gray pinstripe flannel suit has both a casual and an elegant look. The length of the jacket is accentuated by the large patch pockets and long pointed lapels.

Beachwear for men, 1951

Beachwear and leisurewear of the 1950s were influenced by American "weekend" culture. Patterned or exotic-looking Hawaiian shirts were worn over shorts. The buttonless top with a low-cut collar (right) gave a very sporty look.

Jacques Fath, 1954

Jacques Fath developed his creations by draping the fabric directly on the model, which ensured a perfect fit and flexibility of movement. Jacques Fath usually accentuates the waist, but this design shows a more natural line. His collections represented a great variety of individual, glamorous clothes for elegant city women which were very popular with his international clientele.

slightly altered to turn them into civilian clothes, or which sometimes had not been altered at all. Clothes were made from anything one could lay one's hands on. Correct dress was obviously no longer so important at a time when there were fabric shortages; dressing in the height of fashion was not uppermost in men's minds. A combination of pants and jacket, made of different but matching cloth, turned out to be very useful. At the end of the 1940s the American V-line, with broad shoulders and narrow hips, dominated. This gave men's fashion a boost, since it emphasized the figure more and became more versatile. Practicality, exceptional fit, good quality, and durability were more important than a fashionable look.

Eveningwear was still subject to a dress code, but during the day men usually wore single- or double-breasted suits in muted colors, with a white shirt and a narrow, discreet tie. In the United States, however, ties were already patterned or printed with colorful designs. Jackets remained loose, especially as men put on weight as times became easier.

Nylon shirts were more easy-care than traditional cotton shirts. They were easy to wash, quick to dry, and hardly needed ironing. They seemed the epitome of modern times. Hats were a must once again, and were worn with coats as well as suits. Leisurewear in lighter and more colorful fabrics was a relaxed alternative to the suit. Unlike today, when they are worn everywhere, shorts stayed at the beach or in the garden in the 1950s.

The new masters

Many of the great fashion designers of the 1920s and 1930s had been women; in the 1950s men made their mark again, which corresponded to the general social climate. Coco Chanel, however, who started work again in the 1950s, fiercely attacked many of the new designers, Dior in particular. Dior, it was claimed, dressed women like transvestites, turning them into fantasy creatures instead of expressing what women were really like. Chanel was, of course, defending her own territory because her style was no longer as popular in Europe as it had been before the war. Only toward the end of the decade did she achieve new success in the United States.

Elsa Schiaparelli was less successful. Although she re-opened her salon after the war, she did not manage to adjust her designs to the new age. She withdrew from business in 1954. The house of Schiaparelli reopened in 1977, four years after its founder's death, and is trying to continue in her spirit.

Madeleine Vionnet and Madame Grès continued working for a small number of exclusive clients. Neither was interested in the trend toward ready-to-wear lines and therefore they both lost their position in the world of fashion.

After Dior's death, Yves Saint Laurent took over as design director of the famous house and sent out revolutionary signals. In 1958 he launched the trapeze line, the total opposite of the then current fashion for accentuating the waist, and so showed the way forward to the fashion of the 1960s. In 1962 he opened his own house so as to be able to translate his avant-garde ideas into fashion, which he had been unable to do at Dior. Since then he has remained one of the great masters in his field.

Pierre Balmain

Pierre Balmain was born in 1904. His father owned a drapery business. Pierre studied architecture for a while and then worked for fashion designer Captain Molyneux, and with Christian Dior for Lucien Lelong. In 1945 he opened his own house, and in 1953 he designed his first ready-to-wear collection for the American market.

Ingrid Loschek described his creations as "feminine, figure-accentuating clothes of understated luxury." Balmain's work was less sensational than Dior's, but people liked it because he designed wearable dresses in gentle colors and with names such as Jolie Madame. By giving his collections such names he was emphasizing his wish to combine lightheartedness with elegance. Balmain himself compared his work with that of an architect: the one works in stone, the other in muslin; fashion was architecture in motion.

After Balmain's death in 1982, Erik Mortensen, his assistant of many years, became the design director of the house. In 1992 the American Oscar de la Renta took over and continues the tradition; he has opened up new markets.

Jacques Fath

Jacques Fath came to fashion by a roundabout route. After training as an accountant, he went to drama school and drew costumes, and only then did he turn to fashion. He was soon regarded as one of the most promising up-and-coming designers. During the war his wife continued running the fashion house. In 1948 Fath agreed a very well-paid contract for ready-to-wear fashion with an American manufacturer. By doing so he was ahead of his time and had the advantage over many of his colleagues who – being totally committed to haute couture – missed out on a major market. According to Caroline Rennolds Milbank, his designs "were always on the brink of the risqué." Sexy yet elegant, they appealed to a young clientele who wanted a touch of provocative glamor. Fath designed the dress in which Rita Hayworth was married to Prince Ali Khan. Like Chanel and Madame Grès, Fath worked directly on the model and so developed a very special feel for dresses and movement. Folds and asymmetry, points and zigzags emphasized the dynamics of his designs just as much as the color and pattern of his fabrics. His wife closed the fashion house a few years after his early death in 1954.

Hubert de Givenchy

After spells working with Jacques Fath, Lucien Lelong, and Elsa Schiaparelli, Hubert de Givenchy opened his own fashion house in 1952. He soon achieved great fame, not least through his creations for the actress Audrey Hepburn, for whom he also created the perfume L'Interdit. Givenchy not only dressed her for many of her movies, such as *Funny Face* (1957) and *Breakfast at Tiffany's* (1961), but also designed many of the clothes she wore offscreen. In the movies Givenchy was able to exploit all aspects of his art and show that he was the unrivaled

Audrey Hepburn and Fred Astaire in *Funny Face*, 1957

The background to this famous film-musical was the real-life story of fashion photographer Richard Avedon, who also worked as a consultant on the movie. In his search for a new face for a Parisian couturier's collection, a fashion photographer discovers a young bookseller from Greenwich Village. She takes on the role and they go to Paris for the photographs. Audrey Hepburn, who was the fashion idol of that time, played the part. Wearing the clothes of Hubert de Givenchy, she changes from a Cinderella into an elegant woman. The long, narrow skirt, hip-length jacket with bell-shaped back, and the brimless hat dominate the picture.

Christian Dior puts the finishing touch to a wedding dress in 1951

Below: Nadja Auermann in a dress by John Galliano for Dior, spring/summer 1996

Below right: a design by Dior, sketched by René Gruau, 1946

The epitome of haute couture

CHRISTIAN DIOR

(1905–1957)

Christian Dior was one of the greatest French fashion designers of the 20th century. The initials CD, which have come to symbolize the epitome of women's fashion and elegance, set international standards for haute couture. After the deprivations of World War II, in the 1950s Dior created fashion that was both feminine and ambitious. The whole of high society wanted to be dressed by him and followed the dictates of his fashion.

Fashion enthusiast from a good family

Christian Dior, who was born in Normandy in 1905, was the son of the wealthy owner of a chemicals factory. In 1910 the family moved to Paris and lived in a luxury apartment entirely furnished in Louis XVI style. Christian wanted to become an architect, but his family had planned for him an illustrious career in politics. He followed his parents' wish and took up his studies, but he spent most of his time with artists in Paris. Driven by his enthusiasm for Cubism, he set up a small gallery with Jacques Bonjean in 1928 and sold works by the masters of classic modernism. But during the economic crisis of the 1930s his father lost his entire fortune on the stock exchange, and so the gallery had to close too. Within a very short time Christian Dior was almost penniless without even a place to live. He sold the remaining works of art to raise money.

While staying with a friend, Jean Ozenne, Dior started to make fashion sketches of dresses and hats. Being good at drawing, he managed to make a living from this. His hat designs, in particular, caused a stir, and he was soon drawing for the famous milliner Agnès and for the fashion section of *Figaro Illustré*. Michel de Brunhoff, the editor of *Vogue*, gave him helpful advice on how to improve his drawings.

In 1938 Robert Piguet employed the 33-year-old Dior as a designer in his haute couture house. At Piguet, Dior learned the arts of simplicity and omission which were to make his own collections famous. Contrary to the usual silhouette, in which straight lines were used to create a severe type of woman, Dior was already designing evening dresses with small waists and full skirts. After military service, Dior went to work for Lucien Lelong in 1942. The cotton magnate Marcel Boussac soon offered him the chance to open his own house. Three studios were created on the Avenue Montaigne, and Dior employed staff and models.

Birth of the New Look

With his first collection in spring 1947 Christian Dior became famous overnight. The American magazine *Life* gave his fashion the name "New Look." He had rediscovered a long-lost splendor and created a new, elegant woman. In the years that followed Christian Dior was to dictate what women wore as nobody had ever done before him.

In 1947 Dior introduced the Corolle line: rounded shoulders, short waisted jackets, wasp waists, and full calf-length skirts. To go with this he designed shoes with shallow platform soles and straps which crossed over around the heel. Thick high heels completed the look. Clear shapes such as those of the A-line or Y-line were his trump card. Every season he surprised and delighted the fashion world with his new creations. This in itself was completely new at a time when fashions were still changing more slowly than they do today.

Each of his designs required between 10 and 25 meters of fabric, and for evening dresses up to 85 yards. For his full skirts he used fabrics such as taffeta, satin, and

retained the image of the house of Dior, which was based on superior haute couture, but he did not market the ready-to-wear label successfully. This was the area where much was expected of the Italian Gianfranco Ferré when he was appointed design director, especially as he had already made a name for himself with his own ready-to-wear collection.

It fell to John Galliano to bring Dior back into the limelight, when he showed his first collection in 1997, the 50th anniversary of the fashion house. He spectacularly combined free, individual styles – street style, kitsch, and sports fashion – with a return to the opulence of sumptuous gowns of times long past. In haute couture Galliano is provocative and playful in his use of old patterns and fabrics. Time and again he honors the great master by going back to the designs of the 1950s, and so proves his talent for creatively combining the traditional and the new.

The complete anniversary collection, 1957

duchesse satin, which had the necessary rigidity and were quite different from the flowing jerseys or soft wool fabrics used by other couture houses at the time. Initially there was some criticism voiced concerning the waste of fabric and lavish luxury involved, but in the new desire for splendor this fell on deaf ears.

In 1948 Dior introduced pencil-slim skirts with a long back vent to allow movement, and by lining them with dress fabric he created another innovation. The Dior slit was worked out by the talented Marguerite Carré, who was one of Dior's closest collaborators. For Christian Dior haute couture was an art comparable to architecture or painting. The art of the right cut and fit as part of the esthetic creation were very important to him. That is why Madeleine Vionnet and Jeanne Lanvin always served him as mentors.

Expansion in great style
Dior showed seven collections each year: two for haute couture, two for ready-to-wear, and one each for the boutiques, for the United States, and for fur fashions. On top of this the house of Dior received almost 25,000 people every year. To make his name internationally known and appreciated, Dior founded his first

subsidiary as early as 1948. To begin with it was Dior perfumes which scored a big hit with Miss Dior. In 1949 the exquisite ready-to-wear line of Christian Dior Inc. was founded, and in 1950 he licensed his accessories. His first branch was established in London in 1952, and innumerable others followed all over the world. Within ten years Dior managed to build up an empire with an unsurpassed international reputation. Since 1987 the house has been part of the Louis-Vuitton-Moët-Hennessy group.

The successors
The young Yves Saint Laurent had been working for Dior as a draftsman and design assistant since 1954. After Dior's death in 1957 he was appointed head designer of the house at the young age of 21. However, the new star of the fashion world quit the house of Dior as early as 1961. Neither the management nor Dior's traditional clientele could come to terms with the avant-garde designs which Saint Laurent created as a reflection of a new age. In 1962 Marc Bohan succeeded Yves Saint Laurent, remaining at Dior until 1989. He

Spring/summer 1998

Brigitte Bardot, 1956

French actress Brigitte Bardot played a decisive part in shaping the image of women in the late 1950s and early 1960s. This seemingly natural girl derived sex appeal from her naive permissiveness. With her untamed blond hair, pouting lips and large, dark eyes, she was a bewitching mixture of child and femme fatale. Her initials, BB, which read Bébé (baby) in French, underscored this image. She wore thick black sweaters or light tight dresses, in gingham fabric – a pattern of white and pastel checks. She was the first actress not to wear stockings in her movies, and this too was gladly taken up by her contemporaries.

master of a range of designs, from Capri pants and cocktail dresses to flowing evening robes.

Bettina Graziani, the star model of the early 1950s, took on Givenchy's publicity; she modeled his designs herself and also engaged other famous models of the time, which greatly contributed to the success of the collection. Givenchy named a white cotton blouse with flouncy sleeves and embroidery for her. Bright colors and cheerful patterns became his trademark. At times he worked closely with Balenciaga, but he always retained his own style.

In 1995 British fashion designer John Galliano was appointed head designer of the house of Givenchy. A year later, he went to Dior, and later Alexander McQueen took on the job at Givenchy. After initially attempting to give the creations a very British look in his 1998 and 1999 collections, McQueen adopted a more traditional line by using exquisite fabrics for his lavishly cut designs.

Jacques Griffe

Jacques Griffe was born in Carcassonne in 1910. He started his career training with a tailor, then worked with Madeleine Vionnet for a few years before opening his own house in the 1940s. He loved strong colors and fabrics such as moiré and lamé that set off the colors to their best advantage. He was greatly influenced by Vionnet's cutting technique and also used the bias cut, and draped and knotted fabrics. He was among the first designers of the 1950s to create dresses which were not totally tailored but fluid and soft.

Jean Dessès

Jean Dessès became famous for his pleated and draped evening gowns in chiffon, which were inspired by ancient Greece. With his long, flowing dresses, the line of which was accentuated by floor-length shawls, he offered his clients an alternative to the rounded shape of the New Look and found a way of moving on from prewar fashion to modern times.

Cristobal Balenciaga

The worldwide fame of the Spaniard Cristobal Balenciaga was already well established by the 1930s. His haute-couture

Tailored suit by Fernandi, 1954

The tailored suit was the women's equivalent of the standard man's suit. It was a firm favorite when traveling because it was so versatile. With its waisted, double-breasted jacket and shawl collar covering the shoulders, this tailored suit represents the cool elegance of the 1950s. The hat would add an extra touch of severity or playfulness, depending on the wearer.

house continued until 1968, but he reached the climax of his creative work in the 1950s. In 1937 the trained tailor, who already owned a haute couture salon in Madrid, opened a salon in Paris, where he soon achieved great success with his characteristically innovative, elegant, yet highly dramatic style.

For Balenciaga it was always important to retain the artistic character of fashion. From his point of view a designer's duty was not to serve women but to create individual art forms and an individual image of the female body. Faithful to this philosophy, he definitively closed his house at a time when haute couture was beset by increasing problems and many designers were devoting all their energy to ready-to-wear clothes. However, in 1986 the name Balenciaga was revived, and since 1997 the Frenchman Nicolas Ghesquière has continued the fashion house's tradition with his elegant designs.

Trendsetting youth culture

In the 1950s young people began to rebel against an older generation that was preoccupied with restoring prosperity. Since the mid-1940s French existentialism had represented an intellectual counterbalance to a society which it regarded as self-satisfied. This movement set itself against bourgeois values and offered instead an individualistic definition of human life, by which everyone was required to discover the meaning of their existence without reference to traditional values. Jean-Paul Sartre, Simone de Beauvoir, and Albert Camus philosophized about a new awareness of life, and Juliette Greco sang about it. The existentialist attitude was also expressed in fashionable black clothes, especially black polo-neck sweaters.

The American influences that were flooding Europe were less intellectual but even more widespread. Rock-'n'-roll and its idol Elvis Presley were especially important influences on the youth of the Western world. Elvis's provocative movements and glittering costumes fired young people with enthusiasm and caused mass hysteria among his predominantly female public, while some older people considered his act obscene. Other famous singers, such as Little

Richard, Jerry Lee Lewis, and Chuck Berry, influenced the musical taste of the time as well as the clothing styles of their fans.

For many young people rock-'n'-roll meant rebellion against tradition. It was the music of the lower classes and was associated with the forbidden and even the criminal. The charisma of this provocative music had a great deal to do with the unusual, imaginative costumes and the sex appeal of its stars, and young people of all social classes could identify with it. It became as important to look different as it was to behave differently or to make different forms of music. The colorful, glittering costumes formed a striking contrast to the serious suits that all men had been expected to wear up until that time.

Radio broadcasts and records took the new music into everyone's home. But it was television, which dominated the United States and was starting to make inroads in Europe in the 1950s, which was the main reason why this new product of the American entertainment industry was spreading its influence across all social classes. Young people became an important market factor, and no one could ignore them any more.

Movies also disseminated the new lifestyle and the new fashion. *Rebel Without a Cause*, starring James Dean, presented young people's attitude toward life: a gentle outsider with a defiant face questions the apparently superficial and hypocritical values of the bourgeois middle class.

James Dean and Elvis Presley were idols who also represented the growing trend in the 1950s of prolonging adolescence. Like Peter Pan they never wanted to grow up; they no longer accepted the work ethic and the family values of their parents' generation, and rejected the prosperity and decency, banality and boredom of the bourgeois world.

Adolescence was no longer simply a dominant phase in the life of an individual, but an important factor in society as a whole. The adolescent society of which we speak today has its origins in the affluent society of the 1950s and in the protest of the young rebels of that decade.

The female movie stars and role models of this time were very different from those of

James Dean, 1955

In his films *East of Eden*, *Rebel Without a Cause* (1955), and *Giant* (released 1956), James Dean represented the rebel in his outfit of tight jeans, T-shirt or shirt with rolled-up sleeves, and wide, short jacket. The melancholy characters that he played and his death at the age of 24 made him a cult figure for international youth, who also copied his style of clothes.

Bild-Lilli in her 1950s living room, 1959

Bild-Lilli − the precursor of the Barbie doll − was created by the German newspaper *Bild*. She first appeared as a comic-strip character and in the years of German economic recovery represented a new image of femininity. Her immaculate body exuded sex appeal, and her blonde hair, ponytail, high-heeled shoes, red lips, painted eyebrows, and frivolous look represented self-confidence and independence. In 1955 she was made into a doll and a model who wore all the latest fashions of the time in all the latest surroundings. She was shown as a nurse, an air stewardess, and a barmaid, as well as a housewife in a simple woolen suit with her kidney-shaped table and her 1950s dog − a poodle.

Cliff Richard and Doreen Freeman do the jive, 1958

Girls wore petticoats to dance to rock-'n'-roll, while the hairstyle for boys included the kiss-curl. The jive was a very popular, extremely energetic dance.

earlier years such as Greta Garbo and Marlene Dietrich, and in many respects they were also very different from the cool beauties of fashion photography. In the representation of role models in the media there was a great contrast between the conventional, very elegant lady and the daring young woman. Marilyn Monroe, Sophia Loren, and Brigitte Bardot became idols throughout the entire Western world. Unlike the photographic models of the time, they clearly signaled eroticism and sexual attraction. Movie stars had voluptuous figures, emphasized by tight pullovers, and sensuous lips; they walked and moved in a particular way, and had opulent hairstyles, whether long or short. They personified confident, seductive women, yet at the same time seemed to represent a certain childlike innocence. This was the birth of the kind of child-woman who was to have great success in the 60s, personified in literature by Vladimir Nabokov's *Lolita*, which came out in 1955.

Barbie

It is scarcely a coincidence that the Barbie doll was developed in the United States at that time. She came out in 1959 and was soon exported to Europe. She had been created in the early 1950s as a cartoon character in a German newspaper, and her great popularity led to her being produced as a 7-inch-tall and 12-inch-tall doll in various outfits as an advertising gimmick for adults. Toy company Mattel bought the rights and produced an almost identical doll in the United States. Barbie soon made triumphant progress around the world, and against all expectations she was a great success with children: the adult doll allowed more forms of role-play than just the mother-and-baby model.

However, for many adults Barbie represented (and still represents today) an unrealistic image of womanhood; with her exaggerated figure – big bosom, tiny waist, and endlessly long legs – she is more like a bunny girl than a real woman. Nevertheless, Barbie continues to enjoy worldwide success.

From the start Barbie's clothes were perfectly styled, down to the tiniest detail: all her accessories – bra, garters, gloves, purse – were true to life and matched her clothes. The clothes themselves were made for every conceivable occasion: whether it was a morning walk, a college visit, shopping or sport, Barbie and her friends could be suitably dressed. At the same time little girls learned how to dress for specific events, and no doubt they also gained a taste for fashion and consumerism.

Today the doll and her wardrobe are more suited to a modern youth culture and leisure style. Just as Barbie's roles and clothes have changed with the spirit of the times, she is a valuable representation of female images and fashion over the last 40 years.

Jeans and the American lifestyle

Originally considered working clothes, jeans were first worn as leisurewear in the United States in the 30s. By the 1950s they were being exported to Europe, and they quickly became very popular because of their emotional association with concepts such as freedom and manliness.

Jeans suggested a certain American lifestyle, which was very important at a time when people could not travel the world as easily as they can today. Because they were so informal and had their origins in working clothes, jeans acted as a perfect expression of youth protest against the establishment. They were also very practical and hard-wearing. Since then jeans have lost their rebellious connotations and have now become an essential part of most people's basic wardrobe.

Neo-Edwardian fashion and teddy boys

A few young men from privileged social backgrounds rebelled against the bourgeois style of their fathers and the privations of the recent war years by adopting a more opulent style of clothes. This harked back to men's fashion from the time of King Edward VII, with narrow trousers, frock coats and tailored jackets with velvet cuffs and lapels; these were complemented by a monocle, watch chain, and diamond tiepin.

In the London of the early 1950s a new type suddenly emerged: Teddy boys, young men mostly from a working background, who spent their free time on the streets in gangs and derisively copied the Edwardian style. They wore draped, long, dark, single-breasted jackets, with long, narrow drainpipe trousers, and later tight jeans. They also wore a starched shirt, a vest, a narrow tie or bowtie, shoes with thick crepe soles or, later, pointed winklepickers, and to crown it all their hair was brilliantined and shaped into a DA ("duck's ass"). Teddy boy fashion lost its way toward the end of the 1950s: it was overwhelmed by trends in the newly arrived pop culture, though it has been kept alive in some circles as a cult fashion.

Teddy boy in London, 1954

The long, draped jacket, black drainpipe trousers, and smart hairstyle are all unmistakable trademarks of the Teddy boy, or Ted.

Roman Holiday (1953) with Audrey Hepburn, Gregory Peck, and Eddie Albert

A long, full skirt, small neckscarf, and short hair with bangs turned Audrey Hepburn's princess into an ordinary young woman in this cult movie.

SHOES

It is not only clothes that make the man – shoes do, too. However well formed the feet may be, they require the right footwear to give them real elegance. Many women, and even men, become obsessed with shoes, to the point that their shoe cupboards are filled with hundreds of pairs. Real collectors need no excuse to buy an extra pair: they are concerned with the precise coordination of tiny details within their overall appearance, or they want to expand the range of expression in their clothes – a pair of shoes for every mood. Many designs have risen above the status of accessories. They do not need to justify their existence; they were created as works of art and are either worn as such or exhibited in a showcase.

Noble shoes

The precise effect of a shoe has always been determined by the shape of its sole and heel. High heels not only make their wearer look taller; they also increase the wearer's erotic appeal. In the 20th century, and into the 21st, it is mostly women's shoes that have high heels, while in earlier times it was men who wore richly decorated high gold shoes. Up until the 18th century it was usual for men's shoes to have a heel, and at the court of Louis XIV in France, red heels were preferred.

Boot made in Sweden, c. 1910

Their purpose was to demonstrate that the aristocrats did no physical work; they did not have to walk through the dusty streets but rather were driven in comfortable carriages. Even pumps, perhaps the most common form of women's shoes today, were originally worn by men. They were part of a lackey's uniform and acquired their name from the noise that they made on the master's polished parquet floors.

Heel shapes

Even today, shoes continue to stand for wealth and extravagance. André Perugia was one of the greatest shoe designers. His shoes matched the chic and extravagance of French fashion. Paul Poiret took Perugia from Nice to Paris, and society ladies were soon carried away by his shoes. In 1920 Perugia opened a studio in Faubourg Saint-Honoré, where he worked for many other well-known fashion designers, besides Poiret. For his exclusive clients, among whom there were many international movie stars, he created individual designs that were true works of art.

Salvatore Ferragamo made his name at about the same time. This Italian designer went to the United States in 1914 and was soon creating designs for the greats of the movie industry. He was one of the most intriguing and imaginative shoe designers of the first half of the 20th century, and he was ahead of his time in his approach to new materials. The shortage of materials during World War II and the ban on using leather for civilian shoes did nothing to hinder him; on the contrary, it stimulated his imagination. He used cellophane, raffia, and fish skin on his cork-soled shoes and sandals to elegant effect. In 1936 Ferragamo created the wedge heel in cork, and though it was not accepted at first, by the 1940s it had become a very popular shape. In 1938 he created sensational sandals with platform soles, in which the heels were made of cork covered with various colored suedes.

Platform soles were always controversial; some loved them, others found them ugly and ungainly. In the 1970s women wore

them both with baggy pants and with swirling skirts. They reappeared in 1990s retro fashion in many different forms, from pumps to hiking shoes. In 1994 Vivienne Westwood, who is famous for her anarchic, provocative clothing designs, created blue leather platform shoes that were 8 inches high; they even caused as accomplished a model as Naomi Campbell to stumble on the catwalk during her show. Innovative heels were Roger Vivier's trademark. His curved, comma-shaped heels and angular, prism-shaped heels were copied all over the world. Vivier had

Heelless suede pump with polished, gilt cork sole by André Perugia, 1937

studied sculpture, and his shoe designs had a solid, balanced base. He decorated his basic shapes with remarkable taste and playfulness. For the coronation of Queen Elizabeth II he designed elegant shoes with garnet-studded heels. And for Marlene Dietrich he designed strapped sandals with paste beads pinned to the

Rainbow-colored platform sandal with cork sole by Salvatore Ferragamo, 1938

Slip-on shoe of goatskin and velvet by Herbert and Beth Levine, 1954

Leather boot with acid-proof, air-cushioned sole by Doc Martens, 1996

always the chance that she would go over on her ankle, get stuck, or lose a heel. Despite this, stilettos are still worn.

George Bernard Shaw, Irish dramatist and critic is supposed to have once said: "If you rebel against high-heeled shoes, make sure you are wearing a very fashionable hat." Emancipated women of the 1960s and 1970s did protest, but without following Shaw's advice. They rejected high heels and wore flat soles. Audrey Hepburn had shown how attractive these could look by wearing ballet shoes with capri pants and creating a new style. Moccasins with pimpled soles and heels also took off for both men and women. Diego Della Valle was inspired to this type of design by shoes worn by racing drivers.

Men's shoes

Men's shoes were much plainer than women's during the 20th century. Only the multicolored, extremely pointed shimmy shoes of the 1920s were more extravagant. Gaiters and galoshes slowly died out, and in the 1940s and 1950 comfortable, flat shoes were worn.

Various forms of lace-up shoes have always been worn with a suit and were therefore the predominant form for men, along with the classic moccasin, the low-cut slip-on shoe made of fine leather. In the cult movie *Easy Rider* (1969) Dennis Hopper and Peter Fonda replaced the myth of the movie cowboy, yet they stuck with their footwear and turned cowboy boots into fashionable streetwear.

Doc Martens, tough everyday shoes for young people, brought some color into footwear. Workmen's shoes were discovered by the punk fashion of the 1970s, and as shoes or boots they became popular fashion

Platform shoe in imitation crocodile leather by Vivienne Westwood, 1994

heels. After World War II he worked for Christian Dior and complemented the New Look silhouette with his attractive, balanced high-heels.

High-heeled boots have a long history as desirable objects with sex appeal. The earliest 19th-century pinup photographs show women in tight corsets and almost knee-high boots. To this day impractical boots are fetish objects for many people; their appeal lies in their high, pointed heels and in their laces, buttons, or zips, which are just asking to be undone.

In the 1950s high-heeled shoes stole the show. It was felt that a woman in high heels had both erotic appeal and fashion sense. In their most extreme form – stiletto heels, 4 inches high, and pencil-thin – the wearer lived dangerously; there was

items and youth icons. Women took up Doc Martens too; they were worn to contrast with short skirts and to symbolize independence and self-confidence.

Sports shoes

Trainers also became a central element in a really fashionable outfit. The manufacturer's name is noticed before either the material or the design, and the popularity of an individual make is supported by pioneering advertising campaigns. In the same way as names in haute couture, certain sports labels have come to represent a kind of world view, so that it is considered "good form" to wear branded trainers.

Running shoes and sneakers first became acceptable as streetwear in the United States. Even women in business suits wore comfortable trainers on the way to work in the morning, and then changed into elegant pumps in the office.

Works of art

As well as useful and fashionable shoes, there have always been footwear designs that were really conceived as art objects. Most designers created unique models that were inspired either by fine art or by a client's particular preferences.

In 1937 master shoemaker André Perugia created an elegant illusion with his first heelless shoe, which seemed to float because the wearer's foot balanced on a very small base.

In America Beth Levine became famous toward the end of the 1940s. She created objects which at first did not look as if they were to be worn on the feet, as well as unwearable variations such as pumps consisting of nothing more than a sole and a heel. At the same time some extremely elegant designs have come out of her studio in Manhattan, including her 1954 velvet slip-ons and the glamorous sequined pumps made for Liza Minelli.

The miniskirt and the hippie look

Fashion revolutions

1960–1969

Youth as social ideal

The 1960s saw the first postwar generation in Europe reach adulthood. This meant that ideas that had been valid up until and throughout the 1950s changed considerably. Never before had the cult of youth so radically taken over all areas of life. In the Western world, youth now became an absolute model of fashion and of the whole ambit of social life. Here was a powerful young class of consumers who did not relate to haute couture but wanted a fashion that would not only match the spirit of youth but would also be affordable. In this way fashion lost its elitist character and turned into a mass youth phenomenon which also served as a way of expressing political views, especially toward the end of the decade.

This generation no longer followed the rules of bourgeois morality and manners, which they saw as based on double standards. For the first time, the pill removed from liberated sex fears of pregnancy and resulting social disapproval. The market for books and movies on sex education boomed, sexuality came into the public arena, and after the prudishness of the previous decades new norms were created, but also new pressures. Those who wanted to be "in" had to be sexually liberated, and this often meant being sexually liberal.

The elegant lady gave way to the seemingly naïve child-women who looked at the world with great doe-eyes. The maxim was to be young and sexy at any cost; transparent blouses and ultrashort skirts bear witness to this. Twiggy became the first model to cause a stir with her childlike, skinny figure with no obvious feminine curves; she was considered scandalous by many older people.

Linear esthetics

The 1950s had not only favored the New Look, with its narrow waistlines and wide or pencil skirts which for us now epitomize that era. They had also introduced several lines into fashion: the balloon and the A-line, the barrel line and the Y-shape. What most particularly pointed the way to the 1960s was the trapeze line, which, as design director of Dior, the young Yves Saint Laurent had shown in 1958: tent dresses or coats without a waist, narrow at the top, widening toward the bottom, and usually ending just above the knee.

The immensely popular tent dresses of the 1960s were not directly linked to the fashion of the 1920s. Although dresses at the start of the century had also appeared emphatically youthful, they were still elegant and ladylike. Shaped like sacks or flowing around the body, they were at least knee-length, often had a low-set skirt with a graceful outward swing, and were often made of delicate fabrics, lace, and silks in low-key colors. Dresses for special occasions

1960 John F Kennedy becomes president of the United States. The Guggenheim Museum in New York opens. Alfred Hitchcock's *Psycho* is released. The independence of 17 countries marks the end of colonial rule in Africa. International disarmament talks in Geneva.

1961 The government of the German Democratic Republic orders the erection of the Berlin Wall. First manned space flight around the world (USSR). Electrification of Trans-Siberian Railroad. Development and availability of the contraceptive pill. The attempted overthrow of Fidel Castro leads to the first Cuban crisis.

1962 Removal of Russian missiles from Cuba ends the Cuban Missile Crisis. Algeria gains independence. Marilyn Monroe dies. First James Bond movie. Premiere of Benjamin Britten's *War Requiem*. France carries out underground nuclear test in the Sahara.

1963 Assassination of US president John F Kennedy. Development of color Polaroid camera. German artist Joseph Beuys causes a furore with his *Fat Chair*.

1964 Civil rights leader Martin Luther King is awarded the Nobel Peace Prize. Beginning of the Vietnam War. Pop Art makes its way into advertising. The Beatles burst onto the scene.

1965 Bob Dylan and Joan Baez become symbols of the antiwar movement. The international children's aid agency UNICEF receives the Nobel Peace Prize.

1966 After a coup General Suharto

becomes prime minister of Indonesia. David Lean makes the movie *Doctor Zhivago*. The novel *Belles Images* by Simone de Beauvoir is published in France. Mao Zedong launches the Cultural Revolution, mobilizing Chinese youth against the Chinese Communist Party.

1967 Six-Day War between Israel

Confrontation at an anti-Vietnam demonstration in New York, 1968

and Egypt, Syria, Jordan, and Lebanon. Death of socialist revolutionary leader Ernesto "Che" Guevara. First successful heart transplant in Cape Town.

1968 "Prague Spring": troops from the USSR, Poland, Bulgaria, and the GDR occupy Czechoslovakia and bloodily suppress protests against Soviet control. Worldwide student riots, the most violent occurring in Paris. Martin Luther King is assassinated. First performance of the musical *Hair*. Agreement between USA, UK, and USSR to halt proliferation of nuclear weapons.

1969 Neil Armstrong is the first man on the moon. The Woodstock festival. Peter Fonda's *Easy Rider* appears in the movie theaters. "Black is Beautiful" movement in the USA. Willy Brandt becomes chancellor of West Germany.

displayed much splendor through gold and sequin embroidery.

The tent dresses of the 1960s seemed like children's clothes in comparison. They displayed hardly any decorative details or refined cuts, and instead were often cut in straight or A-line shapes from stiff (synthetic) fabrics. It was the large-scale graphical or floral patterns in bright colors that made them effective. They were much shorter than the dresses of the 1920s and generally made a pretty loud impression. They challenged the idea of traditional, ladylike elegance, and that was indeed the intention. The new dresses and coats were meant above all to appear young and unconventional, regardless of the wearer's real age.

Role change

The appearance of the sexes changed once again. While in the 1950s the differences in appearance between the two had been very clear, they now became blurred. Men wore long hair and very tight clothing that emphasized the body; women hid their traditional female characteristics and espoused a seemingly sexless ideal, tending to become more and more childlike and skinny. Short hair and pantsuits, which both became very fashionable at the time, contributed even more to this effect.

Something similar to what had occurred in the 1920s took place. The previous ideal of femininity was abandoned in favor of a more severe silhouette, immediately overturning conventional values. What should those childlike, apparently unfeminine yet sexy creatures who looked nothing like women of earlier decades be called? In the 1920s they were regarded as having turned into men and were spoken of as garçonnes (mannish women); in the 1960s the term "androgynous" was applied to the boyish women of that decade.

Hairstyles

Hairdos were slow to follow this new look. At the beginning of the decade it was the beehive à la Farah Diba that set the trend. Painstakingly backcombed, sometimes enhanced with artificial or real hairpieces, and set with huge amounts of hairspray, it made heads appear large in proportion to the rest of the now fragile-looking body. This

anticipated the trend toward the childlike which was to become even stronger during the decade. John Waters' 1988 movie *Hairspray*, in which the opening shots show young women and men in fashionable

Twiggy in a see-through halterneck dress, 1966

Twiggy poses in a transparent halterneck dress on the hood of a sports car. Born Lesley Hornby, the 15-year-old Twiggy was discovered or, more precisely, created, by her later manager Justin de Villeneuve. The superthin model with the delicate teenage figure was given her characteristic blond short haircut, and the ideal for millions of girls around the world was complete. Twiggy was the first supermodel, and her career lasted four years. Christened the "Face of 1966," she became a symbol of the Sixties.

Vidal Sassoon cuts Mary Quant's hair, 1964

The fashion designer who made the miniskirt popular has her hair cut into the revolutionary five-point-cut by the master of modern hairstyling.

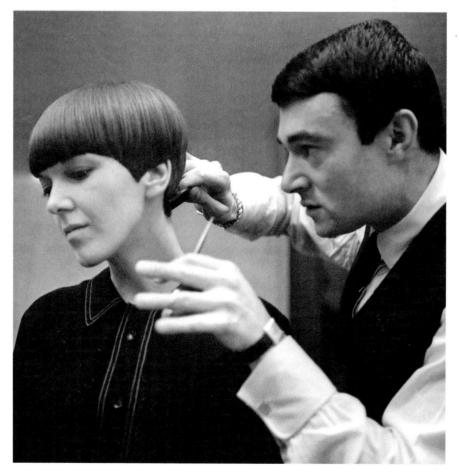

The Beatles during the filming of their first movie *A Hard Day's Night*, 1964

The *Thomas Crown Affair*, 1968

Insurance detective Faye Dunawaye pursues millionaire art thief Steve McQueen, alias Thomas Crown. Its special effects and exquisite, up-to-the-minute costumes as well as its current theme of the battle of the sexes made the movie a classic. It was remade in 1999.

1960s clothes devoting themselves to practically turning their puffed-up hairstyles into concrete with hairspray, is an entertaining parody of this fashion.

Gradually women began to wear their hair more naturally, although still backcombed, which appeared more youthful. In the mid-1960s manes came down once again. London hair artist Vidal Sassoon caused a furore with his smooth, geometric, short cuts. They went well with the futuristic fashion

which came in at the time. Makeup also changed accordingly. The dramatic black-rimmed eyes that had been customary in the first half of the decade gave way to colorful eyeshadow and false eyelashes. The first cosmetic lines purely for teenagers also came onto the market.

Men's hair, by contrast, became longer. The Beatles' mop-tops − which today appear very moderate to us − were seen as quite outrageous then. After the severe short men's cuts of the previous years they were regarded as unmanly and messy, but became an influential ideal for many male heads.

Here too it becomes clear what it was that was influencing fashion. No longer was it the great designers who laid down the lines in fashion but rather pop stars, the movies, and television which were definitively an important factor in fashion.

Men's fashion

Up until the mid-1960s there were no marked changes in men's fashion. From then on suits had a tighter and close-fitting cut, as did coats, which often came with a belt, such as the increasingly popular trenchcoat. Suits could now be worn with a turtleneck sweater instead of a shirt and tie. Worn over a shirt, the sleeveless sweater presented a practical compromise between a thin shirt and a thick sweater.

Suit jackets were fastened in the traditional way with buttons or, very progressive this, with zips. Often they had no lapels but a Nehru-style collar; pockets and belts gave way them a sporty look. Alongside tweed, the traditional, robust material made of fine wool, new fabrics such as corduroy came into use. If worn at all, ties were now more colorful and imaginative than before.

The waistband moved from the waist down to the hips, while the width of the leg went through several changes. In comparison with the wide pants of the 1950s, tighter pants were initially more popular at the beginning of the 1960s. Later, together with the wider jackets, legs became less tight, until unbelievably wide flared pants came back into fashion in the 1970s. The narrow legs were often worn with boots, as ankle boots and longer boots enjoyed great popularity. Jeans, whose revolution had begun in the 1950s, asserted themselves as

the leisurewear above all other in the 1960s. The tight polo shirt became this generation's popular casual shirt.

The hippie look

Standing in opposition to their parents' generation, but also in the face of intensifying international conflict, younger people became strongly politicized. Both in the United States and in Europe there was protest against the hardening positions in the power games of the Cold War. Anti-establishment opponents of the Vietnam War adopted the slogan "Make love not war," and toward the end of decade the wave of student unrest spread from the United States to Europe and Japan.

The hippie look was the visible signature of resistance among the members of protest movements. Women and men went barefoot, had long hair, and wore jewelry, jeans, and shirts in colorful flowery patterns. The women often also wore long, flowing, flowery dresses. Symbolizing peace-loving gentleness and a closeness to nature, as well as the conviction that a life of few needs made more sense than rampant consumerism, this antifashion was an expression of a particular view of the world. It was comparable to that of the beatniks, who had turned against a society based on ambition and who wore emphatically messy, "beat" clothes. Hippies as well as beatniks promoted free love and believed in using drugs to achieve higher consciousness.

Hippies and beatniks, those two great youth movements of the 20th century soon crossed national boundaries and developed into a worldwide trend. This was accompanied by the commercial exploitation of their outward appearance. Hippie clothing in particular soon became fashionable even for those who were not interested in the ideological background. Floor-length skirts, fluttering scarves and bandanas, old-fashioned lacy blouses, and similarly nostalgic clothing quickly appeared in department stores, being cheaply mass-produced and proving highy popular. For a time they dominated the appearance of young people in North America and Europe. Here was another example of a fashion phenomenon that can be observed again and again: developed by a minority, that minority's

clothing is turned into fashion through mass production and largely loses the ideological meaning connected with its origin.

Television and the movies

Although television established itself as a medium in the 1960s and could be found in ever more households, it could not – at least not in Europe – replace the silver screen. Gradually, however, it became an essential part of leisure time and soon resulted in the globalization of knowledge and lifestyles. In matters of fashion, television also began to set trends. The English crime series *The Avengers* was a downright fashion show: Emma Peel, played by Diana Rigg, constantly changed costumes and was always dressed in the latest styles. Her leather outfits are regarded as the first to be inspired by fetishism: they made her appear as an

Men's fashion, 1965

The range of everyday clothes for men. The three-piece glen-check woolen suit on the left has short, narrow lapels, and a jacket slightly fitted at the waist. The polo coat in the center also has a narrow cut. The generous lapels are trimmed with beaver, by the 1960s already almost a relic of the first three decades of the century, when furs for men were customary. Casual turtlenecks were popular among students, who used them to make a statement against the stiff shirt and tie. The single-breasted coat on the right, similar to the Chesterfield, appears more elegant with its slightly slimmer cut and the smooth camelhair wool, and seems intended for the "real" gentleman. The woman in the foreground showing herself most emancipated in pantsuit and toting a cigar, adds a rather ironic note to the picture. Women's suits did indeed follow men's suits in cut and lapel shapes, but could be more extravagant in fabric and pattern.

Jimi Hendrix, 1967

In every respect Jimi Hendrix was the embodiment of the 1960s generation's revolt against the establishment. Famous as the master of improvisation on electric guitar, he openly criticized American politics through his music and demonstrated this nonconformist attitude in his lifestyle. The colorful, richly embroidered jacket that he often wore is an ironic reference to traditional military uniforms and a subtle expression of the anti-Vietnam protest among the young.

Opposite page:
Illustration in *Fashion of the Times* by Antonio, 1967

Antonio worked together with his partner Juan Ramos in Manhattan, surrounded by prominent artists, photographers, and figures from the world of pop. He made his name as an illustrator for *Vogue* and *Harper's Bazaar*. At the beginning of the 1960s he abandoned pure illustration in favor of capturing the decade atmosphere and, as in this image, creating psychedelic improvisations on the themes of music, drugs, and clothes. He had a particular sense for current esthetics and became a central figure of 1960s culture. He also "discovered" models such as Grace Jones.

invincible superwoman and influenced fashion designers of later decades such as Gianni Versace and Vivienne Westwood, who made fetishistic fashion socially acceptable.

Audrey Hepburn was still a very popular movie star, and her slim, graceful figure made her an ideal model for the current girlish but highly elegant fashion. Opposite in image to Audrey Hepburn was Brigitte Bardot, whose fame had been uninterrupted for years. In *Viva Maria* (1965) she played alongside Jeanne Moreau, whose face, although not classically beautiful was highly expressive, and who appeared as a marked contrast to Bardot. Jeanne Moreau often worked with directors Luis Buñuel and François Truffaut, as did the cool, well-proportioned, blond beauty Catherine Deneuve, who achieved worldwide fame through Buñuel's movies *Viridiana* (1961) and *Belle de Jour* (1967), both at the time regarded as scandalous works. Sophia Loren's reputation also reached its high point in this decade. All these stars left their mark on the image of the 1960s.

Apart from actresses, fashion models such as Jean Shrimpton and Twiggy also became role models for women. Now – for the first time – models were so firmly placed in the limelight that they became superstars. In the 1960s, together with fashion photographers and designers, they enjoyed public adulation equal to that of movie stars. As a result the world of fashion became the subject of a number of movies. In *Blow Up* (1966) director Michelangelo Antonioni made a fashion photographer modeled on star photographer David Bailey the protagonist and had top model Verushka play a model.

The print media as well as television also helped to turn public personalities such as Jacqueline Kennedy, wife of the American president, into fashion models. Jackie, regarded as one of the most beautiful women of her time, possessed her own unmistakable style. She loved suits and boxy jackets, straight dresses and pantsuits in strong colors, preferably pink. With these she always wore gloves and a hat: it was she who made the round, brimless pillbox hat popular. Barbie, the fashion doll with the bubble-cut hairstyle that she was given at the beginning of the 1960s, was wrapped in many little dresses and outfits that gave her striking resemblance to the popular first lady.

Music

If pop music influenced the formation of specific youth cultures in the 1950s, the tendency became even more marked in the 1960s. The music of the 1950s and its stars contributed to the acceptance of wide jackets, narrow neckties, suede shoes, and duck's tail haircuts for men, and petticoats and ponytails among girls. In the 1960s the picture was different. For instance, the Beatles began their career in black leather but soon appeared in suits. The Who did wear jeans and T-shirts, but they too preferred suits while on stage. Suits with barrow legs without turnups, patterned jackets with standup collars, and shirts with frills and jabot sleeves were different from everyday clothes and were widely copied by their fans.

Young people who were more politically engaged dressed in jeans and parkas, like their idols, Bob Dylan, Arlo Guthrie, and Joan Baez, singers influenced by American folk music. In 1969, all these musicians appeared at the now legendary Woodstock festival, which is regarded as the symbol of the hippie generation's lifestyle. Famous bands such as The Who and Santana played alongside Janis Joplin and Jimi Hendrix, who both attained the status of cult figures after their early deaths a year later.

Jimi Hendrix's worldwide success as a guitar genius marks the international breakthrough of black musicians and youth idols. His extravagant yet laid-back mixture of clothes, combining uniform, ethnic, and patchwork elements, coupled with wild Afro hair, as well as his distorted version of the American national anthem that he performed at the festival, were enormously provocative in the United States.

New structures in the fashion industry

More and more people at all income levels dressed fashionably, as clothing could now be produced, distributed, and sold at ever-decreasing prices, particularly as the result of intensive trade with low-wage countries. Clothes were no longer acquired for the longer term but had become one-season wonders widely available in stores; they were bought quickly, worn, and discarded just as quickly, to be replaced by something new. However, the quality of these pieces was often correspondingly low.

The first mail order businesses specifically geared to a youthful clientele emerged, and large stores put in special departments for "young fashion." Boutiques appeared, a new kind of store for modern, fashionable clothing. They also differed markedly from department stores or conventional clothes stores in the design of their interiors and the fact that music played continuously.

The large fashion houses felt the impact of these changes. Some adapted to them and expanded their range to include ready-to-wear lines. Although mass-produced by industrial means, they were still created by a fashion designer, were of high quality, and were still expensive. Haute couture, made-to-measure manual work, was no longer the great money-spinner, even if it remained (and still is) important for a fashion house's reputation. By the second half of the 1960s there was hardly a great fashion house that did not offer a prêt-à-porter collection. In addition to the couture displays there were

YVES SAINT LAURENT

(b. 1936)

Yves Saint Laurent is regarded as one of the most important fashion designers of the 20th century, along with Christian Dior, Coco Chanel, and Elsa Schiaparelli. For more than 40 years his designs were among the most influential and most frequently copied creations in the world of fashion. Saint Laurent created the tuxedo for women, he provoked Paris fashion with the "nude look," and his individualistic color combinations had an outstanding influence on the development of tastes.

Yves Saint Laurent at Dior, 1960

Printemps 1958

Sketch of a trapeze dress, 1958

The child prodigy of haute couture

Yves Henri Donat Mathieu-Saint-Laurent, who later simply called himself Yves Saint Laurent, was born on August 1, 1936, the son of wealthy French parents in Oran, Algeria, where he also grew up. Already fascinated by fashion at an early age, he traveled to Paris in 1953 and with his drawings won an award in a design competition of the International Wool Secretariat. After his high school graduation in 1954 he settled permanently in Paris, where he attended a design course at the school of the Chambre Syndicale de la Couture. Only a year later Christian Dior, who with his New Look had led French postwar fashion to glittering success, noticed the young designer and employed him as design assistant.

Following the death of Christian Dior, Saint Laurent, just 21, was appointed chief designer for the house of Dior on November 15, 1957. With his very first couture collection, featuring the trapeze line, he was hailed on January 30, 1958 as the new star of Paris fashion. Many fashion editors are said to have cried with emotion, and a French newspaper ran the headline "Saint Laurent Saves France." This statement was hardly an exaggeration: at the time, nearly half of French fashion exports came from the house of Dior. With the death of Christian Dior, the high point of postwar fashion seemed to have passed, and a young genius of a designer had to take his place.

The Ligne Trapèze already showed with what manual dexterity and knowledge of past fashion the young designer intended to make his mark in fashion history. His designs were as balanced and opulent as Dior's, organza and magnificent embroidery made reference to the house traditions, and with Lily of the Valley, the dress named after Dior's favorite flower, Saint Laurent directly showed his reverence for his great predecessor. However, he dispensed with padding and stiffness, introduced lightness and elegance, and with his widely flaring, comfortable dresses he abolished the feminine tailoring established by Dior and his New Look. Thus he remained within the house's tradition and at the same time

moved it forward – taking a great step, in fact, for the trapeze shape had not appeared in fashion history since the early part of the 18th century.

Parting from Dior

In 1961 the house of Dior broke with the young designer. Prior to this Saint Laurent had been required to do his military service and during that time had suffered a nervous breakdown. Released from the army, and after spending some time in a

Mondrian dress, 1965

clinic, he returned to Dior to find that his position there had meanwhile been taken by Marc Bohan, who on January 26, 1961 showed a collection that was received as enthusiastically as Saint Laurent's trapeze line has been three years earlier.

The house of Dior and Yves Saint Laurent parted at a time when he was not only having personal problems but had taken a new direction in fashion. For in 1960 tradition had embraced the revolution: Saint Laurent had shocked the fashion house's conservative clientele by introducing the beat look and black leather jackets.

Tuxedo for women, 1966/67

The 1960s: revolution with elegance

Together with his business partner for life, Pierre Bergé, who was responsible for the administrative side of the business, Saint Laurent now relied on his own name and founded his own couture salon. His first collection, revealed to the world on January 29, 1962, was a success and, freed from administrative work by Bergé, Saint Laurent was able to introduce the trendsetting designs of the 1960s: his tunic dresses with large-scale Mondrian-style designs in 1965; the tuxedo for women in January 1966; the summer 1966 collection influenced by the artist Andy Warhol; the controversial transparent dress with a silk chiffon bodice covered with nothing more than an ostrich feather and references to student protest in duffel coats and fringed jackets in the summer of 1968. His preference for androgynous shapes was groundbreaking at a time when women more than ever before were seeking emancipation.

Yves Saint Laurent became a revolutionary of the Paris fashion scene by enriching the current tendencies of haute couture with trends from the street. "Turning to the street without ever losing sight of quality, of elegance" was Saint Laurent's unique ability, wrote German fashion designer Jil Sander. Saint Laurent became involved with the bohemian culture of the Left Bank – which at the time was regarded as unseemly by Parisian society – and accordingly christened his ready-to-wear line Rive Gauche. However, perhaps understandably, he never drove his revolutionary zeal to the point of alienating his rich customers and doing himself out of the wealthy audience essential to the success of a couturier.

Yves Saint Laurent and art

Saint Laurent's near-legendary reputation sprang not only from his dexterity and his feel for designs that were often ahead of their time. It also reflected his enormous interest in art that since the 1950s had inspired his work for film, theater, and opera. Whether in Catherine Deneuve's black PVC coat in Luis Buñuel's movie *Belle de Jour* (1967) or designs for Marguerite Duras' *While Days in the Trees* (1965), Roland Petit's choreography (1962–65) or Jean Cocteau's *Cher Menteur* (1980), Saint Laurent was able to realize his ideas in designs for theater and opera just as much as for fashion. Indeed his art-based designs serve him as a reminder, a search for the historical self-confirmation through which he regards himself as a successor to Proust.

Saint Laurent owes his inspiration to contacts in the artistic world, such as the dancer Rudolf Nureyev, artist Andy Warhol, and actress Catherine Deneuve. However, he did not succumb to the simple transfer of artistic or ethnic designs into fashion. His Op Art creations, the safari style that he developed from the late 1960s, the Ballets Russes collection of 1976, the Carmen dresses, also of 1976, and his 1993 homage to Nureyev, who had died of AIDS, sought to emulate the objects of his inspiration without imitating them. Saint Laurent places value on the independence of fashion, which he expressed through an ironic break with artistic prototypes and with a perfect cut.

In the 1980s and 1990s Saint Laurent's designs no longer caused the uproar that they had in earlier decades. Saint Laurent became a fashion classic through major shows in New York (1983/84), Paris (1986), and St Petersburg, Russia (1987). His creations have drawn much praise from such prominent admirers as Miuccia Prada, Christian Lacroix, and Paul Smith,

Prêt-à-porter, 1994/95

among other contemporary designers. Saint Laurent himself admits to feeling apprehensive before every presentation, but by now he has come to appreciate the advantages of being a classic designer: "I am concerned with the perfection of my style, I no longer need to develop it." Today Saint Laurent captivates less with innovative than with classic designs, and his prêt-à-porter and haute couture shows in Paris continue to raise storms of adoration.

Two pairs of twins in Biba, the Kensington boutique, 1966

As an advertising ploy Barbara Hulanicki employed two pairs of twins in one of her Biba boutiques in London. While the twins in the foreground, with their minidresses and bobbed hair, represent the style of the early 1960s, the bellbottoms and the long hair of the pair in the background display a tendency toward hippie fashion, which was also made popular through Biba.

now also two annual prêt-à-porter shows, both in Paris and in Milan, the latter under the name *alta moda pronta*.

The new, young audience demanded affordable clothes and not prohibitively expensive single pieces. The fashion industry met these requirements and even encouraged their development through trends that changed at an ever-increasing rate. To fully exploit the modern, efficient production methods, new markets had to be created; these in turn grew and demanded ever better manufacturing techniques. Thus supply and demand soared to previously

unknown heights. From the manufacturers' point of view the potential of consumerism was now unlimited. Many of the great fashion houses also expanded in order to serve a global market. A good example of this is Pierre Cardin, who took quite new directions in marketing.

Some fashion creators did not join in the development of mass production and instead retreated from the business. Such was Cristobal Balenciaga; for him, fashion could be nothing but an art form, and he rejected the fact of its banality and reduction to cheap trends that became passé almost as soon as they were taken up, simply by pulling out of the open market.

Street fashion

The phenomenon of mass fashion shows that the profile of fashion producers had also changed. It was no longer exclusively the French fashion houses who made or even dictated fashion. From the 1960s on fashion created by youth culture was taken over into haute couture and prêt-à-porter collections rather than trends always spreading from haute couture outward.

Referring to the 19th and early 20th centuries, German sociologist Georg Simmel claimed in 1911 that fashion acts to outwardly mark the distinction between the wealthier strata of society and those economically less privileged. As soon as a fashion has spread and is imitated by everyone, it no longer serves its purpose and it has to be replaced by a new one. In the second half of the 20th century this thesis was only partly valid, as the real innovation often came from the streets and no longer from haute couture.

Carnaby Street and British fashion

Britain was the leading trendsetter of the 1960s. English tailoring had long enjoyed an excellent international reputation for its timelessness and perfection, and in the 18th century the fashion of the English gentry had a strong influence on European men's clothing. But never before had Britain played such a leading role in the dissemination of new fashion ideas as in the 1960s.

The fashion center of the world was now no longer a distinguished fashion house in Paris but a London street: Carnaby Street. Here young shoppers could buy anything "in,"

Four minidresses, from Brigitte, 1967

These straight, single-color dresses in pastel shades sum up all that was typical of the outgoing decade: a moderate length, a belt in a contrasting color emphasizing the waist, small button facings, and a neat, contrasting trim at the neck. The simple cut of the dresses is complemented by feminine-looking accessories such as the beret worn at an angle, conspicuous handbags, and color-coordinated shoes with straps. Although at first glance the young women all appear practically identical, this shot, by photographer F.C. Grundlach makes clear that by this time the minidress had become acceptable for very different types of women.

whether new or old, for secondhand clothes also became fashionable at this time: knitted sweaters in lacy patterns of all colors of the rainbow; crocheted shoulder bags and leather bags with fringes in the Native American style; leather jackets and jeans; flowery dresses, and blouses in loud Op Art fabrics or old-fashioned grandma-style patterns with lots of frills; miniskirts and matching pantyhose in all designs and colors; shoes and boots in patent leather. Anything that the fashionable heart required could be found in Carnaby Street. Fashion-conscious men, too, could acquire a stylish wardrobe here. At the beginning of the decade John Stephen opened the first men's fashion boutique in Carnaby Street. Although he initially kept to the classic model of suit and tie, he updated it considerably by adding more color and flair. At the time men tended to think of brightly colored clothing as being rather feminine. To counteract this Stephen used strongly masculine models such as boxer Billy Walker or prominent musicians from the then popular groups the Moody Blues and the Kinks to pose in his crushed velvet trousers, leather vests, and frilled shirts. By the mid-1960s Carnaby Street was lined with men's boutiques, nine of which belonged to Stephen.

"Swinging London"

During London Fashion Week, which was first established in 1959, British fashion designers display their ready-to-wear and haute couture collections. For several decades British fashion had produced some important designers, such as Lucile, Worth, and Captain Molyneux (even though they all worked in Paris), and royal tailors Norman Hartnell and Hardy Amies. However, only in the 1960s did British fashion become the international avant-garde and a rival to French fashion. Mary Quant, Barbara Hulanicki, who founded Biba, Ossie Clark, and many others who are today unknown became fashion trendsetters not only in Britain but throughout Europe. Anybody who wanted to know what was "in" looked to Swinging London. The English haute couture tradition continued at the same time, influenced far less by young trends of the time than the French fashion houses were, and producing made-to-measure classics for well-heeled older women.

Mary Quant

Mary Quant, born in 1934, is regarded as the inventor of the miniskirt, alongside French couturier André Courrèges. The truth probably lies in a remark by Mary Quant that it was neither she nor Courrèges who invented the miniskirt, but the girls on the street.

Mary Quant found the style of the 1950s too grown-up and too boring. Already in the mid-1950s she had opened her first store in London and, as she could not find the kind of clothes she wanted to sell, she began to make her own designs. From the beginning she was inspired by popular culture so that

Football minidress by Mary Quant, 1967

This minidress in stretch fabric is given a sporty look by the white trim clearly inspired by the shirts of English soccer players. With this design, worn here with dark ballet pantyhose of stronger material than nylon stockings, Mary Quant launched a casual variation of the omnipresent mini under her label Ginger Group.

Tomato Soup Dress by Andy Warhol, 1966/67, in printed paper. Museum at the Fashion Institute of Technology, New York

With his design of his faintly A-line minidress, Andy Warhol delivered Pop Art's message in two ways. First, in his famous graphics, he irritated the observer by elevating a can of soup to the status of a work of art; secondly, his use of paper, a strong but flammable material, can be interpreted as a critical comment on Western consumer society. The tomato soup can, now a museum piece, reappeared in a new edition in the 1990s on dresses by Jean Charles de Castelbajac, which were printed with Warhol motifs.

she could create a fashion that related to young people's lives. In doing this she made a point of referring to English tailoring tradition, which entered her own designs. This double inspiration is characteristic of many current British designers, for the creations of Vivienne Westwood or John Galliano would also be inconceivable without references to both fashion history in general and British tailoring tradition in particular. Mary Quant got her break in 1963, when some of her short tunic dresses were shown in *Vogue*. Her finger was on the pulse of that time. She no longer distinguished between daywear and eveningwear and rejected seasonal fashion

production. Instead she introduced new designs throughout the year. Her innovative ideas, such as PVC raincoats, knickerbockers for young women, and large shoulder bags, rapidly spread throughout Europe.

Quant's miniskirt, introduced in the mid-1960s, was an immediate hit, even though many raged against it and condemned it as indecent. Coco Chanel claimed that the knee was the least attractive feature of a woman and that it was best kept hidden. Nevertheless, as the 1960s went on, skirts for all ages grew shorter and shorter until they barely covered the bottom. The fashion in extreme minis was made possible not least by the invention of seamless pantyhose, which now came onto the market in all conceivable patterns and colors. This eye-catching legwear became a crucial part of the fashionable look.

Biba

Like Mary Quant and other designers of the 1960s, Barbara Hulanicki found the fashion of the 1950s much too "old" and wanted to play a part in revolutionizing it. She founded Biba, the first mail-order business for avant-garde young fashion. Her creations came in gentle colors and were inspired by romanticism and nostalgia, sometimes by exotica, and she stood in clear contrast to the futuristic fashion of many 1960s designers such as Courrèges or Cardin. Her severely cut pantsuits were printed with huge rose patterns or made in figure-hugging velvet; long dresses with wide sleeves had to be complemented by old-fashioned velvet chokers and a mane of hair. Biba was the first to sell dresses in midi and maxi lengths, hitting exactly the right time for nostalgia. However, the department store in the Art Deco style that Barbara Hulanicki opened in 1973 was forced to close in 1975.

Laura Ashley

Laura Ashley's timeless-romantic style also developed in the 1960s. She had begun as a fabric and wallpaper designer, and under the influence of hippie fashion moved over to designing clothes in an ultrafeminine, country-house style. Flowery prints, frills, wide skirts and short, close-fitting jackets characterize the typical Ashley style even today. Today Laura Ashley clothes are sold worldwide and the style continues to adhere only faintly to current fashion trends.

Fashion and art

Op Art, Pop Art, rock music, the Beatles – the arts too were dominated by the experimental, a break with the old, the search for the spectacularly new. Anything that was fast, could be reproduced, and was consumer-friendly was turned into a concept. The different art forms of the time were characterized by a clear tendency to overcome any fixed distinction between high and low culture. Irreverently, the Beatles had a string orchestra play the backing to their music, and the controversial but internationally recognized Pop artist Andy Warhol produced records with Velvet Underground, for whom – as later for the Rolling Stones – he

designed the album covers. He painted tomato soup cans with supermarket-realism and, to the dismay of "normal" educated society, declared the result to be art.

Serial reproduction was elevated to an artistic principle, as were photographic realism and screen printing. The aura of the unique work of art gave way to a new understanding of art and the artist's task in industrial society; subject and technique were made to adapt to the changing world. The happening was a totally new form of representation, which was absolutely in the present; both antimuseum and shocking, it also intended to bring high art and everyday life closer together. The new realism presented lifelike imitations of people and objects, while Victor Vasarely's Op Art confused the eye of the observer by employing optical illusions. Like that of other

Pierre Cardin's Space Collection, 1968

A frequent motif in Pierre Cardin's Space Collection of 1968 was the dresses with windows – cuts and openings over a black background – which emphasized the contrasting colors of the materials.

Cardine, a special fiber developed by Cardin, helped to keep the shape of the openings, whose outline was often complex. The forms of these windows on the overlying material are reminiscent of the motifs on the costumes worn in the popular science-fiction series *Star Trek*, and the colors and designs in hard lines show a similarity to futuristic creations.

The men's collection is characterized by square, one-color suits, with chunky zippers as decoration and large silver belt buckles. The ladies' clothing further included bodysuits, knee-length black boots, and helmets worn over smooth, short hair.

the front of a dress, presented visual surprises and made the dresses appear highly contemporary. Modernity was experienced through the shock of the new and spectacular, and seemed to have become more important than beauty in the traditional sense.

Futuristic fashion

Futuristic fashion emerged as an opposite to hippie fashion, and found its adherents especially among French fashion designers. A similarity to the flower-power style perhaps lay in the imagination underlying the designs, but in form they were worlds apart. At a time when beatniks were attracted by science fiction in literature and film, and the first moon landing was being planned, there was also an attempt in fashion to introduce elements of a utopian, fully technologized world, or of outer space.

André Courrèges vied with Mary Quant for the title of inventor of the miniskirt. It was definitely Courrèges who made the mini acceptable to haute couture, and he who came to epitomize 1960s haute couture. His short dresses with their strict geometrical lines and strong materials, only loosely fitted and often without a waist, won as much praise as his leather and patent leather jackets, his white ankle boots, which were worn all year round both with pants and with dresses, and his astronaut-style headwear under which the wearer's face was hardly recognizable. Courrèges made women's pants the basic piece of clothing for every occasion. However, he no longer followed the lines of men's pants but created hipsters, slimline straight pants which were combined with sharply cut, short tops revealing the waist. He offered tight knitted all-in-one pantsuits and designed all-in-ones with short pants.

Caroline Rennolds Milbank described Courrèges as the Le Corbusier of fashion, pointing to the sense of proportion which Courrèges, trained as a construction engineer, had developed during his apprenticeship with Balenciaga. Absolute simplicity of design together with obvious functionality gave Courrèges' fashion its futuristic appearance. His preferred colors – white, pink, turquoise, ice blue – and simple, clear patterns (wide stripes, checks, or abstract flowers) made his style unmistakable and revolutionized fashion: his clothes appeared as the perfect

Paco Rabanne with a model in a dress made of aluminum platelets, 1968

With his utopian collections Paco Rabanne too showed his enthusiasm for science-fiction esthetics. He joined up aluminum or plastic platelets with chain links to create fashionable dresses in heavy textures and completed the outfit with the quintessential fashion article of the 1960s: pantyhose with totally new optical effects, hints of technology always matching the dress.

artistic tendencies, his vocabulary of geometric forms found its way into fashion.

Yves Saint Laurent caused a particular furore with his collections which borrowed from classic modern art styles and contemporary movements. A famous 1965 collection featured straight-cut jersey dresses made of pieces of material arranged so as to look like pictures by Dutch artist Piet Mondrian. According to Saint Laurent, these severe geometrical forms perfectly fitted the female body. Indeed, the dresses look anything but shapeless. Saint Laurent's series of Pop Art dresses were in turn inspired by the paintings of Andy Warhol and Roy Lichtenstein. Large-scale patterns on straight, short dresses in bright, unbroken colors, or trompe-l'oeil effects such as body silhouette in profile on expression of the age of space travel, which people thought they were living in.

After studying architecture, Paco Rabanne also worked with Balenciaga. With the plastic and metal dresses that he first showed in 1965 he introduced an entirely new material to fashion; it was meant to be contemporary and point to the future but in the end it failed to make an impression. Dresses made of metal plates or rings, or molded in metal or plastic, were his trademark, albeit one that can really only be admired in museums today. For however futuristic they looked (and sometimes they simultaneously recalled the chain mail of medieval armor), his fashion was not as wearable as Courrèges' creations. Nevertheless, the science fiction movie *Barbarella* (1968), based on the comic of the

Paris restaurant of which he had a replica built in Beijing, and is also an interior designer.

He was the first Western designer who later, at the end of the 1970s, was allowed to display a collection in China. His fashion designs reached their apogee in the 1950s and 1960s. Cardin reveled in the space look and designed dresses with round spy-holes at the waist, helmetlike headwear, and boots. He used new materials such as vinyl and let wild zigzag patterns run across his miniskirts and dresses.

The transparent look

The fashion for short skirts and exposed waists soon extended to a fashion for transparent clothes, which in the age of newly developed synthetics were often made

same name, with Jane Fonda as lead actress and "model," was proof of how well Rabanne's extravagant costume designs were suited to illustrating futuristic fantasy.

Pierre Cardin

Pierre Cardin was one of the first fashion designers to interpret the signs of the time correctly. Already at the end of the 1950s he was working for department stores, and he installed departments for his own collections. He made licensing contracts worldwide and so built up a gigantic fashion emporium that sells far more than fashion and cosmetics: ballpoint pens, porcelain, watches, bicycles, chocolate, and much more. Cardin is the owner of theaters and restaurants, including Maxim's, the famous

of plastic or finely woven artificial fibers. In winter 1968 Saint Laurent showed a floor-length evening gown of transparent black muslin. Ostrich feathers attached to the waist hung down to mid-thigh, and there were no other accessories but a gold snake belt. In the late 1960s Courrèges created organza dresses with blossoms or geometric shapes attached at the most intimate points. The most wearable were transparent blouses, which often had frills on the sleeves or at the neckline and which were available in many different designs.

Like flares, ethnic clothing, or PVC dresses, transparent fashion was part of the wide-ranging repertoire of the 1960s, which designers have returned to again and again, most recently in the 1990s.

André Courrèges, winter 1968/69

Among the fashion designers of the 1960s, André Courrèges was probably the one most dedicated to space-age fashion. The models are wrapped in short capes with concealed fastenings and wear astronaut's caps with slits for the eyes and – a Courrèges trademark – white boots. Underneath is a bodystocking, which was also an ideal basic piece that could be combined with miniskirts or pocket belts which resembled loincloths.

Decorative accessory for the gentleman

THE NECKTIE

The necktie is a classic piece of men's clothing that evolved from the protective scarf. Over the centuries the necktie developed into a decorative accessory for the otherwise fairly uniform style of men's clothing in the Western world. While other forms of decoration around the neck are not appropriate for every occasion and do not suit every man, the conventional long necktie is still an integral part of the contemporary suit and takes a wide variety of colors, patterns, and materials.

Giovanni Boldini, **Robert Comte de Montesquiou-Fezensac**, 1897

Below: two examples from an American advertisement for neckties, 1940s

The origin of the necktie

The necktie is not one of the oldest fashion creations in history, as it is among the few articles of clothing that do not serve to protect against cold or other inclement conditions. In ancient China and Rome a cloth was wrapped around the neck to give protection against the cold. In Europe, the history of the cravatlike neck scarf presumably began in Rome.

Already more than 2000 years ago, Roman soldiers wore a focale, a cloth that was dipped in water when it was hot and wrapped around the neck for cooling. The focale continues to live on today in the form of the plastron, a puffed-up silk scarf held together by a pin that is worn particularly in Italy on festive occasions.

The real history of the necktie only began when the function of neckwear shifted from protection to decoration. At what point this occurred cannot definitively be established. One theory has it that in 1660 Croatian soldiers in the service of Austria arrived in France with muslin or linen scarves flung around their necks. The ends were either bunched up into rosettes or were decorated with tassels. The French named these neckties croates, for the Croatians, and the term soon became cravates.

Other fashion historians argue against this derivation of the term, claiming that the word already existed in the 14th century and that, for example, the Italian copperplate engraver Cesare Vecellio referred to the Roman focale as a cravata in 1590. In any case, the cravat spread throughout the land in the century of Louis XIV, either made of simple cloth or even of lace, which was liberally added.

The triumphant progress of the tie was temporarily halted by the French Revolution, when not only were knee-length pants outlawed (hence the term sansculottes) but also the neck was liberated from any restriction. Shortly afterward, around 1800, the dandy Beau Brummel, who had his cravats starched, introduced the tie to London. The cravat must have taken an extraordinary upturn at the time, for French novelist Honoré de Balzac later wrote about the nonsensical fashion for cravats: "Some wrapped whole pieces of muslin around their neck, others virtually covered it with a quilted cushion, to which some handkerchiefs were attached just to top it all off."

Ties and knots

Only in the 19th century did the necktie assume the shape that it has today. Since the 1940s the shirt collar has been turned over the tie. This led to simpler forms. In the 1860s loose loops were superseded by the knot, and the necktie became ever longer. However, the elegant loop did not disappear but lives on as the bow tie, so that the length-knotted tie brought about the cross-knotted tie.

Left: ties from the house of Hermès, 1980s and 1990s

Bow tie with paisley pattern, c. 1966

With its general spread, the necktie became the quintessential sign of masculinity. In a modern society that had replaced archaic rites of socialization with civilized procedures, the correct knotting of the necktie developed into a sign of being a man. Knotting a tie turned into a real initiation ritual that had to be undergone before confirmation, in the army, or at the very latest before marriage. Even though at the start of the millennium the knotting of the tie has mostly lost its status of a cultural technique, Balzac's adage was nevertheless valid for about 150 years: A man's intelligence shows itself in his ability to knot his necktie." This is presumably also a reason for the short life of the clip-on tie of the postwar years; it did not need to be knotted but could simply be hooked onto the front of the shirt collar with a metal clip.

Ladies' neckties

The necktie speaks volumes not only about men, but on occasion also about women. Already in the 19th century, and again in the 1920s and 1960s, a woman's spirit showed itself in her courage to wear a tie. Just as women taking over men's jobs was seen as scandalous, the cross-gender tendencies of female fashion and the adaptation of pants, tuxedo, and necktie were regarded by many as an unnatural appropriation of male symbols. Although pants had already established themselves as workwear in World War I, it still took an emancipated woman like Marlene Dietrich to stake women's claims to men's fashion. However, the necktie for women never succeeded in making a real breakthrough, although designers have, periodically, introduced neckties into their womenswear collections. Perhaps women do not feel the need to adopt the conservative formal wear that so restricts a man's wardrobe. Also, the attraction of the necktie for women is likely to have decreased because today a woman no longer needs a necktie to prove that she is her own person.

Dots, stripes, and paisley

As the necktie is the most important and often the only form of decoration for the man, it is more prone to fashion dictates than the shirt or the suit. For instance, the exotic motifs and loud colors of the 1920s were succeeded in the 1930s by muted colors in the Windsor style, while in the 1940s, particularly in the United States, designs with object-based motifs were extremely popular. The garish designs of the 1970s were followed by more subtle colors and more discreet patterns in the 1980s and the 1990s. Paisley patterns, seen frequently toward the end of the 1980s, were replaced by animal motifs or by geometrical all-over designs.

The cut and the material were also directed by fashion. While at the beginning of the 1970s a necktie as broad as a hand (known as the kipper tie) and covered in large spots was entirely acceptable even for businessmen, a decade later leather ties less than 2 inches wide were worn again. During the 1980s ties settled at an average width of 3½ inches. In Italy, the leader in men's fashion and necktie manufacture, ties since the late 1990s are about 3½ inches wide and about 55 inches long. Silks are the materials most used, with wool or cashmere sometimes used for winter wear. In Italy there is also a trend for dévoré velvet, which gives the tie a three-dimensional appearance.

The choice of color, fabric, and pattern of a necktie, and way that it is knotted depend on the suit and shirt with which it is worn. A wide-winged collar calls for a broadly tied knot, while a button-down collar requires a tighter knot. Generally, with a relaxation in the once-strict formalities of men's dress, there is also greater freedom in the choice of necktie. Although the necktie remains the most important neck decoration for the man – ahead of the bow tie, plastron, and scarf – it is obvious that it is going out of fashion. Already the student movements of the 1960s demanded a slackening of the rules of dress. The most prominent victim of these demands was the necktie, which today is scorned by students and tends only to be worn at business meetings and formal or festive occasions: the phrase "ties must be worn" has largely disappeared from our vocabulary.

Necktie fashion for ladies, 1967

The correctly knotted necktie for a wide-winged collar

Knits and flares

Flower power

1970–1979

Politics as lifestyle

The 1970s were marked by the politicization of public life, brought about particularly by the younger generation. Global problems, such as the East–West conflict and the resulting arms race, as well as environmental issues caused ripples made by the student unrest of 1968 to spread ever further outward – finally reaching the extremist positions taken up by terrorists in Europe.

It was not only the world order that had become problematical; social structure was another core issue in the 1970s. There were several attempts at finding alternatives to the traditional way of life. Drugs, "free love," and communes played an important part in that quest, and the women's movement also had a decisive influence at the time.

In this decade fashion defined itself as a democratic means of expressing opinion. Of course, there were interesting developments in the world of haute couture: many of today's greatest fashion designers, such as Thierry Mugler, Kenzo, Issey Miyake, Vivienne Westwood, and Ralph Lauren, began their careers at this time. However, it was the hippie movement that, with its environmentally aware and antiestablishment clothing, made the greatest mark on fashion in the 1970s and even into the 1980s.

Feminism regarded fashion in itself as an element of the patriarchal system, so that committed women often preferred a kind of antifashion, which expressed itself differently in different countries. The significance of the styles chosen by political and social protesters in the 1970s becomes very clear when one sees how many of its elements were adopted by fashion in general.

Pure nature – handmade

Back to nature. The beginning of the oil crisis was one of the things that prompted young women, and men too, to take up the adage that natural is best and reach for knitting or crochet needles. Anything that could be worn – from the cardigan, the woolly hat, and the giant shawl to the floor-length dress with matching scarf – was crocheted or knitted, as were furnishings such as blankets and cushions, curtains and lampshades. Hints and instructions on making clothes and furniture became a key theme of many columns in fashion magazines.

This all-embracing "natural" ambiance included simple wooden furniture and paper lamps: on the basis of this ethos, a Swedish furniture company was able to launch itself, and is now a firm with international outlets.

The trend for home knitting left its mark on haute couture, too. Sonia Rykiel, today among the most important French fashion designers, became famous at the time through her highly elegant, ultrafeminine, and very fine knitwear. This range had nothing in common with the robust leisurewear and

---

1970 During protests against the Vietnam War, four students are shot dead by soldiers at Kent State University, Ohio. The German terrorist group RAF makes its first active appearance. Invention of the videotape. Marxist Salvador Allende is elected president of Chile.

1971 Idi Amin comes to power in Uganda after a military coup. Willy Brandt is awarded the Nobel Peace Prize. Stanley Kubrick makes the movie *A Clockwork Orange*. Death of the jazz trumpeter Louis Armstrong.

1972 Olympic Games in Munich; Palestinian kidnappers murder two Israeli sportsmen. Worldwide protests against French nuclear trials on Mururoa atoll. In the United States the first computer game is released.

1973 End of the Vietnam War. Following a coup General Pinochet sets up a military dictatorship in Chile. An attack on Israel by Egyptian and Syrian troops leads to the Yom Kippur War. Cuts in Arab oil exports cause an international crisis. Death of artist Pablo Picasso.

1974 US president Nixon resigns after the Watergate scandal. Bob Dylan makes his first tour of the United States in eight years. Itzhak Rabin becomes prime minister of Israel.

1975 Dictator Francisco Franco dies, and Spain reverts to a monarchy under Juan Carlos. Bill Gates founds the company Microsoft. Premiere of

Milos Forman's movie *One Flew Over The Cuckoo's Nest*, starring Jack Nicholson. First Broadway performance of *A Chorus Line*. Socialists win the first free elections in Portugal.

1976 The United States celebrates 200 years of independence, and

Richard Rogers' and Renzo Piano's Centre National d'Art et de Culture Georges Pompidou, Paris 1971–77

Jimmy Carter is elected president. Death of Mao Zedong. Alex Haley's family chronicle *Roots* is published. Volkswagen opens a factory in the United States for the production of the Golf. Death of photographer Man Ray.

1977 Free elections in Spain. Palestinians hijack a German airplane in an attempt to force the release of imprisoned terrorists. Premiere of George Lucas' science fiction movie *Star Wars*. Death of Elvis Presley.

1978 Camp David agreement restores peace between Israel and Egypt. Polish priest Karol Wojtila becomes Pope John Paul II. The punk-rock singer Nina Hagen begins her career.

1979 Islamic revolution in Iran, and Ayatollah Khomeini comes to power. Hostages taken at the US embassy in Teheran. Mother Teresa is awarded the Nobel Peace Prize.

workwear with which anything knitted had previously been associated.

Not only knitted jackets and sweaters appeared, but also knitted suits, even pantsuits in the widest variations. For a while long knitted coats were fashionable, and knitted blazers replaced the somewhat stiffer fabric ones. Knitted dresses and lurex sweaters spelt casual evening chic rather than dressing up, which was looked down on at the time. It was not unusual to find knitted swimwear, knitted shoulder bags and even knitted ties.

Like crochet, patchwork achieves a colorful, simple, improvised, rural look and became increasingly fashionable. Its origins lie in the pioneer days of the United States, when settlers' wives created magical works of art out of the few materials and scraps that they had to hand. Patchwork was born of necessity, but it became so fashionable the world over in the 1970s that people no longer made the effort of sewing together the many little patches since the same effect was now produced as a printed pattern. Wide floor-length patchwork skirts harked back to simpler, supposedly better times and were considered very romantic.

Patchwork also found its way into haute couture. For instance, Yves Saint Laurent made great use of it in his Gypsy collection and even created patchwork fur coats.

Nostalgia and ethnic styles

Grandma shirts and long peasant skirts, gypsy skirts and Indian shawls, Bedouin clothes and Afghan coats: nostalgia style was booming. Everything that was a reminder of the fashions of the 19th and early 20th centuries was highly popular, as was anything suggesting peasant traditions from Europe and around the world. The result was a colorful mix that followed no one style entirely but took distinct elements from all of them. This colorful eclecticism developed in haute couture too. Again, mention must be made of Yves Saint Laurent, whose collections elevated the mix of styles to the level of the luxurious. Among others, his 1976 collection inspired by the Ballets Russes hit the headlines. Velvet and brocade in the colors of gold and precious stones were used to create voluptuous skirts with gold linings, Cossack coats, and traditional

Poncho with hood and knitted hot pants by Jacqueline and Elie Jacobson, founders of Dorothée Bis, from *Elle* 1970

Cheerful and uncomplicated fashion was the declared aim of Jacqueline and Elie Jacobson. They opened the boutique Dorothée in Paris at the beginning of the 1960s and, soon after, a second one under the name Dorothée Bis (roughly translatable as Dorothée II), which they adopted as their company name. Their Total Look consisted not only of clothes mostly made of knitted fabric, such as stockings and woolen caps, but also hats and knitted shirts, which were worn over pants. This ensemble shows tightfitting hot pants worn with matching long over-the-knee socks and a long, stripy poncho. The outfit is completed by sweater and hat of the same color. Typical of the Dorothée Bis range were the only slightly changing colors which featured again and again, the connecting element of the Total Look. From the beginning the company wanted to offer highly fashionable and wearable clothes that were affordable to a young clientele and focused on short-term trends.

Bulgarian jackets. Fur trimmings and hats, gold tassels, and other accessories added a French touch to Oriental luxury, matched by the heavy, sweet perfume Opium which Saint Laurent launched in 1977.

In the 1970s, a simpler style for teenagers with little money was the Indian look: floaty dresses of batiste silk, blouses with embroideries or prints of Indian inspiration, cheap scarves with Oriental patterns, and silver jewelry in an Indian style. All this was produced at little cost and reached every part of Europe, initially via London. Of course most of it was imitation, and some ideas were merely developed further into a European "art nouveau": crushed velvet jackets in simple designs with small pieces of mirror glass set into the embroidery, and "Indian" embroidery on ordinary cotton blouses are two such examples. Followers of these fashions loved incense sticks and anything that gave the everyday an exotic flavor.

Form without norm

From a fashion point of view, this derivation from earlier epochs and other cultures was a manifestation of an age of transition. The 1970s developed no real character of their

The folklore look, from *Elle*, 1970

In the 1960s and 1970s India and Pakistan were not only popular destinations for hippies. The jewelry and costumes of those countries also had a great influence on Western fashion. The long jacket with pants of printed muslin and edging at the seams as well as the thin blouse with wide sleeves have an Oriental flavor.

own; instead they took trends from the 1960s, developing these further and carrying them over into the 1980s, which more clearly stood out as different from, and free of, previous periods. Altogether, fashion became more casual and more influenced by leisurewear. Dress rules disappeared almost completely. Fashion had also become a somewhat antiauthoritarian area.

The importance of casualness in eveningwear can be seen at a glance. In style and overall outline evening clothes could hardly be distinguished from day clothes, except that dresses and skirts were often floor-length and the fabrics a little finer. This departure becomes clear when one considers eveningwear up to the middle of the 20th century. At the turn of the century there were types of clothes specifically intended for the evening which would have never been worn during the day. Even in the evening itself there were very exact differences in the clothes worn, depending

on the occasion. The cut of the dress, the depth of the neckline, the length of the sleeves, sweeping trains, and headwear in a variety of forms, quite apart from the splendor of the fabric, clearly marked a dress as being suitable for the theater, a ball, or dinner party. Even as late as the 1950s there were great evening gowns. These disappeared entirely in the 1970s. A shirt-dress became floor-length, as did the A-line skirt; perhaps both were in a slightly finer fabric than their counterparts in daywear, but otherwise there were practically no differences. Now even in the evening a skirt could be worn not only with a blouse but also with a knitted sweater, perhaps with gold threads worked into it.

Skirts and dresses

In the 1970s, the skirt and blouse became the standard outfit that could be worn on any occasion and at any time of day and that was regarded as highly practical. At first, blouses were usually simple tight shirts or polo shirts, but over time these were joined by more romantic versions.

Around 1970 skirts were shorter than ever before, often hardly even covering the behind. A counter-movement promptly came into existence: the first calf-length skirts – known as midis – came onto the market. They were usually A-line and made of four strips of fabric, so no longer had the totally straight shape of the 1960s. They were often combined with waist-length sweaters or jackets, which were sometimes lined with artificial fur and featured a hood, a particularly popular type of collar or head-covering taken from sportswear and leisurewear.

Initially the midi made little impact, as women had developed a taste for short skirts and regarded them as more youthful than the mid-length skirts whose cut made them appear rather stiff. The floor-length coat was more acceptable, and the contrast between a miniskirt and a maxicoat was considered particularly successful. Skirts with a line of buttons down the front offered a compromise; the buttons could be left undone as far as desired, so that the skirt would appear to decently cover the knee yet at the same time be provocatively revealing. By 1975 very short skirts were no longer fashionable, and the knee-length pleated

Yves Saint Laurent's Ballets Russes Collection, 1976/77

With his Russian collection Saint Laurent was at the very heart of the "natural" trend of the time though he gave it an exquisite note. The wide swinging sleeves, the wide gathered skirt, and the triangular shawl that even in everyday fashion often served as a jacket were based on peasant costumes. Gold embroidery and strong colors such as red, purple, and blue are reminiscent of traditional East European clothing.

skirt had taken its place. By comparison to previous styles pleated skirts looked quite correct and, at least from today's perspective, rather prim and conservative. They were made in jersey, tweed, or check woolen fabrics and were teamed with short knitted jackets, sweaters, or blouses sometimes worn with a sleeveless sweater over the top. Later gathered skirts came in, as well as skirts with intentional creases, sometimes with a saddle, too.

Around this time teenagers – as far as they wore skirts at all rather than jeans and nothing but – took to wearing floor-length skirts. These were designed on a perfectly circular pattern or consisted of four wide A-line panels; a later design consisted of overlapping layers of frills that got progressively wider toward the bottom. Skirts were preferably printed with flowery or patchwork patterns and were sometimes trimmed with lace. Not infrequently they were worn barefoot, even in the city, together with a romantic blouse, a wrap-around scarf, and long, straight hair – a look expressing the trend for nostalgia.

Only toward the middle of the decade did the dress length for fashion-conscious women of all ages finally settle just below the knee. Dresses were also given a different, bell-shaped form.

The development of dresses was similar to that of skirts. Teenagers preferred them floor-length, women knee-length. Particularly popular were shirt-dresses with belts, part of a basic wardrobe. By the middle of the decade they were replaced by jersey dresses. This soft fabric did not constrict the wearer's movement, was easy to care for, and could be used in softly falling, slightly frilled patterns which were considered both practical and attractive. Soon not only skirts but also tops consisted of layers or pleats falling from seams. Like jackets and other items of clothing, they were often unlined, so that they draped softly. The casual look and the gentle feeling on the skin were regarded highly, a preference also met by fabrics such as crushed velvet or soft polyester fibers whose comfort was far superior to the stiff perlon dresses and nylon shirts of the 1950s.

Some summer dresses were wrap-over, sleeveless, or had batwing or crescent-shaped sleeves. Altogether more skin was on show as

Evening dress with bolero by Hubert de Givenchy, 1972

This evening dress in red-and-white printed cotton shows the new midi length, which was regarded as the ideal compromise between mini and maxi. The simple A-line is complemented by the very short matching bolero jacket with short sleeves, making a smart and sophisticated statement characteristic of Givenchy. Since 1968 the designer had created young designs for sale in his store Givenchy Nouvelle Boutique, which matched his taste in extravagant designs especially well.

sleeveless dresses, sometimes with a halterneck, or even cylinders of elasticated fabric – known as boob tubes – were worn.

Blouses and jackets

Shirt-blouses and polo shirts were the usual tops, complemented by T-shirts and romantic grandma-style blouses later in the decade. The latter were quite freely based on the lines of blouses of the turn of the century. They had a high neckline, usually a breast panel set off by frills, and a stiff collar made of the same fabric as the blouse or of lace. The sleeves were often attached in folds, and in the extreme they were real jabot sleeves, long or half-length, ending either in a wide cuff or, depending on the blouse's overall shape, in a round bell. A less extreme, more classic and elegant form was popular to wear with suits, with a soft shape and high neckline and featuring a bow.

ITALIAN FASHION DESIGNERS

The success of Italian fashion in the 1950s and 1960s was guaranteed, especially by names such as Ferragamo, Pucci, Sorelle Fontana, Schuberth, and Gucci. Among today's Italian fashion houses whose stars have long been shining far beyond the borders of Italy are Versace, Armani, Prada – and again, Gucci.

Alta moda in the Palazzo Pitti

Italian haute couture's real success story starts in Rome after World War II. With its worldly atmosphere, the city could hardly keep the tourists at bay, and the American movie industry and fashion turned it into a frenetic business center. The demand for quality products grew. Shoes by Salvatore Ferragamo and leather goods by Gucci came into fashion and thus became the international epitome of Italian elegance. Photographs of artists, movie stars, and Italian couturiers were published around the world.

In 1951 Florence hosted the first fashion show, which Marchese Gian Battista Giorgini organized in his house. Giorgini invited the pioneers of "Made in Italy" to display their collections to a select audience consisting of foreign clients and journalists from the most important newspapers and magazines worldwide. All the great Italian fashion houses of international renown were represented.

So great was the success of the event that it was moved to the White Hall of the Palazzo Pitti, where it was held regularly, timed to fit in with the Parisian fashion calendar. It became the springboard for a new generation of fashion designers. In the 1950s the collections of Emilio Pucci, the man who gave us Capri pants, appeared there, among others, while in 1964 Krizia and in 1966 Missoni displayed their prêt-à-porter collections there.

In the 1970s many long-established studios in Italy had to close their doors. Their creations were conceptually interesting but did not follow prevailing trends, and no longer appealed, particularly to the young. The oil crisis also played its part in forcing the Italians to limit their expenditure.

Valentino was highly successful on an international level, his luxurious and elegantly opulent style appealing particularly to his American customers.

However, several fashion houses discovered another source of income in the 1970s: the prêt-à-porter industry, which produced the secondary collections. The marketing of perfumes, spectacles, leather goods, textiles, household goods, and so on, under their own name also helped some houses in economic decline to take a new upward swing.

Milan and the trendsetters of the 1980s

The success of Italian designer fashion in the 1980s was due above all to clever marketing strategies. One man in particular was responsible for the rise of Milan, traditionally the industrial center of Italy, above Rome and Florence at the end of the 1970s: sensing that the world of designers should be brought together with the textile industry, Milanese businessman Beppe Modenese organized the first fashion show at the exhibition center in Milan.

After this successful dress rehearsal with more than 40 designers from home and abroad, an increasing number of important events of the international fashion scene established themselves in Milan. There

Designs by Sorelle Fontana on the catwalk at the Palazzo Pitti, 1973

could hardly be any better advertisement for Italian creators of fashion.

The 1980s were the decade of great contrast, seemingly a world of excess, but at the same time an arena for a variety of new products and creative tendencies. A great part of the Italian fashion designers' success in this decade went to Giorgio Armani. With elegantly crumpled fabrics he created a style that seduces by simplicity – and blurs the differences between male and female. The Armani woman took on certain clothes that up until then had been exclusively masculine, such as the blazer, while the range of both colors and cuts for men broadened. To imagine men's leisurewear today without the sweaters with the typical eagle logo, the casual leather jackets, and the jeans is well nigh impossible. The particular trademark of Armani design is the classic suit, which has left its stamp on both men's and women' fashion.

The career of the couple Rosita and Ottavio Missoni is another great success story of Italian fashion design. Throwing off knitwear's conservative image, they elevated it to an art form. Indeed, some of their designs have already been exhibited in New York's Metropolitan Museum of Art. Missoni patterns are always unmistakable, even if the cuts and the colors of the collections follow current fashion. Missoni's single colors are created through numerous dyeing processes and, in turn, the exciting wave patterns, zigzags, and lines inspired by African cultures and Op Art are created by a complicated combination of several differently dyed yarns.

Left: Emilio Schuberth with models, 1954

Summer suit by Giorgio Armani, 1996

When in 1989 Gianfranco Ferré was appointed design director of Dior, the French fashion scene in particular regarded this as scandalous – an Italian as a designer with Dior! In spite of many critical voices he was able to prove that the sober functionality and simple elegance of his style and Dior's tendency toward the luxurious could be combined in a successful synthesis. Originally working as an architect, Ferré introduced his own label in 1978 and began with an

internationally noted moda pronta (ready-to-wear) collection. In 1986 he moved up to haute couture, smoothing his way to Paris, where he stayed until 1996. With the death of Gianni Versace in July 1997 the international fashion world lost a highly creative designer. Versace learned tailoring in his mother's studio. In 1978 he founded his own business and in the 1980s became one of the greatest designers on the international fashion scene. The particularity of his style manifested itself in the free combination of the patterns, colors, and shapes of the art styles of different periods – from antiquity via the Renaissance and the Baroque to Futurism. For him fabrics were the way of shaping the body so that its pulsating vivacity comes to the fore. However, as well as the extravagant designs rich in colors and patterns there is a rather purist, reduced line which shows itself in his elegant and timeless, often totally black evening gowns, for instance. What marks all the diverse styles of the Versace company is the deliberate eroticism of the designs, and this applies to both women's and men's fashion.

Another big name in Italian fashion is connected with pop star Madonna. During her concert tour in 1993, Madonna wore Dolce & Gabbana, whose designers went for the secondhand look and therefore gave their collection a nostalgic flavor. Domenico Dolce, whose background is in tailoring, and graphic artist Stefano Gabbana presented their first "slut chic" collection in Milan in 1986. It comes as no great surprise that such a woman as Madonna was taken by Dolce & Gabbana's fashion: after all, both designers celebrate the erotic charisma of such full-blooded women. It was precisely for her that they designed their collections, with the sequined or pearly corsets, black pantyhose, and lacy underwear worn as outerwear. In their clothes the connection between eroticism and glamour takes a central position and moves between fetishism and high-class sensuality.

The great rivals: Gucci and Prada

Part of the great Italian fashion phenomenon of the 1990s were two fashion houses with a rich tradition: Gucci and Prada. Up until the early 1990s Gucci had been particularly famous for its accessories, which encompassed leather goods, moccasins, silk scarves, neckties, and glasses. The company went into decline, but rose like a phoenix from the ashes in 1994 with the support of American designer Tom Ford. He managed to increase the high-class brand's profits within a few years. Ford regarded his revival of 1950s style – mostly in high-

tech materials – not merely as simple imitation but as the reinterpretation of a fashion direction in the spirit of the cool 1990s, and it found great appeal even in the cheapest of mass fashion. In spring 1999 Tom Ford looked back to Gucci's traditions and presented leather, although rather unconventionally for the classy trademark in the form of peasant dresses with provocative leather tops, worn under a fur coat.

Prada too was originally a traditional leather brand until Miuccia Prada, niece of Mario Prada, who had founded the company in 1913, joined it at the end of the 1970s. After successful designs of rucksacks and bags she boldly produced her first prêt-à-porter collection in 1985. However, her great breakthrough came only in 1995. She initially drew the inspiration for her designs from the patterns of plastic tablecloths or curtains of the 1950s. With this she has been successful particularly with the younger generation of women.

In the fall of 1999 Prada caused an international furore with its financial backing of German designer Jil Sander. Prada appears to have understood that those who want to be top players have to be big.

Left: Gianni Versace, spring/summer 1991

Right: Valentino, fall/winter 1998/99

Sonia Rykiel, winter 1976 collection

In Paris, Sonia Rykiel is called the Queen of Knits. It is mainly thanks to her that casual, elegant knitwear gained a reputation beyond sport fashion and today is equal to woven fabrics. In this, her philosophy is as simple as it is revolutionary for the fashion industry. Instead of following the typically short-lived trends of the moment, she always designs her avant-garde knitted clothes in compatible, harmonious colors. In this way many of her designs from older collections can be used in new combinations. As with this suit in a soft, ivory-colored fabric, many of her pieces allow a different look to be created for different occasions. Changing its look through the accessories chosen, the suit can be worn during the day, for example in the office, or also as an elegant evening suit.

Blouses too were wrap-over and had floating, batwing sleeves. Rough painters' overalls might be embroidered and teamed with pants or skirts. Wooden clogs were worn with this combination.

Waist-length jackets in bright colors, sometimes in woodcutters' checks, made of plush or Afghan-style sheepskin, unworsted wool or jersey was appropriate. In the evening the same cut could be worn in more elegant, sometimes shiny fabrics.

Knitted jackets were seen everywhere and on all occasions, elegant or sporty, mostly belted, with pants or replacing the suit jacket, sometimes with hoods or unusual collars which left the bourgeois knitted jacket of old times far behind. Blazers made of corduroy or checked fabric were preferred, trevira in summer, wool mixtures in winter.

Afghan jackets and coats taken from less formal antifashion were soon regarded as progressive. They were made of suede, usually had a tight waist, were often embroidered, and had a shaggy fur lining, cuffs, and collars. Worn with jeans, parkas were also regarded as a rejection of fashion. The thickly padded knee-length jackets in camouflage colors were hard-wearing and functional because of their many pockets, but most especially they had become popular as an expression of protest against military activity in the world.

Pants

In the 1970s pantsuits for women finally became socially acceptable. Pantsuits for day wear were made of corduroy, tweed, or velvet, or even knitted fabrics, while for eveningwear georgette or silk fibers were often used. Yves Saint Laurent broke new ground here too, with his smoking jackets for women which today are an unmissable part of all his collections.

Pants that hung from the hip, with widely flared, often turned-up legs, gave both women and men a figure between slim and lanky and later became for many the essence of 1970s fashion. Toward the end of the decade bell-bottoms were replaced by tighter legs; however, these were balanced by comfortable pleats at the top. The shape of the 1980s was announcing itself. Jeans had long been a fashion item, their cut adapting to the prevailing trend. Denim was now so popular that gradually all pieces of a wardrobe were available in that strong fabric, as were accessories; everything from the denim shoe via the cap to the shoulder bag were produced in this near-indestructible material.

At the beginning of the 1970s, hot pants – short, skin-tight shorts – were a hit with very young, slim women, although the word "shorts," suggesting conservative leisurewear, was regarded as an insult to this extremely tight-fitting piece of fashionable clothing. Hot pants were not limited to summer but, made in warm woolen fabrics, were also worn in winter together with woolen stockings. For the evening appropriate versions in finer fabrics were available. Particularly fashionable was the combination of hot pants, or the miniskirt, with often extremely long PVC boots – an element that was revived in the 1990s fashion.

Accessories

The punchy colors of the 1960s – bright green, yellow, orange – remained fashionable for a while in different variations. Gradually they were replaced by darker, more muted colors. Brown, of all imaginable shades, often still combined with orange and moss green, dominated entire collections and even interior decoration: homes were full of brown, orange, and moss green furniture and materials, while bathroom tiles, floors, and crockery were covered in large patterns in these colors. Aubergine was very up-to-the-minute for a season, and in the middle of the decade all variations of purple became fashionable. Color coordination made its entrance: jacket and skirt, shoes and handbag were preferred in the same color or at least the same shade.

At the beginning of the 1970s platform soles on sandals as well as boots were still regarded as unbeatably chic. Shoes were broad and squarish, and had clumpy heels. Patent leather was frequently used, in all possible shades but especially in white. Over the decade shoes became increasingly slimmer, platform soles disappeared, and heels became somewhat narrower and higher. Buckled T-bar shoes were a rival to pumps, while boots remained fashionable and worn with bell-shaped skirts were a must in winter. Wooden clogs worn with turned-up pants, especially corduroys or jeans, were particularly popular but they were also considered appropriate with skirts. Unlike in the 1960s, pantyhose came in mostly quiet patterns and colors and were chosen to match the dress.

For the first time, glasses became a fashion accessory, no longer carrying a stigma as in the 1950s and 1960s. There was now a greater choice in shapes, and the colors of the frames, such as white, pink, and light blue, and no longer just black and brown as before, also became more modern. Even colored glass came onto the market; it gave the wearer an especially garish appearance, particularly in pink or yellow. The frames and glasses were usually very large and often covered nearly half the face.

Men's hair in the 1970s was still fairly long: it tended to go over the collar. Women's magazines often offered tips for the well-groomed male, with hairstyle suggestions that could of course only be passed on to him by his wife or girlfriend, the actual reader of the magazine. At the beginning of the decade long wide sideburns were very in.

Women too wore their hair a little longer again. The style of the moment for teenagers

and those who wanted to appear really young was long, straight, and preferably blonde. Rather more elegant and adult were hairstyles of medium length: the bob, smooth or curling outward at the ends, or the pageboy, which was especially flattering to broad faces. Blow-dried or air-dried styles took precedence over curlers, which were regarded as square. There was a movement against appearing dressed up: naturalness

Man's suit by Brioni, 1978

Gaetano Savini Brioni has been a couturier since 1944 and has always worked toward combining classic elegance with a fashionable look. True to Roman style, the length and wide lapels of the double-breasted jacket and the conspicuous check pattern make it an up-to-the-minute 1970s creation. Hats had all but disappeared from the everyday wardrobe, but were still part of the outfit of a perfectly dressed gentleman.

John Travolta in *Saturday Night Fever*, 1977

In striking this pose John Travolta personified disco – striding elegantly, reaching for the stars in disco heaven, and wearing a white stretch suit by Norma Kamali, he dances to the Bee Gees with Karen Lynn Gorney in a floaty dress. The British band's double album sold more than 40 million copies and accompanied the boom in tightly cut suits with wide lapels over long shirt collars and with flares loosely covering high-heeled ankle boots. In 1998, as part of the 1970s revival, movie producer Robert Stigwood successfully brought *Saturday Night Fever* to the stage in the form of a musical.

reigned supreme. Even perms had to appear as natural as possible, which is why they were worn as Afros. Although women in photographs of the time now seem obviously styled and much more artificial, in comparison to the 1960s there was a definite trend toward greater naturalness.

Zandra Rhodes' Conceptual Chic collection, 1977

Rhodes' jersey dresses are clearly inspired by punk, but they move beyond it with style and elegance. Instead of holding together scraps of clothing with safety pins, the tear and needle here become a decorative style accessory, while the holes almost have the appearance of Flemish lacework. They reveal the shoulders and are emphasized by pearl embroidery. The carefully draped fabric also shows Rhodes' playful handling of punk.

The change in the ideal of beauty also manifested itself in a change of models: Lauren Hutton took over from Twiggy. With charming imperfections, such as the gap between her front teeth, she embodied the new, more natural ideal of a woman.

Shawls crocheted in thin or thick wool were joined by scarves made of artificial fibers which looked crocheted but which had a silky sheen and a very fine appearance. In the 1970s, both fashionable and more alternative men and women wore endlessly long scarves tightly wrapped around the neck, with the ends, usually lengthened even more by fringes, hanging down to the knee. Colorfully striped, knitted or crocheted, in printed silk or cotton, they were an indispensable part of a fashionable outfit.

Teenagers of the 1970s wore costume jewelry of Indian inspiration, such as silver rings, available in boutiques, but more particularly silver or multicolored necklaces and bracelets. Older people wore classic, timeless pieces or modern designs à la Lapponia, the Finnish jewelry firm that based designs on organic forms combined with geometric shapes.

Separates

The fashion theme of the time was separates, a wardrobe of various items – skirts, blouses, jackets, pants, sweaters – in mutually compatible colors and fabrics which could be combined in many variations. Separates made it easier to dress for various occasions, as often one had only to change one piece and choose the accessories designed to match in order to be appropriately attired.

Haute couture

The 1970s were not strong in haute couture. There were many short-lived trends, while the idea of fashionable clothing and its meaning was questioned and undermined from many different directions. Some of the established fashion houses retreated into the background a little, while a number of newcomers such as Giorgio Armani, Kenzo, Karl Lagerfeld, and Jean Charles de Castelbajac made a name for themselves in the 1970s with ready-to-wear collections.

Jean Muir's luxurious jersey and suede collections reflect the soft style of the 1970s that was regarded as appropriate and comfortable in all variations and for all occasions. She said of herself that her training in ballet gave her a sense of the human body in motion, and she tried to express this in her designs. Using polished cutting techniques she produced soft, flowing, yet always clear and disciplined shapes: dresses, tunics, pantsuits, and coordinates.

Zandra Rhodes' luxury is of a kind totally different from that of Jean Muir or Yves Saint

Laurent. Her fashion can be conceived as a highly refined and even more romanticized version of the ethnic look. She was born in 1940 and trained as a textile designer. Finding no one who would make adequate use of her daring prints, she developed her own design, producing "butterfly dresses," in which fabric and cut merge in a single unit. The finest chiffons and muslins were worked into wide, multilayered skirts or dresses with high waists and wide sleeves. Everything appeared delicate and translucent. Rhodes drew her inspiration from ethnic dresses of Native American, Japanese, or Mexican origin as well as from European fashion history. She designed textiles interpreting the slits of Elizabethan dresses, and others transforming the frills of the 19th century into modern forms.

With her Conceptual Chic collection of 1977 she became famous as the high priestess of punk, even though she herself claims that what she did then was not real punk. Unlike Vivienne Westwood's pieces from that time, Rhodes' designs only play with the idea of punk. She worked holes and tears into her clothing, but seamed these so finely with pearls or held them together so deftly with pins of precious stone rather than with safety pins that the overall impression given by her often colorful creations was not threatening but experimental and, as before, a little romantic. She certainly left her personal mark here too. Since the 1970s Zandra Rhodes has presented herself as an eccentric personality. Hair dyed green or pink, elaborate and very conspicuous makeup, and body painting reminiscent of delicate tattoos were already her trademark in the 1970s and in her view anticipated the punk look.

Punk

Vivienne Westwood's designs from those years best show what punk was. She rejected Zandra Rhodes' commercialized and in her eyes kitsch version of punk. Today she claims that punk had never been a street movement, but a fashion event from the beginning in whose creation she played a significant part, together with her then partner and manager of the Sex Pistols, Malcolm MacLaren.

Even so, it can be said that punk was originally a youth movement that sprang from the streets, regardless of whether it came into existence with or without the support of the fashion world. For unemployed young people with no view of the future it played an important role. Wearing black leather, preferably torn or with holes, pronounced makeup, dog-collars around their necks and chains around their ankles,

safety pins through their ears, and Mohican-style hair dyed in garish colors, punks of both sexes wanted to highlight problems in society by taking a stance of aggressive protest. They shocked not just through their appearance, but also through their political activism.

Punk culture was lived out by many young people in Europe and the States. When punk's critical stance had worn away, it was absorbed as an innovative style by mainstream fashion.

London punk couple, 1979

The mid-1970s saw the development of punk rock as a musical style, attacking everything which was connected with the ideas of bourgeois order. Punk was music from the streets, and its adherents dressed accordingly. T-shirts held together with safety pins and tartan bondage trousers were as much trademarks of that culture as spiky hair and leather gear covered with anarchist slogans.

A tough job under the glare of publicity

MODELS AND THE CATWALK

Only in the very rarest cases are models discovered purely by chance. Models must establish themselves in a hotly competitive market, and they are created: advertising and fashion decide on the type of woman that is needed to match the moment. In the 1980s models became icons of the markets for which they advertised, and through exclusive contracts their fees reached extraordinary heights. The seasonal catwalk shows continue to be central to the image of a fashion house, but there are also new ways of spreading name and logo.

Modeling: the dream career

In contrast to the mannequins who in the first half of the century displayed a couturier's latest range to a selected audience, models in the 1990s and into the 2000s earn astronomically high fees. Over the decades a career in modeling has become one of the most coveted jobs in public life. According to a survey conducted by a German magazine in 1993, 92 percent of all girls between the ages of 14 and 17 wanted to become models. Being beautiful, having your picture taken, and showing off the latest fashions on the catwalk was regarded as an ideal career.

In the early days of haute couture the seamstresses employed by the house or possibly the wife of the tailor-designer would take on the task of presentation. Now modeling demands not only an ideal figure and a photogenic appearance, but also excellent career planning.

American agencies, which from the beginning took care of the financial and contractual aspects of a model's work, played a large part in turning models into professionals. One of the top agencies in the early days was Ford, founded by Eileen Ford in New York in 1946. At the time she kept 20 percent of every modeling fee as commission, and in exchange the women and men on her books were looked after and marketed by the agency. Initially the models at Ford mostly represented the cliché of the young, blond American.

With her exotic and sexy appearance, Wilhelmina Behmenburg Cooper was an exception. She began her modeling career at Ford and in 1967, together with her husband, founded her own agency, which specialized in a more modern type of women. Hers was one of the first agencies to work with non-white models such as Naomi Sims and Iman. Margaux Hemingway was also under contract with her from time to time.

In the 1970s John Casablancas founded the Elite agency, today one of the largest and internationally most important model agencies. Casablancas not only worked with models but also sent out scouts to search for new faces. In this way he could

Twiggy, the photographic model, signs her autobiography, 1974

satisfy the advertising industry's growing demand for types and faces that appeared authentic. However, most young women and men who want to work as models are not discovered but take their portfolio from agency to agency, from casting to casting. Those with the right face and of the type in current demand, or even the potential for creating a new ideal – such as Twiggy in the 1960s – can count on high earnings for a few years.

Mannequins present the latest models of a Paris salon, 1920

Big business – marketing via models

Fashion moves fast, so new faces are constantly required. Rarely can a model stay at the top for more than five years. The fashion world of the 1990s was defined by supermodels such as Claudia Schiffer, Naomi Campbell, and Cindy Crawford. Glamorous and beautiful, they attracted the publicity and were given the idol status that movie stars had enjoyed in the 1950s. It was not only fashion magazines such as *Vogue* and *Harper's Bazaar* that wrote about them, quickly moving from reports on the clothes shown to features on the models themselves. The advertising industry also recognized that models were the fairy-tale princesses of modern times.

Buoyed up by all this attention, models became astute businesswomen who courted the visual media, demanding fees appropriate to their market value. The real money was to be had from advertising contracts. In 1994 Cindy Crawford earned nearly $6.5 million through Pepsi advertisements, work with MTV, and contracts with cosmetics companies. For the fashion designers models became banners of their particular style and brand. In the late 1970s, Gianni Versace was one of the first to hire models under exclusive contract, and in 1983 Karl Lagerfeld sent Inès de la Fressange down the catwalk as the new image-bearer of the house of Chanel. The supermodels were to represent only one fashion house so that purchasers were influenced by the effect of recognition and would transfer their positive association with the model to the fashion house.

Much is spent on such strong advertising effects: in the 1990s, a show with supermodels could cost a fashion house more than half a million dollars.

Fashion show as spectacle

Until the 1960s a catwalk presentation still had something of the intimacy of a salon. The guests, usually a select circle of high society clients, fashion journalists, and purchasers for foreign licensees, were greeted by an employee of the house, who would also call out the name of the creation displayed. At the end the couturier would lead a model in a wedding dress down the catwalk. Rising postwar living standards had given a considerable boost to the textile and fashion industries. They identified new sectors of customers and adjusted their marketing strategies accordingly. Consumers between 20 and 35 years of age were particularly wooed as a moneyed clientele. The emergence of a youthful fashion geared toward these customers also changed fashion shows. In the 1970s the idea of presenting new collections in unusual locations was born. With music and striking lighting effects, the fashion show turned into a spectacle where the production, rather than the clothes, took center stage.

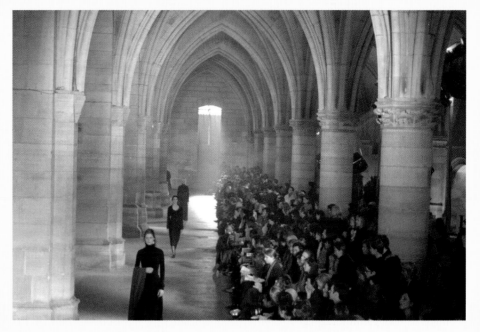

Dries van Noten's prêt-à-porter collection is presented in the Palais de Justice in Paris, 1999

Fashion online

The way that a fashion house presents itself has long been totally focused on the international visual media. Artistic fashion photography is constantly finding new ways of expressing the relationship between fashion and the everyday world. However, the Internet has now assumed a central role. Consumers can obtain information about producers and products, attend haute couture presentations, or meet in the virtual fan club of their favorite model. Agencies display their models' portfolios, and independent models can also be contacted. The fashion houses not only use the Internet as a new way of selling; the medium also offers the possibility of presenting themselves in an entirely new dimension. The live transmission of fashion shows is one of these display methods – but it also enables new trends to be copied at lightning speed. So far only Thierry Mugler has tried to create a completely virtual catwalk, and through this has achieved the fusion of medium and product: his models and his dresses are digitalized, animated fiction.

Gianni Versace with Claudia Schiffer and Linda Evangelista after the spring/summer 1994 haute couture show in Paris

Anything goes

Dress for success

1980–1989

Postmodernism: a multitude of styles

While 1970s fashion was broadly characterized by a desire for authenticity, naturalness, and self-realization, that of the 1980s was marked by the cult of success and achievement that was also manifest in all other aspects of society. Subversive tendencies, such as punk fashion, and the casual look of sportswear added splashes of color to the canvas.

Fashion had finally become international. French haute couture no longer dominated, as countries around the world developed their own styles which spread beyond national borders. Britain, Italy, and Germany were now to be taken seriously as creators of fashion. The United States was supplying up-to-date casual classics, and Japan was coming up with the avant-garde.

Fashion became increasingly playful, and postmodernism, which left its mark on all aspects of art during the decade, also affected fashion. Elements of long-gone fashions were deliberately and quite ironically quoted, also demonstrating a thorough knowledge of fashion history and older techniques. Those references to the past had little in common with the nostalgia of the 1970s, for while frilly blouses and long skirts were no more than faint reminders of 19th-century dress – especially when the necessity of industrial mass production is taken into account – it was now above all the designs of haute couture and prêt-à-porter that reflected the past.

Of course, from its beginnings fashion has always loved a historical quote or the repetition of elements of past styles. However, in the 1980s the approach to historical fashions assumed a new quality. A kind of hybrid historicism emerged during the decade: there was no new Empire style, no neomedieval fashion as such. Rather, suitable matches were sought out from everywhere, were put together anew and shaped into something highly modern. This development in fashion is analogous to those occurring simultaneously in architecture and the arts. As Richard Martin, curator of the fashion department at the Metropolitan Museum in New York, put it, this way the past was not made immortal, but was revived.

This love of the past came through in the decade's penchant for opulent costume dramas, set mostly in the 18th century, the last epoch of splendid fashions for men and women. The movie *Amadeus*, about Mozart, and the movie of Choderlos de Laclos' 18th-century novel *Dangerous Liaisons* practically wallowed in colorful period costumes. Both were great hits with international audiences and influenced young fashion designers such as John Galliano and Jean Paul Gaultier.

Art exhibitions became a fount of inspiration: after the Watteau retrospective, Karl Lagerfeld

1980 Start of war between Iran and Iraq. Death of the Yugoslav president Marshal Tito. Umberto Eco's novel *The Name of the Rose* is published.

1981 Acid rain destroys forests throughout Europe. Pope John Paul II is seriously injured in an assassination attempt. The novel *Chronicle of a Death Foretold* by the Colombian writer Gabriel García Márquez appears, with an initial print run of 1 million copies. Wave of violence in Northern Ireland after the death of IRA hunger striker Bobby Sands.

1982 Israel attacks Lebanon in order to expel the PLO. Worldwide demonstrations for peace and disarmament. Premiere of the musical *Cats*. Falklands War between Great Britain and Argentina.

1983 First reports of AIDS reach Europe. Compact disks (CDs) come onto the market. More mass executions in Iran. The former chief of the Lyon Gestapo, Klaus Barbie, is arrested in Bolivia. Discovery of black holes in space. The first solar power station starts operating in the North Sea. Richard Attenborough's film *Gandhi* wins 8 Oscars.

Erich Honecker greets Gorbachev at the Warsaw Pact Summit, 1987.

1984 Archbishop Desmond Tutu receives the Nobel Peace Prize for his fight against apartheid. Milos Forman's movie *Amadeus* wins eight Oscars. Peace negotiations between opposing parties in the civil war in El Salvador. Famine in Africa, especially severe in Ethiopia.

1985 Summit meeting between Mikhail Gorbachev and US president Ronald Reagan in Geneva. Palestinian terrorists hijack the cruise ship *Achille Lauro* in the Mediterranean. Soviet troops withdraw from Afghanistan. Live Aid, in Wembley Stadium and JFK Stadium, Philadelphia, raises $80 million for famine relief in Africa.

1986 Assassination of Swedish prime minister Olof Palme. Nuclear reactor disaster at Chernobyl, Ukraine. The American space shuttle *Challenger* explodes on takeoff. In his novel *The Beautiful Mrs Seidenman* Andrzej Szczypiorski describes the fate of Polish Jews in World War II. Death of Simone de Beauvoir. Premiere of the musical *Phantom of the Opera* by Andrew Lloyd Webber in London.

1987 Beginning of the Intifada, the Palestinian revolt in areas occupied by Israel. The picture *Irises* by Vincent van Gogh is auctioned in New York for $37 million. Death of Pop artist Andy Warhol. Gorbachev and Reagan sign missile treaty.

1988 Beginning of glasnost and perestroika in the USSR. The United States and USSR agree to dismantling of midrange missiles. Start of nationality conflict in Kosovo. Beginning of democratic protest movement in China. Olympic Games held in Seoul, South Korea.

1989 Fatwa against writer Salman Rushdie is declared by Iranian government. Death of Ayatollah Khomeini. Fall of the Berlin Wall. Massacre on Tiananmen Square in Beijing. Opening of the glass pyramid entrance to the Louvre in Paris. Drug wars in South America. Steven Soderbergh's movie *Sex, Lies and Videotape* wins the Palme d'Or in Cannes. Death of artist Salvador Dalí.

makes references to the work of the great 18th-century painter in his collection. Among his designs is a romantic, white Pierrot ensemble for women which turns Watteau's melancholy *Gilles* into an elegant, androgynous figure.

The end of an opulent fashion that was brought about by the French Revolution also found an echo 200 years later on the catwalks of haute couture. Here modernized elements of the Empire line with its high waists and neoclassical draping, and also Napoleonic fantasy uniforms, were on show. The 1980s' love of history was not limited to the 18th and early 19th centuries, however. On the one hand it reached further back and on the other it remained much closer to its own time: Jean Paul Gaultier reinterpreted the gigantic puff sleeves and the tight vests of the 16th century, while Moschino referred to hippie fashion from only 20 years before. This extremely short time lapse between current and quoted fashion would become even shorter in the1990s; the glance back to the most recent past was seen in a revival of the 1960s and 1970s and it was more wide-ranging than the references to the past that were made in the 1980s. While looking back was an indulgence characteristic of the postmodernist 1980s, it was mostly limited to high fashion. Everyday fashion looked different; here the tendency towards simple, functional elegance made a greater impact. However, the very coexistence of markedly different styles was an essential part of 1980s fashion, which abandoned the idea, strongly held up until then, that there had to be a definite style, a definitive trend. A wide variation in styles asserted itself, and artistic originality consisted of the relevant use of references, through which individuality was not clearly defined but was instead couched in various historical foils.

New image-setters

Pop star Madonna is an excellent and style-setting example of the way in which very different elements can be combined in a highly individual whole. Her first LP, *Madonna*, brought her to fame in 1983, and every single record after that has kept her consistently in the charts.

Madonna's particular effectiveness lies in the way music, movement, and clothes work together in performances and video clips, which are all staged down to the last detail. She plays with all taboos and clichés and shows off her body as both highly sexual and highly controlled. This body is not "naturally female" but the result of aerobics, bodybuilding, and diets – and this is openly displayed. Better than any other star, Madonna embodies the creed of the 1980s that anyone can model themselves into who they want to be, and that diets, training, and physical workouts are sensible means of reaching the goal of becoming one's ideal self – that is, an ideal body.

The ideal of female beauty of the 1980s was no longer a starved little girl like Twiggy or the ladylike beauty of the 1950s, but a sporty, slim, muscular, and ambitious woman

Like A Virgin, Madonna on tour, 1984

By her second tour Madonna was already famous worldwide as a shocking, adored, and outrageous star. In contrast to other great names in the business, she never let herself be pinned to one particular image; indeed, constantly slipping into new and surprising roles became her trademark. In her numerous music videos she appears as fetish girl, punk, or an imitation of Marilyn Monroe.

who was successful at work and in her private life and dressed accordingly, not denying her glamor and her eroticism but deliberately using them. In other words, femininity and eroticism were presented in a well-thought-out way; they were no longer considered natural attributes, unquestionably present.

Madonna represented this aspect of self-creation, too: she decided early on to become a star, and she reached her goal through hard work and single-mindedness. It was this ambition, which manifested itself in many areas and not least in fashion, that made her an icon of the 1980s.

Madonna has influenced fashion since the mid-1980s. At first she appeared as something of a neo-punk "bad girl" with wild hair and a colorful mixture of irreverent styles as she sported crucifixes, leather jackets, leather bracelets, and T-shirts. Later she became increasingly body-focused, more glamorous, and overtly sexual. Corsets, black leather and latex, fishnet stockings, suspenders, and skintight stretch fabric were an integral part of her costumes. The corset that Jean Paul Gaultier famously created for her "Blond Ambition" tour in 1990 caused an outcry. For a while she marketed herself as the modern reincarnation of Marilyn Monroe – her dyed platinum blond hair set off a fashion trend – and constantly made references to the stars and styles of bygone ages, using these to come up with something that was explosive, highly modern, and unmistakably her own.

While Madonna disseminated a hard-edged femininity, male pop stars of the time cultivated a style of sexual ambiguity. Singers as different as Boy George, Prince, and Michael Jackson, with their gentle, high-pitched voices and strongly made-up faces, brought the female side of their personalities to the fore. With flowing clothes or tight, richly decorated silk or leather clothing as well as through expressive dancing they offered a totally new, erotically charged image of masculinity that came across as strongly provocative but which was nevertheless copied, at least in some respects, by many of their fans.

The leisure look

With a great deal of wit Madonna brought fetishism and the frivolous glitter of nightclubs and Hollywood stars back into fashion, but she also contributed to the growing importance of sporty elements in 1980s fashion. These two style directions were not mutually exclusive but complemented each other, as both shared a marked focus on the body.

The 1980s saw a veritable explosion in fitness training. Aerobics became the ultimate fashionable sport, which required the appropriate outfit: shiny leggings, skintight leotards, headbands, legwarmers, and special aerobics shoes, all in fluorescent colors. This sport fashion very quickly influenced everyday fashion, and neither fitness activities nor an appropriate figure were requirements for the people of all ages who wore these clothes in the street. Indeed, combinations of sportswear with pumps or a blazer were no longer considered unsuitable. The trainer turned into the leisure shoe for all, and could be worn with jeans at practically all times.

Not only aerobic studios but also bodybuilding centers mushroomed everywhere. Until then bodybuilding had been regarded as a rather unrefined sport for tough men, and one to be avoided by women if they did not want to turn into a disfigured masculine pack of muscles. Repackaged as body-shaping, it became socially acceptable for women, too. In this way it was possible to shape one's own body to match up to the new, toned, sporty ideal that was so sought after.

Dress for success

Next to sportswear, which was no longer

Calvin Klein Jeans, from an advertising campaign of 1980

Jeans continued to dominate youth fashion. They grew ever more popular as a status symbol after Calvin Klein became the first designer to put his name to jeans. What had previously been working clothes gained greatly in value and, in the eyes of the consumers purchasing a pair of designer jeans, this was part of "belonging." The super-narrow shape, known as the cigarette shape, remained fashionable until the mid-1980s.

Calvin Klein Jeans

Sweatshirt collection by Norma Kamali, 1980

These loosely cut jackets, sweaters, dresses, and suits encapsulate the trend toward a sports fashion which made active women well-dressed without restricting them. Every piece of the collection was made out of the same gray sweatshirt material, a cotton fabric with a fleecy reverse, so that all units could be worn together in different combinations. In this way Kamali wanted to remove the dilemma faced by many women who wanted to be fashionable but also comfortably dressed even in more formal situations. So perfect was her solution to the problem that she was awarded a prize for her Sweatshirt collection.

strictly for leisure time, and glamor for the evening, came another variation – the fashion of the power woman. "Dress for success" was the magic formula. By now women were present in the world of work as a matter of course and continued to climb the career ladder. They no longer fought for equality from women's enclaves; they seemed to have achieved equality and expressed it through clothes which marked their entrance into a man's world. Indeed, for a woman, having a career was made easier by the adoption of appropriate clothes; they appropriated certain forms of men's clothes and therefore made the sexual side of women invisible, instead stressing their equal competence.

Women therefore preferred suits – a long, wide blazer with broadly cut shoulders emphasized by pads, worn with a slimline knee-length skirt or a pleated skirt and high-heeled, simple yet elegant pumps. Now and again the skirt could be substituted by fine and modestly wide pleated pants. For a while Bermuda shorts were in as part of a suit, but they did not establish themselves as

a lasting item of business clothing. Elegant, soft blouses and sweaters in high-quality fabrics completed the outfit.

Dresses were made in soft fabrics, with wide padded shoulders and inset pleats and usually covering the knee. Swinging coats or the indestructible trenchcoat were worn on top.

Dynasty style

The fashion image of the power woman was crystallized in television series such as *Dallas* and *Dynasty*, which in turn of course influenced many 1980s women in their choice of clothes. Here, strongly drawn types such as Alexis in *Dynasty* (played by Joan Collins), were characterized by their clothing. During the day, the "bad" character in this popular US series wore tight skirts, sharply tailored jackets with broad shoulders and a narrow waist to emphasize the bosom. Sometimes the jackets had a little tail. Everything was in strong, vibrant colors, and high-heeled pumps were an essential part of the outfit.

In the evening the 1980s woman showed off in strapless corsages with low necklines

FASHION FROM JAPAN

In the 1970s Kenzo firmly established himself as the leading Japanese fashion designer in the European fashion world with his cheerfully elegant hippie style. Avant-garde designers such as Issey Miyake, Yohji Yamamoto, and Rei Kawakubo with her provocative company name Comme des Garçons soon followed their compatriot to the fashion capital Paris.

Their clothes featured entirely unexpected outlines and spatial effects; they placed the emphasis on unusual fabrics, empathized with the body, and paid no attention to gender – signaling a revolution in the Western understanding of body and clothing.

Kenzo – the most European of Japanese fashion designers

Kenzo Takada, known everywhere simply by his first name, was born in 1939. He first attended the Bunka-Gakuin fashion school in Tokyo, and in the mid-1960s he was drawn to Europe.

In 1970 he opened his first boutique in Paris, where his colorful and unconventional folkloric clothes immediately won over a young audience, who regarded his style as an expression of their outlook on life. Kenzo combined the simple traditional kimono cut of his homeland with elements from South America, the Orient, and Scandinavia. An unusual mix of patterns, intense colors, and large-scale floral patterns were and still are his trademarks – he is one of the few stars of the 1970s whose style is still in demand today.

Apart from ready-to-wear for ladies, Kenzo designs men's and children's fashions as well as curtain and furnishing materials. Since 1992 this designer has always presented his collections one month ahead of other designers.

Rei Kawakubo – the unexpected beauty of imperfection

When Rei Kawakubo, the woman behind the Comme des Garçons label, presented a collection in Paris for the first time in 1981, it was a shock to the whole fashion scene. While the European fashion world was wallowing in glittering colors and full-bodied femininity, this Japanese designer showed clothes that appeared meager and seemingly shapeless. The fashion press claimed that watching her show was like witnessing a funeral march after a nuclear attack.

Rei Kawakubo, born in 1942, is now one of the great figures in today's international world of fashion. After studying art, she worked as a stylist in Tokyo in the 1960s. She soon began to design clothes. At the end of the 1960s she created the Comme des Garçons label, and founded the company of the same name in 1973. In 1975 she showed her women's collection in Tokyo for the first time.

Comme des Garçons ("Like Boys") is not a programmatic announcement of gender equality or sexlessness, but is instead the perfect label for fashion which deliberately confronts and questions Western images of the body. Rei Kawakubo's monochrome and amorphous-looking creations met the desire for something completely new. Along with the widespread rejection and lack of understanding that the fashion creator was initially faced with after her Paris presentation there was also some palpable enthusiasm among the fashion commentators. The sharpest among them understood that somebody had developed an entirely new esthetic here.

Rei Kawakubo opened her first store outside Japan in Paris in 1983. By the end

Kenzo, prêt-à-porter, fall/winter 1999/2000

of the 1980s she already owned 94 outlets around the world and 222 in Japan alone. Even today every store is designed in Japan and reflects the house's purist philosophy down to the tiniest detail. Nothing distracts from the clothes, and Kawakubo provided the example for

Left: Issey Miyake, fall/winter 1999/2000

Right: Comme des Garçons, spring/summer 1997

presenting them simply on long railings along the wall.

She winds and drapes layers of different material around the body; sometimes the needlework and the seams remain visible. She constructs the dresses architecturally and pays attention to the space that her shapes create. Her dresses are not decorative, nor do they directly flatter the female figure.

In 1982 Kawakubo showed lace sweaters with irregular, apparently moth-eaten holes. Her 1997 collection consisted of dresses incorporating puffed-up lumps, bumps, and other protuberances in all kinds of places which questioned everything usually seen. It also made clear that this fashion designer cares not for traditional beauty or even about the expression of a harmonious body, but for the creation of unique forms – which nevertheless should not stand in contradiction to the body.

Her first collections were restricted exclusively to gray, beige, and in particular black. When the designer, who herself wears only black, introduced colored clothes for the first time in 1989, this again created quite a stir on the fashion scene. Since 1978 Rei Kawakubo has also designed men's collections, which are usually presented by non-professional and often not-so-young models, underlining her lack of interest in the extreme extravagance of mainstream fashion.

Artists and actors are also enthusiastic about the Japanese designer's fashions: Dennis Hopper, Robert Rauschenberg, and Francesco Clemente have strutted down the catwalk for Comme des Garçons, and the stores, appearing like cool galleries, exhibit the work of artists, and photographers like Cindy Sherman.

Issey Miyake – fashion artist

Issey Miyake never speaks of the clothes that he designs as fashion – he creates like an artist, he says. For this the manually highly skilled Miyake uses various natural fibers and synthetic fabrics, which give him an enormous sense of freedom in working on his clothes. Indeed, freedom of body and spirit is what he intends his designs to communicate to the wearer.

Issey Miyake was born in Hiroshima in 1938, initially studied graphic art in Tokyo, and showed his first fashion collection there in 1964. In 1965 he moved to Paris to attend the Ecole de la Chambre Syndicale de la Couture. Afterward he worked at Laroche and Givenchy in Paris and later as a stylist for American designer Geoffrey Beene. In 1970 he was drawn back to Tokyo, where he founded his own studio. He began to export his prêt-à-porter collections in 1972 and presented his first Paris show in the same year.

Yohji Yamamoto, fall/winter 1984/85

Miyake's style is influenced by Japanese clothing, but he has also drawn inspiration from the West. For instance, he has chosen to work with the pleats invented by Mariano Fortuny at the turn of the 20th century – but Miyake's pleated material is not silk, like that of his famous idol, but made of synthetic fabrics and colors.

Issey Miyake uses materials totally alien to the fashion world: synthetic fibers or wire constructions recall the armor of the Samurai, while paper or basketweave transform dresses into virtual works of art. Origami folds are carried over into clothing, and gigantic blankets are draped as coats and jackets and tied like old Japanese clothes.

Apparently shapeless pieces such as the series Pleats Please, which has been presented for years and represents something like a uniform for artists and intellectuals, are to be wrapped around the body any which way. Miyake often does not make it clear how a piece is to be worn, so that the wearers play some part in the creation of the piece. In this way the fashion designer makes room for individuality in contrast to the increasing tendency to standardize fashion.

Yohji Yamamoto – poetry in black

Yohji Yamamoto was born in 1943 in Tokyo, where he studied law as well as fashion design. In 1977 he presented his first prêt-à-porter collection in Tokyo. In 1981 he had his first show in Paris, and in New York the following year. Since 1984 he has also been designing men's collections.

His garments are loosely cut and often voluminous; sometimes they appear to be carved out of stone, at other times they are fluid. Often they offer possibilities for different use: jackets are reversible, an extra pocket or laces fulfill not entirely obvious functions. Yamamoto wants to give the body space to move through his clothes. Materials cut against the grain and used at an angle make it possible for the "master of cuts" to achieve just that.

In 1989, Wim Wenders made a movie about this Japanese fashion designer. *Notebook on Cities and Clothes* praises the monochrome and purist severity of Yamamoto's fashion as well as its sculptural quality.

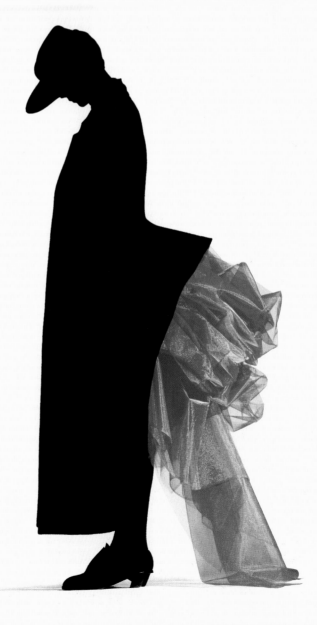

Men's fashion, 1989

The man in this outfit comes across as particularly style-conscious and rather conservative. In the 1980s previously unacceptable combinations of patterns and labels were permissible. Here a loosely cut woolen tartan jacket by Paul Smith is worn with a silk waistcoat with a floral pattern. The shirt and necktie are striped differently, which in earlier times would certainly have been considered daring. The velvet trousers are by Moschino. This correct, always formal, yet colorful style was fashionable for years as the preppy look.

Characters from the series *Miami Vice*, 1983

Miami Vice not only signaled the fashion of the 1980s, but also encapsulated the decade's attitude to life, with its dreams and aspirations. Men's fashion was a balancing act between formal business clothes and casual wear. Suits – in sporty white or highly elegant in silvery gray – were the ideal clothes for a successful American, whether detective or manager. Men were perfectly coifed, the hair worn not too short and blow-dried, a perm supporting the dynamic effect. Popular series like *Miami Vice* were followed throughout the Western world and spread the American way of life: it was consumerist and demanding of certain luxuries but actively worked to achieve positive results; good always triumphed over evil and traditional role models were confirmed repeatedly, so that the viewer was not upset or disturbed but was convinced of the system's security.

or skintight dresses with seductive slits, complemented by appropriately elaborate hairstyles with dark curls.

The opposite of this femme fatale type was the positive character with well-groomed blond hair. The real lady wears rather more modest colors, and her always elegant dresses emphasize the figure less.

In parallel, men's fashion of the time was strongly influenced by the crime series *Miami Vice*. The two heroes were always immaculately dressed, Tubbs in dark suits and neckties, and Crockett always in casual white trousers and T-shirts in pastel shades of turquoise, pink, or lavender. His clothes reflected the colors of Miami, where the series was set. At the same time it turned into fashion: having long been regarded as unmanly and effeminate, soft colors for men gradually became widely acceptable. *Miami Vice* also popularized a Versace invention: men could now wear a T-shirt instead of a shirt with a suit and appear not only correctly dressed but highly fashionable and sexy.

The pleasure of self-presentation

The trend toward the fashion cocktail, in which all sorts of styles could blend together, carried broad potential for human self-presentation. The pleasure of inventing oneself is regarded as typical of the 1980s, the decade of unlimited narcissism. What was new about this was that not only the chosen few wanted and could indulge in these pleasures – everyone was swept away by them. This went hand in hand with the lack of pursuit of political goals for the good of society, in contrast to the previous decade. In this respect, only the peace movement was still an active force, but it was no longer a characteristic attitude of millions the way the hippie movement had been. A kind of political apathy had spread, and instead, according to fashion historian Eva Karcher, "a new class as synthesis of all imaginable style methods" emerged.

Anyone could become anything or at least pretend to. An avant-garde of fashion or art no longer existed: "Today avant-garde meets the taste of the masses" – which of course is a contradiction within itself. A clear indication of this loss of individuality and all-embracing commercialization is the mainstream's exploitation of punk, which is diametrically opposed to punk's characteristic expression of protest and hate against that very mainstream.

Apart from the punks there were the preppies, young people of both sexes with noticeably neat haircuts, flat loafers, correct suits and skirts, who cultivated a

certain snobbery and in – most probably unconscious – imitation of the dandies of the 19th century attempted to be something of an elite by emphasizing their difference from others' excesses.

Disco culture, which had found its ideal expression in the late 1970s with movies such as *Saturday Night Fever* and *Grease*, continued its boom. Appropriate clothes were designed with artificial disco lighting in mind; made from fabrics such as satin or threaded through with lurex, they would glint and sparkle to great effect. There was practically a specific disco-style for women, but strangely not for men, even though John Travolta's white suit and black shirt with outward-turned collar in *Saturday Night Fever* had caused great uproar.

The new outline

Shoulders in women's clothing became increasingly wider and were interpreted by many observers as an indication of fashion becoming more masculine, for up until then only men's jackets had shown such padding. It was only men's broader shoulders and narrower hips that traditionally had been emphasized. The new suits suddenly gave women a similar outline.

However, this was not completely new. In fact, in the 1930s Elsa Schiaparelli had introduced short ladies' jackets which had wide padded shoulders and were worn with narrow skirts. Then too this was regarded as masculine, even though the jackets were often richly embroidered and made of very luxurious, colorful fabrics – especially the evening jackets along the lines of tuxedos, which Elsa Schiaparelli brought into fashion and which to us do not seem at all unusual. Prewar fashion had adapted this trend, but in comparison with 1980s fashion it seemed boxlike and a little shapeless and out of proportion. The severe lines of the 1980s were modified quite considerably by soft fabrics, and the proportions were better than they had been before the war. The broad-shouldered blazers harmonized with the slightly longer and often wider skirts and the elegant shoes.

Fashion historian Ingrid Loschek claims that in the 1980s the body was disowned by outsize blazers and sweaters. Without a doubt the overlarge, overwide clothes

Missoni, spring/summer 1984 collection

Voluminous sweaters and jackets dominated fashion in the 1980s, giant pieces of clothing which offered practically live-in comfort. It was the Italian knitwear firm Missoni, among others, that launched this type of clothing for the upper body. The large knitted areas were now designed by computer, by which new and highly differentiated variations of patterns could be produced. Apart from the jacquard patterns there was also a range of sweaters with figurative motifs knitted into the piece, directed by men's favorite sports. Sweaters like these were also available in less expensive polyester versions. However, Missoni has always been renowned for the high quality of its products and materials. The bold colorings too, sometimes inspired by medieval paintings, were a mark of quality and changed little over the years. Missoni was founded by Ottavio and Rosita Missoni, the husband-and-wife team who had been producing fashion designs since the 1940s. In 1997 their youngest daughter, Angela, took over the design independently and continues to present multicolored knit collections, for women too.

smothered the body. However, this was counterbalanced by eveningwear, which emphasized the figure with slit skirts and strapless tops, tailored jackets, and by the fashion for sportswear, which also often focused on the body.

To some extent the oversized clothes so popular in the 1980s could also be regarded as a cozy cover offering the body a comfortable nest and allowing it to move freely and naturally. The natural fabrics that came back into fashion supported this image, as did the crumpled look – which equated the naturalness of a fabric with its tendency to crease elegantly – that emerged in the middle of the decade.

American fashion

American fashion had always tended toward the sporty and the functional. Already at the turn of the century many designs from European haute couture were adapted to more down-to-earth American tastes. Traditional English sportswear also made itself more appealing, and its style influenced emerging American traditions. An independent American fashion had been developing since the 1940s.

Pantsuit in cotton and organza by Donna Karan, 1985

This pastel pink pantsuit in a fluid, semitransparent material is characteristic of Donna Karan's style in the mid-1980s, which the sharp-edged padded shoulders and the wide lapels are also part of. This style was aimed at the success-oriented working woman who nevertheless did not want to forego a classic, feminine appearance. The wide pants, loose, fluid, and transparent, are in ironic contrast to the correct, almost businessmanlike look of the jacket. This elegant pantsuit thus becomes an evening suit of the kind worn by Marlene Dietrich in the 1920s as a pajama.

Donna Karan's creative ideas are often shaped by her examination of how life can be made easier through clothes. In this she is thinking of the young urban professionals, independent city women. This style has dominated her designs since she took over the studio of Anne Klein, who died in 1974. Only in the 1990s did she change her style. On one hand she has gained new sources of inspiration through an interest in esoterics, which find expression in loose, casual, and above all, more sensual clothing. On the other there is the new, young DKNY line which is making its mark in high-class jeanswear.

It took off in the 1970s and finally achieved international success in the 1980s; it can now be regarded as a serious competitor to European prêt-à-porter. Indeed, the 1980s can be described as the great era of American fashion: it ideally matched the spirit of the decade, which was characterized by sport, success, and ambition.

Donna Karan

The worldwide success of American fashion designer Donna Karan began at this time. Since 1984 she has been designing fashion, under her own name, that underlines the trend for success and that completely satisfies demand for discreet, always correct, but also comfortable yet distinguished clothes. Even into the 21st century, her fashion can be regarded as the epitome of that particular style and its descendants.

No experimentation unsettles the typical Karan customer; she can always rely on the label. With Karan – slim jackets, narrow but never really tight skirts, fine woolen sweaters, and simple blouses with fashionable touches, and feminine, flowing evening dresses that exude effortless elegance, with

everything in muted colors – a woman is always suitably dressed, never overdressed, for both work and social occasions.

Calvin Klein

Calvin Klein, born in 1942, has been one of the greatest internationally renowned American designers since the mid-1970s. After initial successes with sportswear and jeans, he expanded his collections in the 1980s to include classic-casual-elegant business clothes in linen, silk, and fine wool. Straight, well-proportioned jackets, blazers with wide shoulders, and casually elegant coats are characteristic of his style.

Ralph Lauren

Ralph Lauren was born in 1939 and began his career as a glove salesman before moving on to designing neckties and scarves. At the end of the 1960s he created the Polo line, casual men's fashion based on the style of English country clothes; this was joined by a women's collection in 1971.

Lauren's designs for Norfolk jackets, blouses with ribbons, checked skirts, and so on, are intentionally traditional and conservative and gain their effectiveness from clearly American notes. Prairie fashion or clothing in denim, cotton, or wool that is a reminder of the era of pioneers have made him one of the America's favorite designers; he appears to maintain both technical product quality and traditions of countryside and family. This is also expressed in the interior decoration of his stores: wood and leather, fireplaces and heavy chintz give the impression of timeless values and unshakable reliability.

The end of haute couture?

In the 1980s haute couture was scarcely of any importance in the development of new lines, silhouettes, colors, and shapes. The influence it once wielded in the creation of styles was passed to prêt-à-porter. Haute couture no longer created the necessary turnover, as production for a small number of rich clients was no longer worthwhile. The real money was now made from licenses, by which the name of a house is marketed through cosmetics, accessories of all kinds, shoes, pantyhose, or bags.

However, haute couture remains one of the most important advertisements for a large

Thierry Mugler, advertising campaign
1984

In the mid-1980s Mugler staged a
contemporary office situation to
communicate the image of his designs.
Surrounded by computers, scanning
an endless list, this businesswoman is
taking her lunch break. Her apparently
uninterrupted commitment to the job
as well as her laid-back posture refer
to the conventional cliché of the
businessman, which is clearly satirized
here. Nevertheless it is now common for
women to work in jobs previously
considered to be the preserve of men.
Mugler's business look is a suit with
skirt of Italian length, ending just above
the knee, and a white collar and cuffs
which provide a contrast to the dark
jacket. The severe cut also corresponds
to the formal work setting, but it is
Mugler's style to introduce a definitely
female note through the particularly
tight cut, which he achieves in more
elaborate dresses with padding at the
hip and shoulder-revealing tops.

fashion house, and the catwalks are
celebrated accordingly. They have turned into
gigantic shows at which much imagination
and talent are unveiled even though the
pieces presented do not always lead the way
in fashion as haute couture once did. They
serve the reputation and add value to the
label – and more than ever, it is the label
that influences customers, in the area of
young fashion as much as in the luxury sector.

Christian Lacroix

Christian Lacroix, born in 1952, was one of
the few newcomers to haute couture in the
1980s. He opened his fashion house in
1987 and immediately attracted notice with
his colorful, slightly exalted, yet ladylike
designs that often appear theatrical and
highly ornate and draw much inspiration
from Provençal and Spanish folklore.

Thierry Mugler

Thierry Mugler was born in Strasbourg in
1948 and trained as a dancer. From the late
1960s he designed for various companies;
he presented his first collection at the
beginning of the 1970s under the title Café
de Paris. Soon after that, he launched prêt-à-
porter under his own name.
His fashion is strongly styled. Very narrow
waists are emphasized by side inserts in
contrasting colors, busts are like sculptures,
and skintight pants or skirts constitute a
futuristic, hyperfeminine style that often
draws on fetishism and makes women
appear dominant. Mugler's perfume Angel
came onto the market in 1993 and was
advertised by Jerry Hall, ex-wife of Rolling
Stone Mick Jagger and a supermodel of the
1980s who is still in demand today.

Jean Paul Gaultier

Jean Paul Gaultier is universally described as
the enfant terrible of French fashion. He was
apprenticed at the houses of Cardin and
Patou, and introduced his electronic jewelry
and his first own women's collection in
1976. Since 1984 he has also been
designing men's collections. The title of the
first, L'homme objet (Man as Object)
parodied the image of the woman as the
(erotic) object of men (and fashion
designers). Et Dieu créa l'homme (And God
Created Man) played on the title of a famous
movie of the 1950s (And God Created
Woman) starring Brigitte Bardot, and with
consistent irony introduced the first skirts for
men. Gaultier's men's collections nearly
always play with clichés of femininity, taking
them over and inversing them completely.
Hardly any other designer is so little
intimidated by what is generally regarded as
bad taste, even kitsch; no one plays so
unashamedly with gender and creates
something so refreshingly new at every turn.
Gathering, transforming, blending, that is

Jean Paul Gaultier, prêt-à-porter 1988/89

This extraordinary dress clearly refers to the hoops and crinolines that were abandoned at the beginning of the 20th century. It exemplifies Gaultier's fondness for referring back to long-gone epochs. Such designs rely for their effect on the modern interpretation of the historical element, rather than its function, whether in a traditional or contemporary context. It is precisely as a prêt-à-porter garment that the dress is given a special note – for some it is provocative, for others humorous. Nevertheless, in prêt-à-porter, which still represents fashionable and reasonably affordable clothes, an idea as clearly formulated as this can become a trend.

Gaultier's creative process, says the fashion historian Farid Chenoune; in his work the influences of haute couture, the street, and the fleamarkets cross over.

Some of his collections appear as if the clothes do not fit the models; others are held up by braces. The corsets that Madonna wore for her 1990 "Blond Ambition" tour were created by Gaultier; over them she wore a man's suit, which for the fashion designer was the "perfect expression of contemporary fashion." In his shows men pose in little hats with veils or in tulle tops covered with paste gems, while women wear jackets like 19th-century men's hacking jackets or coats reminiscent of oversize microchips from electronic equipment.

Gaultier's first women's perfume, launched in 1993, came in a flagon shaped as a female torso, a reference to Elsa Schiaparelli's flagon for her perfume, Shocking, which was based on Mae West's vital statistics. He followed this with a men's scent in a flagon shaped like a male torso, which is sold in a metal box.

New classics: Karl Lagerfeld

Karl Lagerfeld, born in 1938, was only 16 when he won a fashion competition with his design for a women's coat. The eccentric Lagerfeld, who always sports a Mozart-style ponytail and a fan as well as an elegant suit, has over the years revealed himself as something of an all-round genius. He designs for various labels: Chloé, Chanel, Fendi, and since the mid-1980s also for his own line, Karl Lagerfeld. He taught at the School of Applied Arts in Vienna, is a photographer and a brilliant fashion artist, collects fans, and is well versed in European art history.

From the mid-1980s, Lagerfeld gave the house of Chanel, which by then had gained a reputation for producing boring clothes for wealthy older ladies, a new image. He made its style younger while retaining the traditional elements of the typical Chanel style. He shortened the skirts, used leather, combined sparkling bustiers with short Chanel jackets, and decorated models with embroidery and accessories more reminiscent of Elsa Schiaparelli than Coco Chanel. The same applied to his hat creations in the shape of small pieces of furniture, fruit, or cakes.

Playful elegance, lightweight yet precise perfectionism, wit, and a strong sense for the spirit of the time characterize Lagerfeld's many different designs for various houses.

Giorgio Armani

After designing men's clothes for Cerruti, for more than 20 years Giorgio Armani has been creating distinctive clothes for modern, working women. Armani's style perfectly suited the spirit of the 1980s. Armani succeeded in bridging the gap between business uniform and leisurewear, as Caroline Rennolds Milbank has noted. His unlined jackets, which have no stiffness, are of unparalleled elegance. They are combined with softly falling skirts or pants in fine fabrics such as high-quality wool or heavy silk.

Armani places particular value on the comfort and the simple elegance of his creations. He deliberately does not follow fashion trends but continues to offer quality clothing in the flawless design of Italian tradition for both men and women.

Gianni Versace

Gianni Versace, born in 1946, learned fashion and tailoring from his mother, who was a seamstress. He presented his first collections for women and men in 1975 under his own name.

In the 1980s Versace became one of the leading figures in international avant-garde fashion. Together with his brother Santo and sister Donatella he built up a successful fashion emporium operating worldwide. Donatella gradually took on responsibility for individual lines, so that, after Gianni was murdered in 1997, she was able to continue his work.

Versace is reputed to have said of himself that he drew much inspiration by observing the women in a neighboring brothel. His dresses appear accordingly colorful and flashy, vulgar even, and tend to suit very young, slim women. Actress Elizabeth Hurley caused a sensation when she appeared at the premiere of the 1994 movie *Four Weddings and a Funeral* in a black leather Versace dress held together at the sides by giant safety pins and revealing much bare skin. Low necklines were as much part of Versace's style as waist-high slits and the typically Baroque patterns which he developed himself. The head of Medusa was a central feature of his designs from an early stage.

Portraits of pop stars, fake leopard-skin prints, even putti, sea shells, and many other Baroque motifs decorate Versace's slim, silky, flowing dresses as well as his shirts for men. *Vogue* covers printed on his designs make of his fashion creations a continuous readable self-commentary. At the beginning of the 1980s Versace introduced a metallic material that has the appearance of a living snakeskin and which has proved very popular for the creation of evening gowns.

Versace's style was highly contemporary. It was a blend of the styles of many eras, and it was hard to tell whether his style was making fun of itself or of its wearers, who relied on the renowned designer for tasteful clothes without noticing that they were part of his playing with tastelessness.

Simultaneously kitsch and ironic, this fashion veritably screamed that drawing clear borders between taste and kitsch had been impossible for a long time. Postmodernism

lives on these constant mergers and contrasts between sense and nonsense, kitsch and art, splendor and purism. Versace's fashion does not push these contradictions aside, but rather makes a point of developing and displaying them.

Versace revolutionized men's fashion. As a fashion writer put it after his death, "he understood men's glamor as nobody before." He gave men the courage to wear colorful, figure-hugging clothes, and restored to men's fashion a splendor and an exaggeration that it had not displayed since before the French Revolution. Shirts were printed with Baroque motifs in fluorescent or pastel colors, while pants were usually skintight and no less ornamental. Versace loved to dress men in leather and silk, lacquer and metal, and he liked to show much male skin.

Gianni Versace, spring 1984

Gianni Versace is often quoted as saying, "I do not believe in good taste," an attitude that allowed him all possible variations of his glamorous, richly ornate style. These long jackets, in lightweight fabrics and ending flush with the Bermuda shorts, are decorated with colorful appliqué and achieve different effects depending on the ground color, black or white. Both models wear blouses with broad padded shoulders, in line with the 1980s' trend for oversize clothes, which found its way into more elegant attire. In a combination such as this, the Bermuda shorts, previously reserved for leisurewear, were also acceptable for the office or the evening – though the style did not outlast the 1980s.

IMAGE AND STRATEGY

How is a label created? Why does it sell? For internationally renowned designer companies as well as for the majority of customers, it is no longer qualities such as cut or fabric that influence a purchasing decision, but the company's appearance in the media. Through advertising and the projection of an image, a connection between a lifestyle and a certain label is made in the mind of the consumer, who aspires to make that lifestyle his or her own by wearing particular pieces or accessories from the chosen designer's collection.

Advertisement for Vers le Jour, the perfume by Worth, 1919

Label as lifestyle

Ever since the concept of fashion was established and ever since certain styles and lines have been associated with the name of their creator, it has been necessary for fashion houses to create an image and maintain it in ever-wider public circles. It has always been of the greatest importance for couturiers, from Charles Frederick Worth to the fashion designers who created the great gowns of the post-World-War-II period, to advertise in fashion magazines and to present their house as the epitome of elegance and quality.

The creations were usually pictured so as to be easily recognizable, and were often presented in an ambiance appropriate to their exquisite elegance that would transport the wooed observers into a world of which the clothes appeared to be a natural part. Accessories and items such as perfume had always been among the products of any house conscious of style and quality. The intention was to suggest to clients that they could rely on a label in all questions of outer appearance.

However, the idea of an organized marketing system was only thoroughly realized in the 1960s. Pierre Cardin created a whole "world for living" that took in not only clothes but also interior furnishings, leisure gear, and even a restaurant chain, so that it became possible to stay within the security of one and the same style in every conceivable situation.

The fashion designer: the symbol behind the label

A new stratum of customers who lacked the financial means to wrap themselves in expensive haute couture creations still demanded fashionable clothes. In 1966, as a compromise between made-to-measure designer tailoring and cheap confections that attempted to copy trends dictated by haute couture, Yves Saint Laurent created the prêt-à-porter line Rive Gauche; aimed at a younger market, it came as a refreshing change in the fashion world. Saint Laurent wanted to establish a label that was contemporary and appropriate to new social realities of the postwar period.

The fashion house and its designer were intentionally used as image carriers of the young label. Saint Laurent exploited his worldwide reputation as an avant-garde fashion creator, which had stuck since his unwelcome designs for Dior in the early 1960s, to launch clothes that were more wearable and less expensive than those of haute couture.

In 1971 he posed naked for a photograph advertising his perfume YSL and with that overturned the idea of advertising as the concrete promotion of an article. This campaign, in which the picture is only an indirect link between a company's image, established in other ways, and its products, pointed the way for a new type of fashion advertising. Designers such as Jil Sander, and to a greater extent Calvin Klein, for example, founded their success on this method. It also developed the working image of a fashion artist: he or she was now no longer simply the creator of the clothes, but also an integral part of their marketing – he or she became the symbol of the label to be sold.

Creating an image

This meant that the way that designers worked was totally redefined, too. Suddenly it was important not only to guarantee a certain standard of quality, but also confidently to project one's own image. From the beginning of the 1970s, following the model of prêt-à-porter, more and more designers built up their own labels, such as René Lezard or Esprit.

In the mid-1970s, Luciano Benetton made the jump from family business to label with a successful image-forming campaign. With his strategy of letting the customer take part in the world of Benetton, he became a pioneer in image creation. The presentation of the clothes in small boutiques was a sensation in itself: Benetton lost the image of a mass producer, and the goods took on an intimate, exclusive character which had until then been reserved for the stores of famous designers. Above all, Benetton exploited the reaction of its target audience.

As a manufacturer of quite classic clothes and basics, Benetton never pretended to be a trendsetter. It was nevertheless important to spread the concept of simple and functional clothing for everyone. The slogan "United Colors," the leitmotif of the early campaigns, smoothed the way for the label. It communicated a simple, direct

Issey Miyake, spring/summer 1998

UNITED COLORS
OF BENETTON.

message: photographs of children of different races were intended to appeal to an open, tolerant society and to show Benetton as a representative of a harmonious, conflict-free world. By acquiring a Benetton sweater, the buyer would gain a part of this world for himself or herself.

The attempt to alter this image of the cosmopolitan company at the beginning of the 1990s with the introduction of photographs of birds covered in oil or a dying AIDS sufferer caused great controversy, and the name Benetton was on everyone's lips. At the same time, other fashion houses advertised their lines with pictures that critically examined reality in other ways by using fictional situations to refer to drugs and violence.

Marketing a formula lifestyle

Advertising stirs up emotions, and the need for all-encompassing advertising strategies is satisfied by a wide variety of means. What should remain in the consumer's mind is the association of the emotion with the label which is advertised. In its elaborate shows, haute couture displays clothes that are generally considered to be unwearable and that are intended only to create an image that serves the marketing of prêt-à-porter or licensed articles. Exactly the same applies to clothes manufacturers at all levels, who depend on the recognition effect: a single accessory from a renowned firm should be enough to express and uphold that house's particular style.

The presentation of label as lifestyle and the deliberate marketing of a label to its target group was also an important part of

Above: United Colors of Benetton, a poster from Benetton's advertising campaign

Right: Levi's on the Internet

the success of Hugo Boss. At the beginning of the 1980s, the success-oriented decade of the yuppies, the company Holy hit the nerve of the time with its Hugo Boss label. Up until then Holy had been a smaller company producing uniforms and business clothes, which then expanded to include classic men's clothes. With Boss the company scored one of the great successes in fashion history. The label stepped into the foreground; the designer and producer of the clothes remained hidden.

Intensive work went into the label's development. The name of Boss alone stands for success, dynamism, and a cosmopolitan outlook on life – all attributes embodied by the target group.

This was visualized by the beaming male model of the 1980s who presented Boss outfits and became a figure with whom a whole generation of men could identify. In this way, Hugo could be introduced to the market as a trendy young label complementing the classic Boss line, while Baldessarini represented the upmarket segment of the company.

Internet service

It is arguable that the value of design, a simple development of form, has decreased. The strategy and marketing of a product have moved center stage, pushing aside the product in favor of the world in which it is set. The customer chooses brand X because he or she accepts, or embraces, the lifestyle which is connected with it as his or her own, or at least aspires to attain it by acquiring the product.

At a time when it is important for many companies to go online, the visual communication of an idea becomes increasingly important. Today, clothes are not only advertised but also sold through the Internet. The American jeans company Levi's offers its Internet customers the possibility of having jeans made to measure. Although individual cut and fit are provided only with certain lines, there is still the potential for making the product an individual one.

In the world of online shopping, a company's image is of paramount importance, and it must already be established outside the ambit of the Internet so that the customer will search for and find it online. The image that a label projects on its website must coordinate exactly with the image that it has elsewhere.

Retro look and the cult of technology

Fin de siècle

1990–1999

Changing perspectives

A new generation came to define fashion in the 1990s: these children of the swingers of the 1960s, now aged between 15 and 30, issued lifestyle statements in order to formulate their fresh attitude to life. Techno music and synthetic fibers demonstrated that the green surge of the 1980s had ebbed: while respect for the environment was second nature to many, others were bored by recycling. There was the realization that many, apparently natural, materials had been so heavily treated with chemicals that they really could no longer be described as natural. Many of the new synthetic fibers, however, caused fewer skin irritations and were biodegradable.

Recession, unemployment, war, and nationalism on the one hand, a heretofore unimaginable globalization of politics, culture, and technology on the other, defined contemporary perspectives and turned cool into a seemingly essential attribute, at least in the urban environment. The media and communications industries became areas of professional activity of the utmost importance to daily life: perception was defined by a multitude of technologically produced images which sometimes allowed virtual reality to merge with actuality.

Fashion innovations

Fashion was also subject to fluctuation: in the 1990s reference to earlier styles became even more dominant than it had been in the 1980s. Fashion trends which started in the 1980s continued into the 1990s. They did not bring about any new looks, but they spawned a series of spectacular variations on existing shapes and styles. For example, young fashion revived the 1960s and 1970s, while John Galliano's haute couture for Dior was a reinterpretation of the 1920s.

Revivals followed each other at an increasingly rapid rate and the intervals between cycles became ever shorter. Dress codes relaxed, and many people could go to work dressed in leggings or jeans. Dressing up for the theater is no longer compulsory, here too the motto is anything goes as long as you like it. Sportswear has become generally accepted and represents a large slice of a market within which distinctions are made between the everyday and the elegant, between outdoor and street styles. With this democratic fashion it is possible to combine various levels of design, such as Reebok trainers with Armani spectacles, or informal pants with a blazer.

Fashion for different age groups

Whereas at the beginning of the century the age at which items of clothing, certain styles, outlines, colors, and fabrics could be worn was clearly prescribed, the strict distinction between ages began to melt away in the

---

1990 Mikhail Gorbachev is awarded the Nobel Peace Prize. Reunification of Germany. Beginning of Turkish persecution of the Kurds. Albania's borders are opened. Yugoslavia fragments; Slobodan Milosevich becomes president of Serbia. The hole in the ozone layer is discovered. Iraq invades Kuwait. Nelson Mandela released after 28 years in prison.

1991 Civil war in Yugoslavia. The Gulf War: the USA and its allies launch Operation Desert Storm. The end of apartheid in South Africa. Discovery of a 5300-year-old body in Ötztal, Austria.

1992 EC economic treaty signed in Maastricht. Airlifts to embattled Sarajevo and the Somalian civil war zone. Islamic fundamentalists assassinate the president and prime minister of Algeria; the military take over. Bill Clinton is elected president of the United States. UN environmental summit held in Rio de Janeiro. Billy Wilder awarded the European Felix movie prize for his life's work.

1993 Czechoslovakia divided. Peace Accord of Mutual Recognition agreed between Israel and the PLO, determination of Palestinian autonomy. Bosnia becomes involved in the war in Yugoslavia.

1994 After 14 years, a project to restore Michelangelo's frescos in the Sistine Chapel is finally completed. Tunnel link between France and the United Kingdom opens. *Pulp Fiction* awarded the Palme D'Or at Cannes. NATO intervenes in the war in Yugoslavia; end of war. Peace talks between the IRA and the British government.

1995 Christo and Jeanne Claude wrap up the Reichstag in Berlin. Outbreak of ebola fever in equatorial Africa. Sarin gas attack on the Tokyo subway network: 12 dead, 5000 injured.

Yitzhak Rabin, Bill Clinton und Yasser Arafat after signing the Gaza-Jericho Accord, September 9, 1993

1996 Dutroux scandal in Belgium. Emergence of BSE cattle disease. La Fenice opera house in Venice destroyed by fire.

1997 British crown colony Hong Kong restored to Chinese rule. The world mourns Princess Diana, killed in a car crash in Paris. James Cameron's epic *Titanic* is the most expensive movie ever made.

1998 Hurricane Mitch devastates Central America. Unrest in Indonesia; President Suharto resigns after 30 years of military dictatorship. The Lewinsky affair rocks the White House. General Pinochet arrested in United Kingdom. US embassies in Kenya and Tanzania are bombed.

1999 War in Kosovo. Seizure of Kurdish leader Abdulah Öcalan in Kenia triggers worldwide Kurdish protests. The medical organization Médécin sans Frontières is awarded the Nobel Peace Prize.

1920s. Jeanne Lanvin's dresses for mothers and daughters were still mutually distinct, yet clearly tended toward a blurring of differences. The 1920s trend for youth and androgyny generally favored the removal of distinctions between fashion for young and old. This development was revived in the 1960s and, by the 1980s, there was barely a difference to be seen in the style of dress of people of various ages. Children, adults, and the elderly wore virtually the same styles: leisure clothes, jogging pants, leggings, trainers, jeans, T-shirts, and brightly colored skirts.

Although this continues to apply in principle, a differentiation between youth fashions and clothes for working adults seems to have reemerged. For instance, the 1970s fashion revival – platform shoes, flared pants, bare midriffs, figure-hugging tops in the typical colors orange, green, or brown – has found acceptance only among very young men and women. Those who were themselves young in the 1970s and wore these styles at the time prefer not to wear them today.

The women of that generation tend to wear classic suits. Knee-length or shorter, the figure-hugging skirts and narrow blazers worn today are similar to the suits of the 1980s, except that they are more restrained and elegant. Pantsuits enjoyed a boom in the second half of the 1990s which almost completely displaced skirt suits: frequently made of materials containing stretch fibers, narrow pants and jackets are extremely comfortable and can be complemented by a waistcoat to make a three-piece suit.

Pantsuits in the classic colors gray, black, or blue (also checkered or pinstriped, depending on the year and the season) have become almost indispensable as a basic wardrobe item. Pants have replaced skirts to such an extent that the clothing industry has had to make the greatest efforts to increase the skirt's popularity and sales.

In general, skirts are worn short to just below the knee, although increasingly they are floor length and close fitting, made of bright orange, kiwi green, lemon or beige stretch material, perhaps printed with a leopard-skin or tartan pattern, decorated with slits or zips and, since around 1996, are frequently combined with padded waistcoats. On the other hand, colorful, full

skirts made of lightweight fabrics and worn with embroidered T-shirts or blouses – a style which emerged in the 1980s – have been reserved for women of middle age (and middle income). Yet again, transparent clothes are for very young men and women, or for people who would like to look young, and whose needs are catered for by the chains that have established themselves by selling cheap, trendy clothes for young people under 20 or 25. Individual pieces from such collections – a skirt perhaps, or a blouse – are often also worn by older women. The gray zone now tends to be middle age where the upper and lower limits are not fixed.

Fashion today

What is it that counts as fashion today: the creations exhibited twice yearly in haute couture shows or the clothes which are available in every department store and in every price band? Do these two areas have anything in common? Is fashion about

Alberta Ferretti, spring 1997

The lingerie look – foundation garments worn as outer garments, and sheer fabrics and lace worn in layers over simple underwear – was an unconventional style of the 1990s and generally aimed at younger women. The trend was inspired by such designers as Alberta Ferretti, famous for her delicate chiffons. She opened her first shop at the age of 17, which expressed her philosophy of a mood-dependent "emotional" dress style.

GERMAN FASHION

There was a time when Berlin competed with Paris: German fashion designers recognized that the concept of "fashion for the masses" was a recipe for success. By producing variations on French haute couture designs, they enabled the less well-off to stay in step with the splendor of the German metropolis. German couturiers were talked about not because of their experimental and bold creations, but because of their sense of style and their marketing skills. Today, the boundaries of fashion are fluid and the big names in the industry have established themselves in the global market.

The birth of ready-made clothes

When we speak of German fashion today, names like Karl Lagerfeld, Jil Sander, and Wolfgang Joop come to mind. Yet German fashion was making history back in the 19th century. Instead of attempting to outstrip haute couture, Paris' great innovation, the mass production of clothes was taken as an opportunity to reach a broad public. To safeguard the industry's success, all foreign fashion trends – not only the French – were carefully observed, and often copied or adapted.

In 1836 Hermann Gerson, "supplier to the imperial throne," founded the first company to mass-produce elegant evening dresses. Daywear, coats, and suits soon followed. He succeeded in combining profitable manufacture with interesting fashions. The Gerson establishment remained one of the most prestigious in Europe until the 1930s; it acquired international flair by introducing designs by Paul Poiret, whose creations mirrored Gerson's ideas about modern clothes.

During the 1920s, Berlin was not only the capital of Germany; it also enjoyed a reputation as the heart of the roaring twenties. Intellectuals, painters, musicians, and aristocrats from around the world met in the city to enjoy the fruits of modernism and to bring about Berlin's cultural blossoming. During this period Berlin also became a center for fashion, the creations of its designers being considered uncommonly chic.

Fashion in distress

During World War II, European haute couture stagnated and almost ceased to exist. As elsewhere, rationing became a way of life in Germany, and there were more important things than fashion to think about. Elegance, so familiar during

Berlin fashion 1922

the 1930s, was once again reserved for a narrow stratum of society. Foreign influences were now frowned upon, and the barrier between German fashion and Paris became insurmountable. Fabric was scarce, and most clothes were made either of bed linen, old uniforms, or parachutes. The National Socialist Party dictated that modesty was to be the first commandment of fashion, and that German women were to be neat and well groomed. Women who still possessed opulent and extravagant clothes were not encouraged to wear them. Functionality triumphed and, in order to have any chance of survival, clothes had to be hard-wearing. By 1941, when all the fashion design salons in Berlin were combined to form the Berlin Fashion Company, which was permitted to work for the export market only, Berlin had become a nonentity in the fashion world.

Time to catch up – the 1950s

In the early 1950s Germany had much to do to catch up with the rest of the world. Fashion was needed to bring luxury and impose some shape on a new way of life. New centers of fashion emerged in Germany: Düsseldorf became a center of

Heinz Oestergaard, 1960 collection

international trade, Berlin's clothing industry prospered once more, and Munich was notable for its fashionable elegance.

One of the most successful fashion designers of that period was Heinz Oestergaard. He opened his fashion house in Berlin and had his own philosophy: "Naturally I have a particular fondness for the grand evening gown, but I dedicate all my care and attention to 'little' dresses, garments in which women can feel well dressed throughout the day." He espoused a practical elegance which sold well in the form of good-quality, mass-produced garments. In pursuance of this logic, Oestergaard closed his house in order to concentrate on producing "fashion for everyone" for Quelle, the mail-order company, and to design a uniform for the German police force.

Willi Bogner's name became synonymous with sportswear. He had been responsible for dressing the German 1936 Olympic team and, in the 1950s, he set the trend for superior, mass-produced sportswear which could easily be adapted to suit the requirement of frequently changing lines.

Berlin-born Heinz Schulze-Varell trained with Gerson and made his name in the 1930s with his couture salon and with his designs for movie costumes. After the war he moved to Munich, where he became a renowned creator of extravagant and superbly feminine garments.

The superstars

During the 1980s, the most glittering personality of the designers' decade was Karl Lagerfeld. Although he began his career on French soil at the age of 16, he has always been regarded as a German fashion designer. It was while working for Fendi, Krizia, and Chloé that he became a European fashion phenomenon whose reputation as an innovator brought him all the way to Chanel: as design director he has been rejuvenating the classic rigor of Chanel since 1983, thereby returning the

house to public attention. Furthermore, a new line, launched under the name KL by Karl Lagerfeld, is now marketed by Quelle, the mail-order company, for whom he also acts as a consultant. Lagerfeld, the "chameleon of fashion," has a glamorous, frequently playful style that is not restricted to one sector of the fashion market. His motto is "Creativity, like the market, is a battlefield. One period of rest and it's all over."

Hamburg-born Jil Sander is known as the architect of fashion. Good-quality fabrics, her most important building blocks, have absolute priority. In 1967, the former fashion editor opened her first boutique in Hamburg, thus launching her unstoppable global career. Jil Sander's creations are characterized by her purist approach – clear tailoring, usually suffused with understatement, and good-quality materials. Her range also includes cosmetics, shoes, bags, and other accessories.

Hugo Boss, the label created by the company Holy, has also followed the tradition of high-class mass production. Holy markets its clothes under three labels, providing something for every type of man. Clothes marketed under the Baldessarini label have an exquisite touch: every piece is hand-finished. The Hugo and Hugo Boss labels represent classical yet relaxed elegance; this menswear is not characterized by daring experimentalism.

The aim of Wolfgang Joop, by contrast, is to seize on short-lived trends and transform them into garments for men and women that exude a cool elegance. Nevertheless, some of his collections have featured brightly

Karl Lagerfeld with Amber Valetta, Naomi Campbell, and Kate Moss, at a Chanel show, 1997

colored stylistic hybrids that have broken away from a sometimes rather uniform, urban style.

Much of today's fashion comes from licensing: cosmetics and accessories convey the names of German fashion houses to the far reaches of the world.

Hugo Boss, spring/summer 2000

Jil Sander dress, 1994

Advertisement for Rocky jeans, 1997

Reminiscent of a photo of US soldiers putting up the national flag on the island of Iwo Jima, this scene portrays a pair of jeans as the unifying symbol of identity for both sexes.

Christian Lacroix, haute couture, 1995/96

A countermovement, with a return to subdued colors and simple, unpretentious cuts, was initiated by Christian Lacroix, who presented his first collection in 1987 and immediately became a star. Inspired by various elements, such as Mediterranean national costumes and the opulence of ancien régime dress, the creations by this designer from the south of France are characterized by variety and pastiche; rarely is a garment made in a single fabric and rarely does a design refer to only one style. Fine fabrics, bright colors, and an emphasis on the body's outline determine his designs and restore glamor and luxury to the world of fashion. These designs often appear a trifle theatrical: Lacroix, who studied the history of art before launching his career as a fashion designer, also likes to design costumes for the stage. As to the role of fashion, his maxim is not liberation but freedom, and one of his best-known statements is: "My designs should contribute to people becoming what they have always wanted to be: cheerful!"

affordability and wearability, or is it an art form that follows its own rules? Is fashion what is disseminated by the fashion magazines? If so: which magazines? Is fashion only what is worn by the very young or can it also be what women over 40 wear? Can we even distinguish between fashion and nonfashion any more?

What is clear is that haute couture, prêt-à-porter, department-store clothes, and street fashions are drifting ever further apart; it could even be said that they have become entirely separate from one another. The catwalks feature skirts for men, although these are in fact very rarely worn by ordinary people, and then only for special occasions like the Love Parade. Culs de Paris, clothes with hunchbacks and bumps, or simply breast-revealing dresses are to be seen only at fashion events, never in real life.

In practice, people are seeking wearability, figure-enhancement, and also a certain amount of decorum – and they want to look good. The way we view things is being changed in the couture salons, where the female form is used to create new sculptures that scarcely relate to actual bodies and conventional beauty – or on the contrary, the relation to the body has become so direct that young bodies shaped by diets and exercise become the garment and are revealed, rather than covered up, by the fabric.

Fashion in the 1990s and into a new millennium seems to be composed of this kind of diversity. It can no longer be tidily divided into fashion and nonfashion. Garments purchased in boutiques or department stores and discarded after a season's wear are as much fashion as are the creations of great designers. With so much diversity, there been no common thread for some time. Fashion continues to serve as a means expressing individuality, and also of marking social differences and boundaries.

However, fashion's actual forms have been changing at an increasing speed. They seem to have become more arbitrary and exchangeable, so that people are no longer obliged to adhere to a consistent type, and they have brought an element of playfulness to fashion. In reality, however, the actual choice of dress, jacket, or shoes is extremely important in the presentation of a look.

Change is in the nature of fashion, but it cannot happen without content. Content is no longer as standardized as it was in the 1950s; it can be chosen with a degree of relative freedom. It is therefore impossible to state that fashion in the 1990s and into the 2000s has a single direction. It plays with androgyny, and it deepens the gulf between the sexes. It is sporty and ladylike, ragged and glamorous, disheveled and dressy: it is all those things, consecutively, concurrently, simultaneously. Fashion, which coincidentally

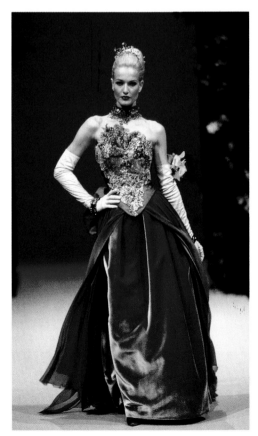

emerged at the same time as capitalism, has finally collapsed just as the heart of capitalism – the notion of consumerism as lifestyle – has ceased to beat. Even art – regardless of whether it is painting, literature, or fashion – has long ceased to be independent of commerce and no longer denies this.

Label as fetish

The sense of a garment as a consumer-product rather than a functional item is clearly demonstrated by our era's obsession with labels. It can at times seem that labels have displaced content. Open any fashion magazine today and the advertisements for the better-known companies present themselves as artfully constructed images at the center of which the garment no longer lies. Artistic licence was applied during earlier periods of fashion photography as well, especially in the 1950s, but the pictures tended to be precise representations of the garments worn by the models.

Nowadays it is often necessary to read the caption in order to find out what the person in the image is wearing: the dress is by Versace, the shoes by Prada, the coat by Missoni . . . The image itself exists as an esthetically autonomous construct, which also has the function of selling the clothes that it illustrates: a function which it conceals and which is only apparent in the accompanying words, usually climaxing in the name of the label. The label may represent a particular style and quality, but above all it stands for social distinction, for the image that the individual wishes to portray by this choice of dress.

It is often impossible to tell whether a T-shirt is the product of a famous designer or a no-name brand; however its provenance is made apparent when the name of the manufacturer is emblazoned across the front. This in turn leads to an inflationary trade in labels. It has become difficult to find items of clothing that do not feature the name, or at least the initials, of the designer or manufacturer, since mass-producers have adapted to this trend by making garments sporting their own, ostentatiously placed brand names, in an attempt to suggest quality and exclusivity. However, this can only be successful with the uninitiated, since

for real fashionistas it is not just any old name that counts, but the right name.

The techno trend has added irony to this label fetishism by spawning what might be called dayflies, limited-edition labels which become desirable objects due to the small numbers available. Of course these labels have little more than an esthetic function since, if they exist for a limited period only, they cannot produce the effect of recognition – all that remains is the graphic symbol and the wearer's declaration that he or she dresses independently of tradition.

Fashionable understatement

The exclusivity that is the preserve of wealthy fashion aficionados can now be guaranteed by the new modesty that emerged in the early 1990s and that frequently sports a very expensive price tag. In contrast to the 1980s, today's wealth is not paraded but concealed in the detail. Suddenly, conspicuous

CK One, the fragrance by Calvin Klein

Calvin Klein's first unisex fragrance "For a man or a woman," aimed to portray a new kind of sexiness – away from the blunt and direct eroticism of the 1980s and toward something approximating a certain demeanor. Global openness based on the maxim that "everything is possible, nothing is fixed" was accentuated. Sexual ambiguity and androgyny fused to create a neutrality and passivity previously regarded as unusual – at least in advertising.

Prada, fall/winter 1998/99

Miuccia Prada's designs are simple and natural – a tendency emphasized by the use of leaves on some of the other pieces in this collection. This white silk dress is sparsely structured by means of geometric seams and represents the restrained, minimalist esthetic of Prada, whose designs have also been described as inverted luxury. The unusual and surprising combination of fabrics in her costly garments may not be apparent at first glance, which is why Prada appeals to lovers of understatement. It is not surprising therefore, that a fifth of this Italian designer's turnover comes from Japan, a country whose traditionally rigorous and purist designs have had a strong influence on the West.

he maintains the simple form of the classic suit while substantially refining it with regard to fabric and perfect workmanship. The cost and time required for a dandy's dress were at least as much as that required for an ostentatiously dressed woman, yet it was less obvious; made invisible to the common eye, it was apparent only to the connoisseur. The same principle applies to the clothes of Jil Sander, who has made the cool art of omission her guiding principle and who designs unadorned garments, the quality of which may only become apparent when the fabric is touched or the garment worn.

When it comes to the restrained presentation of ostensibly unspectacular clothes, the Italian company Prada has set standards enthusiastically adopted by many others. Subdued, even somber colors, apparently simple cuts, fabrics that look felted when they are new, garments that appear to be much too small for the wearer, are the dominant characteristics of this fashion. It is presented by unkempt, pale models who seem dissipated and unfit despite their youth and who bear absolutely no relation to the magnificent ideals of beauty of the 1980s.

The models used to present the Austrian Helmut Lang's minimalist designs look the same. This trend can be regarded as a fin-de-siècle phenomenon which seems more justified than ever given the current global political and environmental situation. Yet it also begs the question of whether this new trend really has to be linked to a historical situation or whether it is not in fact the product of a sated society in search of new esthetic pleasures that contrast explicitly with the ostentatious glamor of earlier fashion trends.

Apart from the fact that splendor still thrives alongside this avant garde – just think of Versace or Dolce & Gabbana – this new modesty tends to require the use of costly fabrics and is so expensive to buy that it has brought about a new understanding of beauty; it is regarded as a distinguishing mark of those whose refined taste (and comfortable income) enables them to wrap themselves in the apparently inconspicuous products of luxury labels.

The new modesty in fashion is mirrored in a new physical type of woman whose appearance has had an increasing influence

ostentation and glamorous fashion ceased to be the marks of fine taste, that role being taken by the illusion of meagerness instead.

In terms of fashion history there are parallels to be drawn between this process and the dandyism of the mid-to-late 19th century. Dandies did not wish to look poor; quite the opposite. Yet they turned menswear, which over the years had become less elaborate than womenswear and thus appeared more modest, into a high art of subtle differentiation. A dandy understates:

on fashion photography and who has gradually supplanted the radiant beauties of the 1980s. Kate Moss rang in a new era. Emaciated, pale, and with the air of a neglected child, she fixed empty eyes on the camera and signaled that the era of the magnificent supermodel and glamorous fashions was over.

Such images embody the current social preoccupation with youth, disillusionment, and apathy as well as violence, drugs, and abuse, and transform these into a new esthetic standard which contains aspects of the punk era. Kate Moss' high cheekbones and large mouth have set precedents; many models now have a similar look, and the Slavic type has also become very popular.

These young women are often carefully made up to look as if they are not made up at all and have stumbled, unwashed and uncombed, into the studio after a night of unbridled excess. When visibly made up, it is to look as if they had just been beaten up and were parading their bruises, or they are fitted with headdresses to transform their faces into entirely artificial living images. Finally, piercing and tattoos have also attained popularity as a rejection of the image of feminine loveliness.

Retro fashion

Young fashion in the mid-1990s was dominated by a revival of 1970s styles. A toned-down version also found its way into general fashion. The fashionable image in boutiques and department stores, in fashion magazines, and on the street has long been determined by this trend. Shoes were generally broader and almost square, with wide, boxy heels and, often, platform soles. T-shirts, blouses and sweaters became tighter and shorter, jackets were closely tailored and never straight, as was still the case at the beginning of the decade. The same applied to the more figure-hugging and shorter coats.

Pants were either very narrow and unpleated or loose, and then frequently flared. Long waistcoats worn over miniskirts were in vogue once more, as were frock coats for women: the general influence of menswear was noticeable. Subdued colors dominated. What made these new garments different from their 1970s prototypes were the new

The skirt for men, 1999

Since Jean Paul Gaultier launched his men's skirt in the 1980s and was himself occasionally seen in a kilt, this garment has made repeated appearances at the major fashion shows. Although generally unassuming as an item in itself, it is astonishing when worn by men. At the end of the 1990s this traditional piece of female clothing was offered not only by avant-garde gentlemen's outfitters, but even by trendy, mass youth market outlets. As with skirts for women, there are few guidelines as regards the type of top that can be worn with a man's skirt, although men are advised to maintain the androgynous effect. Like no other item in men's collections, the skirt is a challenge to gender clichés and even today demands courage from the wearer.

materials. The synthetic fabrics of the 1970s were replaced by highly refined hi-tech fibers that could achieve a variety of effects: rubber or leather, silky or with a metallic sheen, and all beautifully soft and utterly wearable – everything is possible and greatly expands the spectrum of natural fibers.

Grunge

In parallel to the 1970s revival a new style emerged: grunge. Flimsy floral dresses that did not quite seem to fit the wearer were combined with heavy-duty boots. The smooth femininity fashionable at the time was countered by an eclectic, very young, and very individualistic femininity that (allegedly!) ran counter to society's norms – although it was immediately absorbed by the mainstream. In fact, grunge, which was featured in all the fashion magazines, even managed to draw politics into the fashion scene when President Clinton issued a

Space-age fashion, 1999

The manifestation of the virtual world in the real world seems to have been brought about by clothes made in synthetic fabrics, artificial-looking makeup, and incongruous combinations, such as sportswear and prêt-à-porter, hi-tech and fine fabrics. Borrowing from the futuristic designs of Pierre Cardin and André Courrèges, astronauts' hoods reemerged, as did an adaptation of space boots with a strongly shaped sole. The padded collar of the shoulderless polyester top is held together with velcro, and the variable skirt is only fitted to the waist and is constructed from two projecting lengths of padded material. Although the clothes reveal large areas of the body and, with the featherlike appliqué on the top, contain references to the exquisite elegance of 1950s evening dresses, the overall effect is of a woman equipped for her daily struggle in the cyberspace of the third millennium and a universe away from the conventional image of feminine beauty.

Eenie van de Meiklokjes, presenter on the VIVA music channel, 1999

The role of television as transmitter of fashion has become even more important since the birth of television music channels. By being living exhibits of short-lived fashion trends, the presenters are like the stars that they introduce. The combination of youthful avantgarde and commerce brings forth personalities whose dress style, haircut, mannerisms, and language become the subject of imitation. The channels ensure that each presenter has their own authentic, individual, and eminently marketable style. One variant is the loud, colorful, and not exactly sporty image of Eenie van de Meiklokjes, who has a preference for a form of elegance which is not created by independent label T-shirts but by a wardrobe full of basics like Levi's jeans and Kookai blouses which she combines in a way that is reminiscent of the 1930s with prêt-à-porter by Vivienne Westwood, Gaultier, or W.&LT.

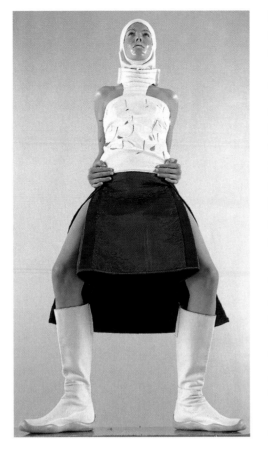

warning about grunge's glorification of drugs and declared that he was minded to forbid its further dissemination.

Girlies

Whereas 1980s style was largely defined by stars like Madonna and soap operas such as *Dynasty*, style in the 1990s was set by the MTV music station and early evening television programs aimed at teenagers, which developed stronger styles of their own. The predominant mid-1990s type was the girlie. She too was modeled to a great extent on the style of the 1970s; her wardrobe would include short skirts or tight, often flared, pants, short tops that occasionally reveal a pierced belly button, or short summer lingerie dresses definitely worn with platform shoes.

Hair was died pale blond or pinkish-red, worn shoulder-length, and layered close to the head with the ends casually blow-dried outward. Long, straight hair also went with this style, either messily pinned up or braided. Under no circumstances should the hair look dressed.

Girlies were cool: they knew what they wanted and they took it. At least, that was the impression that they gave. They believed feminism to be an utterly outmoded concept

and considered themselves completely emancipated in a world designed to be fun and to be speedily conquered.

Techno

A variant of the 1970s revival was the techno trend. Techno took up many things which were once the sole province of minorities and creatively adapted them: skirts, albeit still rare, cropped, bleached hair, and earrings for men, sometimes accompanied by an equally bleached goatee. Clothes were inspired by the 1960s and 1970s without being slavish copies and were eclectically combined with other styles: a little bit of punk, a pinch of girlie, elements of the fetish scene, and many new items rooted in technology, website design, and the world of consumerism.

Accessories were again highly ranked and were characterized by key concepts of the 1990s: communication and mobility. At the end of the decade wristwatches could receive short messages; cellphones became a basic piece of equipment for young people; those in work may also need a notebook. All had to be carried in conspicuous bags, the form, material, and label of which continues to change seasonally.

Haute couture and prêt-à-porter

The often humorous eclecticism which characterized 1990s youth and street

fashions did not necessarily stop at the doors of the great fashion houses, although with them it might take quite different forms. Vivienne Westwood and Jean Paul Gaultier continue to play their own idiosyncratic games with fashion history and frequently achieve unexpected and utterly original effects. Gaultier works with extreme notions of masculinity and femininity, which he confuses, thus returning to the theme of androgyny. His collections have characteristic titles like Les Andro-Jeans. He designed the famous costumes – corsets and suits – for Madonna's 1990 "Blond Ambition" tour. Time and again he has made ethnic and cultural motifs his own and gives his collections names like Les Rabbins Chics (The Chic Rabbis; 1993/94), Les Vikings (The Vikings; 1993/94), and Le Grand Voyage (The Great Journey; 1994/95), which included elements of Tibetan and Mongolian ethnic dress. Following many successful years in prêt-à-porter, he finally presented his first couture show in 1997.

Vivienne Westwood's collections also move freely within the full spectrum of European cultural history. She is undoubtedly the most creative, innovative, and influential fashion designer of our time, whose sense of humor and mastery of her craft are utterly convincing. Her clothes are not androgynous but brazenly display classic feminine erotic clichés (and, since her first menswear collection in 1990, masculine ones as well). She caused a frenzy with her penis-shaped ladies' shoes – an ironic allusion to Sigmund Freud's interpretation of the shoe as symbolizing the penis.

Glamor

The French and Italian haute couture and prêt-à-porter establishments that pander to the new modesty are but few. They continue to value wit and color, ostentatious theatricality and sexy glamor: even Rei Kawakubo, founder of the Comme des Garçons label, has begun to use color in her collections, although the garments are autonomous sculptures that do not show a traditional relation to the body but whose rough cut and deformations demonstrate her critical stance toward the esthetic of dress and its sexual component. In 1997 many salons featured the most beautiful,

Dolce & Gabbana, 1997
Cast as Cruella de Vil in the movie of *101 Dalmatians*, the actress arrives at the premiere dressed in sophisticated, vaguely sinful evening attire. The Italians Domenico Dolce and Stefano Gabbano were able to give their imagination free rein when they designed this elaborate costume. The Dalmatian print and gently transparent dress reveal a lace body that only just covers the bosom. The sparkling coat is trimmed with a fur collar and cuffs which show off a flashy necklace. The overall effect is typical of the design duo. D&G is synonymous with the eroticization of luxuriant femininity through the use of flamboyant, color coordinated accessories, references to the fetish scene, and an aura of elegance like that which surrounded the stars of early Hollywood movies.

delicate, colorful, and transparent evening dresses under which nothing but bare skin could be worn. Gianni Versace's creations, always colorful, became more elegant and restrained in his last collections, although they continued to send obviously erotic signals. Chanel showed modern elegance, Yves Saint Laurent remained faithful to his opulent style, and many of the other old houses continued to offer the world splendor and riches.

The first show presented by the Italians Domenico Dolce and Stefano Gabbano was held in Milan in 1986. Since then, Dolce & Gabbana has become a very fashionable label. They love the sensual femininity of Sophia Loren and Anna Magnani, and their designs play with old-fashioned feminine markers like corsets and full (or very tight) skirts, romantic florals, animal prints, diamanté and embroidery, exaggerating these to such an extent that the effect can be described as ironic glamor bordering on kitsch.

Since 1994, Gucci has also joined the greats of Italian fashion. The company once produced expensive accessories: bags, luggage, shoes, silk scarves, ties, wristwatches. Constant quarrels undermined the morale of the fashion house and it had

VIVIENNE WESTWOOD

(b. 1941)

British designer Vivienne Westwood today enjoys international acclaim as an eccentric genius. Together with her partner Malcolm McLaren she entered the fashion business in the early 1970s, initially with copies of Teddy boy suits, followed by biker and sadomasochist (S&M) outfits and punk fashions. Her first catwalk show, in 1981, featured the Pirates collection and launched Westwood's career as a couturier: within the space of only three years she was counted among the world's foremost designers. Since then, the fashion shows of this former schoolteacher, supplier of grandiose ideas, and holder of the OBE have become the high point of every fashion season.

First lady of punk

Vivienne Westwood, who caused a sensation in mid-1970s London with her punk fashion designs, is today a celebrated fashion queen. Her clothes are not to everybody's taste – some find them decadent, grotesque, unwearable – yet fashion aficionados cannot wait to see the next ensemble with which she will amaze her public. This self-taught, eccentric Englishwoman has shown courage, and often makes a direct hit in her battle against the "taste dictatorship of the masses." She senses what the next trend will be long before it becomes commonplace, and insiders regard her as a paragon of inspiration. Her liking for the unorthodox, together with daring and a strong element of recklessness enable her to bring onto the market styles whose shock effect would frighten her competitors from a commercial point of view alone.

"I was very working class"

Vivienne Westwood was born near Manchester in 1941. Her lower-middle-class upbringing was hardly spectacular. In 1958 she moved to London with her parents, became a primary school teacher, married Derek Westwood, the manager of

a rural dance hall, and became a mother. Shortly afterward, she left her husband and began a new life.

Let it rock

Her new companion Malcolm McLaren, a student at Croydon Art School and a friend of her brother's, was a vehement critic of the flower power movement, which he regarded as a mercilessly commercialized and empty lifestyle. Together they sought new forms of expression, discovered the conformist charm of the 1950s and in 1970 opened a small shop at the cheap end of the King's Road, where they earned their living by selling nostalgic fashions. Vivienne, by then the mother of two boys, would take apart old Teddy boy suits in order to copy them – a fascination with originals which she retains to this day. Whatever subject she tackles, she must always get to the bottom of it.

"Too fast to live, too young to die"

The trend exhausted itself after two years and the couple found new clients in the biker scene. In 1972 they renamed the shop Too Fast to Live, Too Young to Die and began to stock martial leather suits, brightly colored African suits, and T-shirts with pornographic slogans, thus coming into conflict with the law. Their reaction was swift; they renamed the shop SEX, made their T-shirt slogans even more provocative, and enhanced their stock with the addition of rather taboo S&M scene garments. As the protagonist of "rubber clothes for the office," Vivienne Westwood appeared in public wearing a leather miniskirt, torn T-shirt, chains, padlocks, and stiletto heels: a provocation to "good taste" if ever there was one. She enjoyed going to the extreme limits of offensiveness and her clients were delighted: Westwood's "catalyst shirts" sold like hot cakes. The concept of punk was born.

Vivienne Westwood wears a plastic carrier bag as a headscarf, 1994

Queen of punk

It was during this phase that the work of the dynamic Westwood-McLaren duo began to diverge: in 1974 he became the manager of the New York Dolls, and she created a sensational outfit made entirely of red rubber and vinyl. However, they did not become famous until they began to represent the legendary punk band the Sex Pistols in 1975, whereby McLaren acted as the manager and Westwood as the costume designer who gave them S&M outfits and aggressive accessories. The Sex Pistols' first performance, held on the occasion of the reopening of the shop under the name Seditionaries, hit the mood of the moment because the pair had not merely understood the message of the "fuck-off" generation, they themselves were promoters of the movement. Photographs of the time show today's top designer as

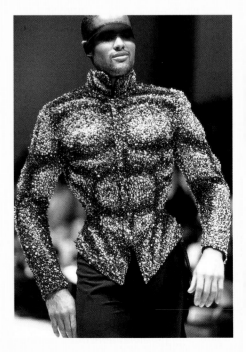

Left: salesclerks Jordan and Paul Getty outside Westwood and McLaren's boutique SEX in London, 1974

Right: the Martyr of Love collection, 1996

the prototype of punk woman: bottle blond punk hair, pale face with dark lips, short kilt teamed with huge lace-up boots. "I did not yet regard myself as a fashion designer at that time. We were looking for motifs of rebellion to shock the establishment. The result was punk."

World's End: the end and a new beginning

Three years later, the rebels' subculture was disintegrating and the cult band Sex Pistols was finished, Sid Vicious dead from a drug overdose. In 1980 Vivienne Westwood abandoned punk and, a little later, separated from Malcolm McLaren. She energetically began to ransack the history of clothing for new ideas and became interested in the dress of outcasts, rebels, Native Americans, and pirates.

The couple changed the identity of their shop at 430 King's Road one last time, calling it World's End. Here, the floor was crooked, the monstrous clock on the facade showed 13 hours and sped backward, while the Queen of Punk began work on Romantics of the High Sea, the first of the two final catwalk shows that she was to organize with McLaren and with which she would conquer the world of fashion. The collection was fantastic, precious, and colorful. A particularly lovely bright orange suit with gashed sleeves, black and yellow polka dot waistcoat, and a two-cornered hat found their way into the collection of London's Victoria and Albert Museum, as have around 30 examples of Westwood's work. In 1982 they took their second collection, Nostalgia of Mud, straight to Paris – the first Britons since Mary Quant to show their designs in the French capital. However, their paths separated shortly afterward. Only Westwood's hand is visible in the Witches collection of 1983, a synthesis of ethnic and mass-produced styles.

"Creativity comes from technique." Vivienne Westwood's strength comes from the combination of nonconformity and professionalism with which she develops and realizes her own ideas. The starting point and pool of ideas for her work is the inexhaustible fount of historical material from which she takes her inspiration while remaining independent of the countless current trends, because, as Westwood herself says "Nothing is more old fashioned than zeitgeist."

In 1984, at the height of the fashion for power dressing, she shocked with the extremely feminine silhouette of the unusual padding around bosom and derrière of her minicrinis, which, combined with platform shoes, had a magnetic effect on the viewer. In 1987 she turned corsets into a respectable item of women's outerwear, and in 1990 she had them printed with scenes from *Shepherd Watching a Sleeping Shepherdess* by François Boucher (1703–70), one of her favorite paintings. Her version of the bustle known as a cul de Paris appeared in the Erotic Zones collection of 1994 in an evening dress in which the bustle, in puffed-out fabric, was transferred upward so that it did not cover the buttocks. This is exemplary of her concept of absorption and transformation. In Vive la Cocotte (1995/96), she played with the semiotic repertoire of the demimonde, and in 1997 she turned her wit and esthetic instinct to the traditional dress of the Scots by transforming men's outfits into coquettish and erotic women's suits. Her designs always play a subversive game during which she uses irony to countercheck historic or traditional processes. When she is asked about the wearability of her clothes, her response is that it is not courage that is required, "only the willingness to be better and more individually dressed than others," and that nothing could be worse than "sloppy mediocrity."

Since the early 1990s she has also challenged men to be strong and sexually attractive. In 1990 she went to Florence to show her first menswear collection, Cut and Slash, and the fashion shows that she has been staging in Milan since 1996 have been a great success. Again, the clothes are modeled on the courtly fashions of centuries gone by when

Anglomania, fall/winter 1993/94 collection. Linda Evangelista wears a Highland outfit.

handsome men could strut like peacocks and pretty pageboys be coquettish flirts. The high point thus far was the 1996 Martyr of Love collection which featured a strongly tailored jacket entirely covered in pearls and sequins by the corset-makers Pearl. In the past, men had much greater opportunity to express themselves through their clothes, says Westwood. She is merely attempting to "bring some of that back," although, naturally, in her own, caricaturing way.

Rank and honor

Vivienne Westwood is today one of the undisputed greats of fashion. The honors that have been heaped upon her speak for themselves: she was voted British fashion designer of the year in 1990 and 1991 and was awarded the OBE in 1992, when she also became an honorary member of the Royal College of Art. In the late 1980s she began to accept guest professorships, first for three years at the Academy of the Applied Arts in Vienna, where she met her second husband and partner Andreas Kronthaler, and then in 1993 at the Academy of Art in Berlin, where she continues indefatigably to stimulate students to ever greater achievements. In the meantime she has become the owner of retail outlets in London, Paris, and Tokyo, deals in her own, officially recognized tartan, the MacAndreas, and has recently brought her own fragrance lines onto the market. Despite all this, the black sheep image persists, and she is often the subject of newspaper headlines.

Left: spring/summer 1999

W.&L.T., fall/winter 1999/2000

The Belgian Walter van Beirendonck markets his emphatically urban label W.&L.T. (Wild and Lethal Trash) with the slogan "kiss the future." This outfit, consisting of cargo pants, mohair sweater, and outsize PVC bag, is suitable for the active city-dweller who is constantly on the move: it is comfortable and hard-wearing, adorned with the visible symbols of expensive understatement, and suitable for any occasion.
W.&L.T. veers between the retrospection of the fashion of the flower children and futuristic designs, featuring as it does long denim dresses with chunky sweaters on the one hand and a myriad of seemingly functional applications and accessories on the other. Beirendonck is one of many contemporary designers who have taken up the theme of the millennium in their designs.

John Galliano, prêt-à-porter spring/summer 1998

John Galliano, designer director at Dior, developed a prêt-à-porter interpretation of sportswear, an almost unrecognizable version of current sporty fashions. He characteristically bases the set pieces of his creations on a variety of epochs and styles, which he frequently presents in unusual settings. For the spring/summer 1998 show he had a building site set up in the Trocadéro in Paris in which the models gathered around a 1950s automobile for a group photograph. Materials like velvet, silk, and fur are combined with modern synthetic fabrics, models wear 1920s wigs, and evening gowns are worn with costly baseball caps. This mixture of styles is ennobled by the name of Dior and permits an audience used to exclusive, correct elegance to enjoy the freedom of stylistic incongruities.

to be sold. Shortly before his murder in 1994, Maurizio Gucci, owner of the company and grandson of founder Guccio Gucci, appointed the American Tom Ford as design director, since when the house of Gucci has not looked back. Tom Ford determines the house's fashion flair with his rigorous designs which are reminiscent of the styles of the 1960s and 1970s, although made of modern hi-tech materials: hipster pants, military-style blouses, and stretch dresses and, for men, stretch satin suits.

Belgium, newcomer to the fashion scene

Belgian fashion came to the fore in the late 1980s when six graduates of Antwerp's Academy of Art got together to stage a fashion show in London. Since then they have gone their separate ways. Ann Demeulemeester, with her avant-garde classicism, is the most spectacular of the group though her restrained manner also makes her appear the least sensational. Most of her work is in black and white, with the rare addition of a colored accent such as the red items featured in the 1996/97 or 1998/99 collections. For her, fashion begins with the naked human body, which she aims to provide with the best possible clothing. Her garments are designed not just to look good, but to feel good too. Huge men's jackets, outsize, loose pants that seem to be slipping off the hips, astonishing drapings on apparently simple dresses, or ties that are worn on the bare skin beneath

transparent tops, bear her unmistakable signature. Skinny, slightly androgynous women like Patty Smith and Ann Demeulemeester herself are the physical types that best suit these garments, notwithstanding the designer's statement that her work is not exclusive to a single type.

Dries van Noten's designs are characterized by the combination of ethnic elements with classic European forms, such as jackets. He is also notable for his use of rich fabrics.

Dirk Bikkemberg started out with unusual collections for men before he began designing for women – initially very masculine garments, later adding lurex, corsets and decolletés in unexpected places.

Martin Margiela turns his garments inside out and reveals what usually remains concealed: lining and seams, reinforcements and inserts. With respect to this unconventional work, which provokes an artistic reflection of clothing and fashion, he shares some qualities with Rei Kawakubo, with whom he has also staged a show.

Walter van Beirendonck is fascinated by virtual reality, as is reflected in his fashion designs. He has now started to sell his designs on the Internet, where they can be virtually combined and changed, thereby providing the designer with an insight into his customers' attitudes. His youth label is called W.&L.T., short for Wild and Lethal Trash – a perhaps slightly overconsciously provocative rejection of the concept of fashion as beautiful pretense. His work is not

Alexander McQueen, brocade dress
1996

The graceful elegance of the brocade
and the extravagant cut of the dress
with the pronounced collar stands in
uncomfortable contrast to the injured
face of model Devon Aoki and her
hard, one-eyed look. British fashion
photographer Nick Knight creates
artistically heightened images of
modern reality by digital means.
He believes that the insoluble
contradiction between beauty and
destruction, innocence and violence
is a part of this reality. He does not
concentrate on a single aspect of a
fashion shot – a pretty model in an
exquisite McQueen design – but
endeavors to build into the picture
an emotion which originates far beyond
the subject that is photographed.
This shot, for *Visionaire* magazine,
therefore goes way beyond fashion
photography, yet still does justice to the
fashion designer, since the critical view
of beauty and glamor that it expresses
is shared by Alexander McQueen in his
unconventional designs.

just for the beautiful and slender, but also for men who are as corpulent as himself.

A new generation: the British are coming

A new generation has taken over at many of the great, old fashion houses – probably most spectacularly at Givenchy and Dior. The design directors, who determine the houses' lines, are young, avant-garde, and British: John Galliano, known for his fantastic and diverse creations, spent a year with Givenchy before going to Dior in 1997 where he greatly modernized the fashion house.

His successor at Givenchy was 27-year-old Alexander McQueen, a self-confessed "big mouth" who manages repeatedly to shock the world of fashion. His early provocative designs for Givenchy attracted a great deal of attention, and he followed up his uncompromising line with his own label.

The house of Chloé made Stella McCartney its head designer. The daughter of ex-Beatle Paul McCartney designs delicate, girlish dresses in the lingerie style.

Full circle

The return of the British to the fashion scene completes the circle: haute couture was launched 100 years ago by an Englishman in Paris, Charles Worth. Today it is once more inspired by British designers. Although Paris is still regarded as the capital of fashion, "fashion" no longer means "French fashion." In the best possible way, fashion in the 20th century and into the 21st has truly become an international phenomenon.

GLOSSARY

Accessory Something worn or carried to complete a fashionable appearance; for example, a handbag, shoes, a scarf, or jewelry.

Afghan coat Embroidered goatskin or sheepskin coat, popular in the 1970s, when it was part of the ethnic and folkloric style.

Aigrette Head decoration consisting of a bunch or plume of feathers attached to the hair or hat; launched by Paul Poiret in the 1920s.

A-line A-shaped line of a dress or coat, created by Christian Dior in 1955. The narrow shoulders and hips are accentuated by a dropped waistline and flared skirt. In 1998/99 a less extreme form of the A-line reappeared in haute couture, notably at Chanel.

Alta moda pronta Italian prêt-à-porter.

Ankle boots Boots reaching to the ankle and fitted either with zips or laces. They can be either flat, with a sporty look, or feminine, with stiletto heels.

Avant-garde Literally, the advance guard; in fashion terms, experimental and unconventional designers who often establish new trends.

Baby doll Nightwear consisting of panties and top; originally a puff-sleeved loose top and shorts. It became fashionable in 1956 thanks to the film *Baby Doll* and its star Caroll Baker. It was reinterpreted by couturier Jacques Griffe in 1957.

Balloon skirt Full skirt, lightly gathered in at the hem. It was used by Madame Grès in 1950 and by Hubert de Givenchy in 1957. It was briefly revived in 1987 when the form was applied to cocktail dresses and appeared once again as part of the retro look of the late 1990s.

Bermuda shorts Short pants reaching to just above the knee.

Blazer Single- or double-breasted, hip-length man's jacket without a waist seam.

Blouson Hip-length jacket with a drawstring through the hem. A popular style of jacket since the 1950s.

Bob Short hairstyle with bangs and a side parting, developed from the pageboy cut and fashionable in the 1920s. Bob wigs were worn to match evening gowns.

Bodystocking Figure-hugging suit, similar to sheer or knitwear pantyhose except that it covers the entire body. Launched by André Courrèges in the late 1960s, the bodystocking became a staple of disco wear in the late 1970s, when it was made in shiny, opaque fabrics.

Bolero 1. Short jacket with long sleeves, reaching almost to the waist. 2. Small round hat with upturned brim. Originally part of traditional Spanish dress.

Boutique Type of small clothes store that first appeared in the 1930s as an outlet for accessories distinct from outlets for haute couture. It the 1960s boutiques were central to the marketing of young fashion. Today they are usually associated with expensive prêt-à-porter.

Brocade Heavy silk jacquard fabric with silver or gold threads in the weave. A well-known example of brocade weave is the Renaissance pomegranate pattern.

Bubble cut Short hairstyle with large curls usually produced by a permanent wave; popular in the 1960s and 1970s.

Bustle (Cul de Paris) A pad suspended from the waist and worn over the buttocks beneath a gathered skirt. Popular from the late 19th to the early 20th centuries as a means of creating the illusion of a slender torso and pronounced derrière. See also Cul de Paris.

Butterfly sleeve Short sleevelike shoulder valance.

Caftan A long, loose dress with long sleeves and a belt, derived from a type of man's robe worn in eastern Mediterranean countries.

Cape Hooded cloak with slits for the arms and a neck fastening.

Capri pants Narrow three-quarter-length pants with vents below the knee. Popular in the 1950s, they reappeared in the 1980s and 1990s.

Chanel suit Simple yet elegant women's suit named after a style created by Coco Chanel. Typically made of tweed, it is single-breasted, sometimes with a small collar, and often adorned with gilt buttons and contrasting trimmings, small pockets, and a loosely fitted skirt. Worn with a blouse with ties at the collar (Chanel blouse) and long gilt chain necklaces which may also be worn as belts. This ensemble forms the core of the Chanel style.

Charleston Short, slightly flared, waistless sheath dress with narrow shoulders.

Check Various checkered patterns based on Scottish tartan. Popular for jackets, checks also became fashionable in the 1990s for sumptuous dresses and long skirts, such as those designed by Jil Sander.

Chiffon Fine, sheer fabric, usually made of natural silk or synthetic fibers, produced by twisting yarn alternately to the right and left. Chiffon has a fine, irregular surface and a sandy texture.

Chiton silk Finely pleated silk fabric developed by Paul Poiret for his Greek-style gowns.

Cloche hat Brimless bell-shaped hat in vogue in the 1920s.

Clogs Shoes with thick cork or wooden soles. Highly fashionable in the 1960s and 1970s, they were popular again in the late 1990s as slippers or sandals.

Cocktail dress Short evening dress, reaching to the knee or just below, that became popular after World War II and that has never gone out of fashion since the 1950s.

Collection A selection of sample designs consisting of various pieces which are presented seasonally (spring/summer and fall/winter) by a couturier or that represent a particular theme.

Coordinates Fabrics or items of clothing that can be mixed and matched.

Corfam Soft, supple, and porous synthetic leather.

Corsage Tailored, sleeveless, often reinforced, low-cut bodice or separate top.

Corsetry Generic term for very tightfitting, sometimes elastic ladies' underwear, including bras, corsets, corselettes, and stomachers. Jean Paul Gaultier and his famous client Madonna turned corsetry into respectable outerwear.

Cossack shirt Smock shirt based on Russian traditional dress with a low stand-up collar, full sleeves, and embroidered trim. Fashionable in the 1960s and 1970s for both men and women.

Crepe de Chine Sheet silk fabric.

Crepe soles Soles made of a thick layer of solid rubber. Crepe became popular in the 1920s when it was used to sole golfing shoes.

Crinoline Stiff underskirt made of horsehair and linen or cotton, or steel hoops (a hoop skirt) worn in the past to puff out a skirt. In more recent times crinolined dresses with a circular decolleté, tight bodice, and full skirt have been designed in imitation of the crinoline style of earlier periods.

Cul de Paris Type of bustle that emerged around 1785. Variations on it have been used by contemporary designers, among them Vivienne Westwood.

Cutaway Also known as a morning coat. Black man's jacket with coattails that sweep backward in a semicircle from the button fastening. It is worn on formal occasions with a dress shirt and gray pinstripe trousers without turnups.

Drainpipe trousers Tightfitting trousers with narrow, straight legs.

Empire line Line of a dress or coat featuring a high waistband just below the bust. It was fashionable during the Empire period in France (1804–14) and has been repeatedly revived in the history of fashion.

End-and-end weave Flecked pattern produced by alternating light and dark warp and weft threads in black, gray, or brown with white.

Fashion show The presentation of fashion on a catwalk.

Flared pants Pants that are tightfitting from waist to knee, and flared from knee to ankle. Very fashionable in the 1970s and revived in the 1990s.

Fleece Lightweight, voluminous napped fabric made of various fibers. It has excellent heat-insulating properties; since 1980, when the microfleece was developed in the United States for use in extreme climatic conditions, it has proven to be a comfortable, hygienic, and easy-care material for everyday wear.

Frock coat Man's formal coat in dark cloth with straight coattails. It has been adapted for womenswear in the 1990s.

Gauze Fine fabric made of natural fibers, used, among other things, as a base for embroidery.

Georgette (georgette crepe) Heavy, rough-textured, transparent, synthetic fabric named for dressmaker Georgette de la Plante and used for evening dresses since about 1912.

Girlie look 1990s trend featuring, for example, revealing dresses made of transparent fabrics and worn with heavy lace-up boots or similar.

Grunge American youth style of the late 1980s. Central to grunge culture were bands like Nirvana and Pearl Jam, whose dress style of torn jeans and shabby sweaters, lumberjack shirts and parkas, influenced their fans.

Gypsy look Part of the folkloric look which appeared in 1976; also known as the Carmen look. Typical are flounced skirts and low-cut necklines, blouses bound below the bust and heavy silver jewelry.

Halter neck Top with straps that are tied at the back of the neck.

Harem pants Wide pants gathered in at the ankles in the Turkish/Arabic style. They were first made respectable by Paul Poiret and were again popular in the 1970s as part of the folkloric trend.

Haute couture Clothes made to measure by leading designers, and usually forming part of collections for a single season whose first showing is regarded as determining general fashion. Haute couture was founded by Charles Frederick Worth in Paris and became established during the second half of the 19th century. In the early 20th century, it was dominated by Paul Poiret, then by Coco Chanel during and after World War I. Several haute couture houses were established in the 1930s, most notably that of Christian

Dior, elements of whose style were very distinct. During the 1960s, haute couture began to follow the requirements of young people and increasingly came under the influence of prêt-à-porter.

Hippie look Unconventional, colorful combination of clothes that emerged in the United States during the mid-1960s. Typical were jeans with floral appliqués, colorful embroidery, frills, items of traditional dress such as Eskimo hats, ponchos, cheesecloth tops, and Afghan coats. The hippie look has repeatedly been revived and modified, as has the music of the period, and couturiers have also made use of this trend (for example, Dolce & Gabbana in 1994).

Hipsters Pants that hang on the hips rather than from the waist, worn with a cropped top (boleros were worn with St Tropez pants), and particularly popular during the 1960s, 1970s, and 1990s. Today hipsters are a staple of the girlie wardrobe and, when worn with a cropped top, may reveal a pierced navel.

H-line A slightly tailored variant of the princess line, with a dropped waist accentuated by a belt, slender bodice, and narrow hips, introduced by Christian Dior in 1954/55.

Hobble skirt Ankle-length skirt created by Paul Poiret in 1910, with a hemmed or fur-trimmed border and so narrow below the knee that the wearer could take only small steps; to prevent the fabric from being torn, foot-cuffs (a wide ribbon used to tie the calves together) were worn under the skirt.

Hot pants Extremely brief shorts that barely cover the bottom; very fashionable in 1971/72. In Italy, they had already been introduced by Krizia in 1970, and in France by Dorothée Bis. They were also worn under open, button-through skirts.

Jabot Decorative frill attached at the chest or the base of the neck, similar to an ascot tie.

Jeans Pants for men and women traditionally made of blue denim, but now available in a range of colors and styles; originally introduced by German-born Levi Strauss around 1850 in the United States as hard-wearing work trousers for gold-diggers. The craze for jeans reached Europe in the 1940s and they have been a staple of casual dress since the 1950s.

Jersey A soft, elastic knitted fabric in wool, cotton, or rayon. It became popular for workwear in about 1880. In 1916/17, with her beige cotton jersey dresses and jackets, Coco Chanel introduced the fabric into haute couture.

Kimono A loose calf-length robe with wide sleeves, open at front and tied with a belt, similar to a caftan and forming part of traditional Japanese dress.

Knickerbockers Pants gathered below the knee.

Label Trade name under which a collection is sold.

Lace Delicate openwork fabric woven in decorative designs. It can be made by hand or by machine, most usually in cotton, linen, or silk.

Lamé Fine, gleaming silk fabric woven with metallic threads.

Leg-of-mutton sleeve (gigot sleeve) Type of sleeve that is full at the shoulder and very narrow between elbow and wrist; widely used around 1900.

Lingerie Collective term for fine nightwear and underwear.

Lurex Fabric made from aluminum thread coated with gold-, silver-, or copper-colored plastic.

Maxi Length of dresses and especially of coats reaching to the ankle. It followed the mini in the 1970s. Maxicoats were worn over miniskirts or hot pants.

Midi Length of dresses, skirts and coats reaching to the calf. It was introduced in about 1966 during the miniskirt craze. Initially only acceptable for coats, it appeared in 1970/71 in button-through skirts which could be worn buttoned or unbuttoned, sometimes over hot pants. The midi finally became established in 1973 when nostalgia became a fashion trend.

Mini Length of dresses and skirts generally measuring about 20 inches from waist to hem, or stopping at least 4 inches above the knee. The first mini garments emerged in 1959 and became established in the early 1960s. Mary Quant is regarded as the inventor of mini and Courrèges adapted the look for his haute couture designs in 1964. It was very much back in fashion in the 1990s as part of the girlie look.

Moiré Rib-woven fabric with a watered effect. Originally made of silk, now more frequently found as acetate, moiré's main use is for eveningwear.

Muslin Very fine, soft, lightweight woolen or cotton fabric, named after the city of Mosul on the Tigris river.

New Look Trendsetting style, regarded as a new beginning for Parisian haute couture, launched by Christian Dior in 1947 and continued into the mid-1950s by Dior's design director Marc Bohan. The style's emphatically feminine look, with narrow, rounded shoulders, narrow waist, and full calf-length skirts came as a contrast to the designs of the 1930s and 1940s. Despite criticism regarding the use of expensive fabrics, the look was extremely successful and can be regarded as a reaction against the privations endured during World War II.

Norfolk jacket Hip-length jacket in the English country style with patch pockets, box pleats and belt in the same fabric.

Nylon Generic term for synthetic polyamide fibers. Developed in 1937 by the American chemist W. H. Carothers, nylon came onto the European market after World War II, mainly for pantyhose and ladies' underwear.

Organza Fine, rigid and translucent fabric made of silk or synthetic fibers.

Outsize Garments designed to appear several size too large for the wearer. The outsize look, fashionable in the 1980s, has been revived by Jean Paul Gaultier, among others.

Oxford bags Extravagantly baggy man's pants popular with students of Oxford University in the 1920s. They came back into fashion in the late 1990s.

Pageboy Short ladies' hairstyle typical of the 1920s; launched by Coco Chanel and popularized by movie star Asta Nielsen.

Paisley Pattern of Oriental origin typified by a curved cone motif. Named for the Kashmiri-style shawls that were made in the Scottish town of Paisley from 1802 onward.

Paletot Single- or double-breasted coat with lapels and pocket flaps at the waist, generally adapted to suit the fashion of the time.

Parka Knee-length jacket, usually made of robust cotton, with large pockets, a drawstring hem and a hood. It was originally designed as a weatherproof coat for soldiers, which is why the prototype was olive green. Adopted by the mods in the 1960s.

Patchwork Fabric made by sewing together small pieces of material. Particularly popular in the 1960s when the gypsy look was fashionable and there was a sense of nostalgia for simple, country clothing. The term also applies to fabrics that have a patchwork-pattern print.

Peep-toe Basic shape of a flat or high-heeled shoe in which the upper is cut away to reveal the toe (the toenail of which may be brightly varnished).

Pencil line Line characterized by a narrow, straight skirt which appears to taper down to the hem and which is often fitted with a Dior slit to allow freedom of movement. Christian Dior introduced it in 1947 under the name Ligne Huit and it was developed as a contrast to the Ligne Corolle of his New Look.

Perlon Polyamide fabric developed in Germany in the 1930s. It is more stable than nylon but not as comfortable to wear and has therefore been replaced by other synthetic fabrics.

Petticoat Rigid underskirt with flounces or frills, sometimes multitiered.

Pillbox Small, round brimless hat worn perched on the back of the head and popularized by Jacqueline Kennedy, wife of US president John Kennedy, in the 1960s.

Pinstripe Classic pattern of fine stripes, usually pale stripes on a dark background. Usually seen in woolen cloth traditionally used for men's formal and business wear. At the end of the 20th century it was taken up by such designers as Yohji Yamamoto and Dolce & Gabbana.

Piping Narrow decorative strip of fabric sown onto edges and seams of garments.

Plastron Wide silk cravat or bib on blouses and shirts.

Plissé A fine pleated finish given to fabrics by mechanical means. Various types of pleats are used to give structure to fabrics.

Polo shirt Short-sleeved shirt made of knitted cotton fabric, with a line of buttons at the collar, which is typically soft and flat. It appeared in Britain, along with the game of polo, in 1869, and is now a main item of sportswear and leisurewear.

Polyester Synthetic material that is frequently used to make textiles. The fibers are hard-wearing but are not breathable. The first polyester fiber was produced in Britain by Whinfield and Dickson.

Prêt-à-porter Fashionable, original ready-to-wear clothes created by couturiers and independent designers. It has become a fashion trend in its own right, bridging the gap between haute couture and mass-produced ready-made clothes. The fact that haute couture, prêt-à-porter, and ready-made affect each other is regarded as a positive stimulus. Since the 1960s, new trends have increasingly been set by prêt-à-porter. It developed from the studios of Parisian couturiers who staged presentations in prêt-à-porter salons in the 1930s.

Princess line Line of a dress or coat with no waist seam, tailored by working in the vertical seam so that the outline is narrow at the top and balloons out toward the hem. The line discreetly flatters the figure, and it became the standard cut for many royal garments. The princess line was launched by Charles Frederick Worth in 1863. The princess-line dress is regarded as the precursor of the more relaxed form of later garments and was revived, especially for coats, in the 1930s and 1950s.

Pumps Originally a man's shoe, the pump is now a popular ladies' slip-on shoe without laces or straps that is available with high, medium, or low heels.

Punk look Antifashion style featuring unconventional hairstyles (such as the mohican cut) and hair colors, leather jackets, torn jeans and T-shirts, studded belts, safety pins worn as facial jewelry, and so on. The style and the youth movement that inspired it emerged in London in the early 1970s. Initially a social protest, but even haute couture now makes repeated use of punk elements.

Radical look Consciously unkempt, unconventional dress style, particularly fashionable between 1967 and 1973. Characterized by faded jeans, shabby sweaters, old waistcoats, Oriental jewelry and fleamarket bargains.

Rayon Synthetic silk made by the same process as viscose.

Ready-made Mass-produced clothes. The term was increasingly applied to the manufacture of womenswear after 1900, and became completely established after World War I.

Redingote Type of tailored coat cut in a princess line, with a high, narrow waist, full skirt, and flat collar, often worn with a belt.

Retro Fashion that consciously imitates the styles of the past.

Revers Lapel on a jacket or a coat.

Robe de style Evening dress of the 1920s, associated particularly with Jeanne Lanvin. Modeled on historical prototypes, it had a princess-line bodice and a full, bouffant skirt.

Satin Soft closely woven fabric with a shiny surface, made of silk, nylon, or rayon.

Sequins Shimmering metal or plastic platelets used to decorate garments.

Sheath dress Figure-flattering, close-fitting, straight, collarless dress of various lengths; also an evening dress with low neckline and straps. In fashion since 1918, it became known as the Jackie-O dress (after

Jacqueline Onassis) in the 1960s and experienced a revival in the late 1990s.

Shirtwaister Casually elegant, button-through dress based on the style of blouses and men's shirts. Worn with upturned collar and a belt.

Silk (silk crepe, silk jersey) Soft, sheer fabric woven from the fiber made by silkworms for their cocoons. Different manufacturing techniques produce various types of silk.

Skirt suit Woman's two-piece suit consisting of a skirt and jacket and worn with a blouse and waistcoat.

Spencer Waist-length jacket, originally worn only by men.

Sportswear Collective term for comfortable, casual daywear and weekend wear based on various forms of sportswear and active-wear. Heavily influenced by fashion trends, it covers almost anything from bomber jackets to safari shirts.

Stretch fabric Elasticized textile made of various materials. Elastic fibers appeared after World War II as a result of developments in the manufacture of chemical fibers.

Swagger coat Generously cut hip-length jacket or knee-length coat.

Sweatshirt Pullover-style top, usually long-sleeved, and made of comfortable, perspiration-absorbent cotton, fleecy on the inside. Originally the top half of a tracksuit, it has been an extremely popular item of leisurewear since the early 1980s.

Teddy boys British youth subculture of the 1950s whose rebellion against the neo-Edwardian style was expressed by long jackets worn over drainpipe trousers, narrow ties, pointed shoes, and coifed hair.

Trapeze line Line of dresses and coats, characterized by narrow shoulders, a high waistline, or no waistline, and a full skirt. First introduced as

the tent line during World War I, it was Yves Saint Laurent's first major haute couture success when he relaunched in 1958 under the name trapeze line.

Trench coat Single- or double-breasted, belted, all-purpose coat with wide lapels made in such hard-wearing fabrics as gabardine or poplin. The fact that they were widely worn by movie detectives contributed considerably to their popularity.

Trevira Polyester fabric developed in Germany and used there since the 1940s, much valued for its crease-free properties.

Trompe l'œil Pattern, weave, or appliqué that creates an optical illusion. Elsa Schiaparelli, and later Yves Saint Laurent, used this device.

Tulle Net or lace fabric named after the French town of Tulle, where plain strips of bobbin lace were produced in the 17th and 18th centuries.

Tunic Simple type of dress or pinafore modeled on the short dress worn in ancient Rome; the armholes either form part of the side seams or are attached at right angles to them.

Turban Originally an Oriental headdress made of long pieces of fabric wrapped around the head and decorated by Poiret with an aigrette, turbans are also associated with the privations of the war years. Simone de Beauvoir was a famous wearer of turbans.

Tuxedo Man's jacket with tails and black silk lapels. Part of evening dress, it is worn with evening pants and a starched dress shirt and customarily complements a woman's evening gown.

Tweed Fabric made of rough, carded yarn, patterned by the use of different colored yarn. The fabric originates in Scotland and

is named after the river of the same name. Harris tweed is particularly well known. The popularity of tweed was greatly enhanced by Coco Chanel's use of it for suits.

Twinset Matching cardigan and sweater.

Velvet Fabric with a soft, deep pile, which originated in 14th-century Italy.

Vienna Workshops (Wiener Werkstätte) Cooperative of artists and applied artists, founded in 1903 and disbanded for economic reasons in 1932. It included an influential textiles and fashion department whose aim was to produce esthetically sophisticated, beautifully designed clothes suited to the fabrics in which they were made. Initially its style was influenced principally by local trends but was later dominated mainly by international influences.

Vinyl Hard-wearing synthetic material that was taken up by fashion designers in the 1960s and that is also used for weatherproof garments.

Wasp waist Colloquial term for the unnaturally slim waists made possible by corsets at the beginning of the 20th century, and revived in the New Look and the designs of Hubert de Givenchy.

Y-line Line of dresses introduced by Christian Dior in 1955/56, characterized by necklines with wide lapels or other V-shaped tops on otherwise figure-hugging dresses with narrow skirts.

INDEX OF FASHION DESIGNERS

Adrian, Gilbert (1903–59) American designer who was extremely successful in the 1930s and 1940s when he designed costumes for Hollywood actors such as Rudolph Valentino, Joan Crawford, and Greta Garbo. He also influenced European fashion trends. 33, 40

Amies, Hardy (b. 1909) British designer and dressmaker to the British royal family. His international reputation, which continued into the 1980s, rested on his astute commercial sense and his high-class, distinctive country-style clothes and classic eveningwear. 41, 65

Armani, Giorgio (b. 1934) The Italian master of the understatement began his career with Cerruti. He opened his own house in Milan in 1970, since when his Emporio Armani line, with its eagle logo, has become synonymous throughout the world with elegant purism, restrained use of color, minimal decoration, and perfect cutting. 80, 77, 94, 98

Ashley, Laura (1926–85) Disregarding contemporary trends, this British designer launched her highly successful business in 1954. Her furnishing fabrics, linens, interiors and romantic "nonfashion" – striped or floral, flounced, calf-length cotton dresses – were an inspiration to conservative designers like Ralph Lauren. 66

Augustabernard (trade name of Augusta Bernard) The urbane elegance of her Paris salon, which was launched by Mainbocher when he was editor of *Vogue* and which closed in 1935, was highly regarded during the interwar period. Despite this, her creations were overshadowed by Madeleine Vionnet's designs. 20, 29

Balenciaga, Cristobal (1895–1972) The Spaniard closed his house at the outbreak of the Spanish Civil War, but took the brilliant red and black colors and the dramatic dignity of Spanish paintings with him to Paris, where he became a trendsetter with his asymmetric sack-line dresses, three-quarter-length sleeves, and pillbox hat. He also trained Givenchy, Ungaro and Courrèges. In his view, haute couture was the art of combining in elegant harmony an understanding of the body's architecture with the master-craftsman's precision. 36, 50, 51, 64, 68

Balmain, Pierre (1914–82) After studying architecture, this French couturier made his debut at an haute couture salon in Paris in 1945. He dressed the more important members of the European aristocracy and showbiz stars, who appreciated the ladylike glamour of, for example, a white ball gown of tulle and lace, or a silk evening gown adorned with rococo embroidery. His designs are characterized by tailored lines, accentuated waists, and slightly enlarged shoulders. 43, 47

Banton, Travis (1894–1958) Following a period as an assistant to Lucile, this American designer became head costume designer at Paramount Studios and created, among others, Marlene Dietrich's look in *Shanghai Express*. He used the sheen effect of fabrics, which was so important to the camera, for his designs for private clients. 33, 40

Barton, Alix (Madame Grès) (1899–1993) France's last grande dame of fashion used sculptural working methods to create her designs. Working with gently flowing fabrics, she draped them like ancient Greek robes directly on the body, rather than cutting them to a pattern. This was in marked contrast to the working methods of Fortuny, whose references to Greek antiquity were limited to external appearances. 38, 39, 46, 47

Beirendonck, Walter van (b. 1956) Together with five other graduates of the Antwerp Academy of Art, he has successfully been making a name for Belgian fashion design since the 1980s. His clever, youthful prêt-à-porter designs have moved away from the basis of the ideal body and are marketed under the programmatic label W.&L.T. (Wild and Lethal Trash). 110

Bérard, Christian (1902–49) This French theater set and costume designer's daring and colorful illustrations for fashion magazines exerted a tremendous influence on designers like Schiaparelli and Dior. 22, 42

Bikkemberg, Dirk (b. 1962) Since 1985, the house of this graduate of the Belgian school has produced casual and cool streetwear with military references, exaggerated details, a sometimes bold combination of materials, and astonishing accessories. 110

Callot Sœurs (trade name of Marie, Marthe, Régine, and Joséphine Callot) Between 1895 and 1937, the sisters maintained a salon in Paris whose magnificent reputation was based on evening gowns in heavy fabrics adorned with Oriental motifs. 37

Cardin, Pierre (b. 1922) French couturier who began his career at Schiaparelli and Dior. From 1950 he revolutionized haute couture with abstract, circular shapes, sculptural dimensions, colors and forms taken from Op Art and Pop Art, and new materials such as vinyl for his space look. The worldwide licenses that he issued for his prêt-à-porter clothes were the prototype for modern marketing strategies in the industry. His empire encompasses furniture and design studios, a theater, and the restaurant Maxim's. 64, 66, 69, 93, 106

Chanel, Coco (Gabrielle Chanel) (1883–1971) The French fashion designer began her career as a milliner and opened her first couture house in 1910. With pragmatic verve she created understated, casual elegance for the modern, independent woman who liked to be appropriately dressed at all times. In 1915 she made fashionable the practical pageboy haircut and, in 1926, the "little black dress" as an indispensable item of the basic wardrobe. With her long strings of fake pearls she introduced costume jewelry to fashion and in 1954 she designed the now famous Chanel suit. The fragrance Chanel No. 5 achieved cult status. She moved among the artists, writers, and composers of her day and was regarded as a brilliant, albeit difficult, competitor to Patou and Schiaparelli. 10, 22, 25, 28, 38, 46, 62, 66, 83, 94, 101

Clark, Ossie (1942–96) This British designer, regarded as an eccentric star of the 1960s, propagated an unorthodox style that was in opposition to good taste and "for a future that never comes." He worked with the wildly patterned textiles designed by his ex-wife Celia Birtwell, which he preferred to cut on the bias, and was successful until well into the 1980s. 65

Courrèges, André (b. 1923) This designer, known as the Le Corbusier of fashion, began developing the legendary Courrèges style in 1962: for both haute couture and prêt-à-porter, he produced architecturally structured clothes based on geometric forms in balanced proportions He was instrumental in introducing the miniskirt and invented the futuristic space look consisting of a suit worn with flat-heeled boots and a helmetlike hat. His basic color was white, although when his designs took on a softer and more romantic look in the 1970s his range expanded to include a few pastel shades. 65, 66, 106

Delaunay, Sonia (1885–1979) French-Russian artist who, together with her husband Robert, created a style of painting that incorporated geometric elements and bright colors which she then transferred to her angular dress designs in the 1920s. She combined fashion and poetry by printing or embroidering texts onto fabrics. 30

Demeulemeester, Ann (b. 1959) This award-winning Belgian designer has a preference for black and white, although she occasionally uses color to add accents. She launched an androgynous, outsize look in soft, tactile fabrics that tend to conceal the female form rather than accentuate it and caused astonishment with details like a tie worn beneath a translucent top. She also designs eyewear and accessories. 110

Lagerfeld, Karl (b. 1938) The German couturier with the ponytail and fan trained with Balmain and Patou before concentrating on prêt-à-porter, which he did even at Chanel, where he has been design director since 1984. At Chanel he has designed creative and avant-garde clothes; he loves surprising details, with which he has modernized the classic Chanel look, and is regarded as a technical innovator as well as the discoverer of numerous star models. 23, 80, 83, 94, 100

Lanvin, Jeanne (1867–1946) French fashion designer who set a trend when she began to design clothes to suit particular types rather than ages. Her mother-and-daughter collections made her famous, as did her penchant for positive-negative patterns, the classic fragrance Arpège, and the heavily decorated robes de style which she produced in conscious opposition to the 1920s trend for simplicity. 17, 28, 29, 38, 49, 99

Lauren, Ralph (b. 1939) American designer whose international fame rests on his Polo line, which combines conservative and timeless elegance with high-quality fabrics and which is inspired by English country life and American pioneer style. 72, 92

Lelong, Lucien (1889–1958) In 1923 the Frenchman established a house which specialized in the art of understatement and clever finishing. In later years Dior, Givenchy and Balmain, among others, designed for him. 41, 43, 47

Lepape, Georges (1887–1971) French graphic designer and fashion illustrator who in 1911 produced drawings, in the Art Deco style, of Poiret's designs. 14, 15

Louiseboulanger (trade name of Louise Boulanger) (1878–1950) The Frenchwoman opened her salon in Paris 1927. She was noted for the original cut of her elegant taffeta evening gowns and such details as the fringed hem. 29

Lucile (Lucy Duff Gordon) (1864–1935) During her long and successful career, which continued until 1920, the Englishwoman designed colorful foundation garments, transparent tea gowns, and romantic evening dresses. She brought the fashion show to England and dressed Sarah Bernhardt, among others. 65

Mainbocher (1891–1976) The American was an established fashion illustrator and journalist before he began designing unusual and theatrical evening gowns. His fur-lined evening jacket and the blue dress that he designed for Wallis Simpson's wedding to the Duke of Windsor made him famous. 36, 41

McCartney, Stella (b. 1971) The daughter of former Beatle Paul McCartney made a convincing debut as Chloé's design director with her first prêt-à-porter collection Tough and Tender, in which she combined grunge with feminine and classic elements. 111

McQueen, Alexander (b. 1969) The British designer's clever techniques, incongruous combinations of lace and plastic, and unexpected erotic peepholes in his designs made him the shooting star of the fashion industry. He has been design director at Givenchy since 1996. 50, 111

Missoni, Ottavio (b. 1921) **and Rosita** (b. 1926) Together with their three children, the Italian designers run an international company characterized by colorful knitwear with unusual wavy or patchwork patterns. 76, 91, 103

Miyake, Issey (b. 1935) The works of art that the Japanese designer produces are based on the structure of the fabric, which firmly relegates the body and personality of the wearer to a position of secondary importance. His work has a geometric and sculpted look, and since 1988 pleats and complex wrappings have dominated it. 16, 72, 89

Molyneux, Edward (Captain) (1891–1974) From 1919 until the 1950s, the salons of the Englishman in Paris were synonymous with conservative chic. He dressed the celebrities of his time and designed movie costumes. 41, 47, 65

Mortensen, Erik (b. 1926) The Danish designer worked for Jean-Louis Scherrer until he took over as designer director at Pierre Balmain after the latter's death in 1982. While maintaining the traditionally extravagant style of the house, he brought it up to date with modern details. 47

Morton, Digby (1906–83) After working for Lachasse, the Irish designer began his own business, producing classic eveningwear and somewhat vernacular knitwear and tweed combinations that proved particular popular in the United States. 41

Mugler, Thierry (b. 1948) The expressive and intelligent style of the enfant terrible of French fashion has been a source of fascination since 1971. However, he is not averse to quoting from fashion history, thereby developing dramatic yet architecturally well-considered and perfectly finished pieces. Typical of him are caricatures of erotic clichés: for example, exaggerated shoulders and hips that make the head and waist appear very small. 72, 83, 93

Muir, Jean (1933–95) From the 1950s the English designer produced relaxed and sophisticated pantsuits, tunics, and dresses in fabrics like jersey and suede that flow gently with the body. She was also known for using stiffer fabrics, which she subjected to intense processing in order to make them suitable for her designs. 80

Patou, Jean (1880–1939) Despite his undoubted innovatory influence on fashion, the French couturier always stood in the shadow of Chanel. He was the first to mark his clothes with initials, and he found early social success in the United States. Movie star Louise Brooks was one of the most famous fans of his casual and functional designs, which always appeared feminine and elegant thanks to his accentuation of the waist. 28, 34, 37, 43, 93

Perugia, André (1893–1977) The career of this successful French shoe designer began in the 1920s with designs for Poiret and later for Fath and Givenchy, all of whom valued the marvelous workmanship of his products. He was particularly renowned for the creation of one-off artistic pieces. 54

Piguet, Roger (1901–53) The Swiss-born designer moved to Paris in 1918. There he ran his own house from 1937 to 1951, designing fine evening gowns as well as cleverly cut suits. He sometimes worked for Balmain, Dior, and Givenchy. 48

Pipart, Gerard (b. 1933) After training with Balmain, Fath, and Patou, the Frenchman with the elegant, worldly style became Nina Ricci's design director. Under his aegis Myriam Schaefer designs the house's prêt-à-porter collections. 37

Poiret, Paul (1879–1944) The French pioneer of colorful Art Deco fashion design rejected corsets and instead launched a more natural form of female beauty. Inspired by the Vienna Workshops, antiquity, and Oriental elements as well as the artists of his time, he created softly fitted gowns and introduced the turban, tunic, and kimono to fashion design. 10, 21, 28, 38, 39, 40, 54

Prada, Miuccia (b. 1949) In 1978 the Italian designer took over the running of the family firm, which was founded in 1913, and made it hugely successful commercially with accessories and unspectacular yet interestingly detailed prêt-à-porter. The company expanded quite considerably when it acquired an interest in Jil Sander in 1999. 63, 76, 103

Quant, Mary (b. 1934) In the 1960s the British designer successfully fought against the elitism of haute couture and for affordable young fashion inspired by popular culture. She and Courrèges are regarded as the inventors of the miniskirt. Her short pinafore dresses, vinyl garments, cheeky hats, and psychedelic pantyhose designs caused a sensation. To a large extent she was also the originator of the modern fashion show as an event with music and drama. 57, 65, 68, 109

Rabanne, Paco (Francisco Rabaneda y Cuervo) (b. 1934) When the Spanish designer began his own business in 1966, he was already a successful designer of buttons and costume jewelry for Balenciaga, Dior, and Givenchy.

His architectural training and interest in art may have made him more receptive to the possible use of unusual materials. His fascinating designs, in which metal and plastic platelets, crepe paper, feathers, chains, and strips of woven imitation fur were used, were a visual delight, although not very comfortable to wear. 68

Renta, Oscar de la (b. 1932) Following an apprenticeship with Balenciaga, the fashion designer founded his own house in 1965 and successfully produced opulently decorated gowns, extravagant designs based on abstract art, and baroque gypsy and flamenco collections. 47

Rhodes, Zandra (b. 1940) The bird of paradise of British design used handkerchief points, pinked edges, toggles, and fringes to achieve her unmistakable look; she died her hair to match. Unlike hardliner Vivienne Westwood, she romanticized and blurred the elements of punk. 80

Ricci, Nina (Marie Ricci) (1883–1970) The working methods of the Italian-born designer who settled in Paris in 1905 were very similar to those of Madeleine Vionnet. Technical finesse and distinguished, highly feminine elegance characterized her house, which her son took over in 1945. She set the international standard for stylish haute couture and sophisticated fragrances. 37

Rochas, Marcel (1902–55) The French couturier was known for going against trends and forecasting new ones with his theatrical gowns. He anticipated the innovation of wide shoulders and long skirts of the New Look, the pantsuit for women, and patch pockets on skirts, and was a major influence on later generations. 36

Rouff, Maggy (Maggy Besançon de Wagner) (1897–1971) The French designer opened her own couture house, Maison Rouff, in 1925 and handed over control to her daughter in 1946. It was well known for its broad range of practical daywear and sophisticated urban elegance. 29

Rykiel, Sonia (b. 1930) Colorful, angular eyewear became the French designer's trademark, as did practical and comfortable antifashion in sensuous fabrics in discreet colors. She set trends with creations like external seams and asymmetric contours and continues to design fashionable knitwear. 72, 78

Saint Laurent, Yves (b. 1936) The influential Frenchman began his career in 1954 at Dior, where he successfully continued the master's style, and also where he radically broke with him. In 1958 he invented the Trapeze Line for androgynous "little girl" dresses and coats. After setting up his own house, he caused an uproar in the 1960s when he introduced the tuxedo for women and the nude look in the form of a black, muslin piece with ostrich feathers on the hips. Bold patterns on angular tailoring made reference to modern art, and in the 1970s innovative combinations of color and gold reflected the influence of folkloric styles. In 1999 he passed the creative direction of his prêt-à-porter line to Alber Elbaz and now dedicates all his time to haute couture, which for him is the bastion of fashion's values. 49, 56, 62, 68, 73, 78, 80, 96

Sander, Jil (Heidemarie Jiline Sander) (b. 1943) In 1968 the qualified textile designer opened her first boutique in Hamburg and has ever since remained true to her purist style of cool elegance. She rejects any form of decoration, and her preferred colors for a basic wardrobe in high-quality fabrics are white, brown, gray, and black. 23, 63, 77, 100

Schiaparelli, Elsa (1890–1973) She was born in Rome, and her career began in Paris in 1922 when she produced a trompe l'oeil sweater. Her eccentric style, based on precise workmanship and the use of witty surprises, remains a major influence on fashion to this day. She invented the pagoda sleeve, embroidered the waist of a suit jacket to make it appear as if it were encircled by a pair of hands, designed a bug necklace and a hat in the shape of a shoe, was the first to use synthetic fabrics and colored zippers as decoration, and launched the

famous perfume Shocking, named for shocking pink, her favorite color, with which she even died fur coats. In her pursuit of a synthesis between fashion and art she draw deeply on Cubism and Surrealism. 30, 33, 35, 38, 46, 62, 91, 94

Schuberth, Emilio (Emil Friedrich Schuberth) (1904–72) The German fashion designer's heyday was in the 1950s, when his salon in Rome produced exquisite and sophisticated creations in the style of Dior. He dressed such women as Sophia Loren. 76

Schulze-Varell, Heinz (1907–85) The native of Berlin laid the foundations of his career with an haute couture house in 1934 and became head of costume design at the German movie company Ufa. Ignoring fashionable trends he pursued a ladylike and elegant style based on elaborate tailoring, even when he relocated to Munich after World War II. 101

Stephen, John He became the trendsetter of the Swinging Sixties when he opened a number of boutiques on Carnaby Street in London. He revolutionized the concept of the man's suit by using color and glazed fabrics in an innovative way and persuaded prominent figures from the world of sport and popular music to model his clothes.

Versace, Gianni (1946–97) The great Italian fashion designer loved opulent eveningwear as embodied by his exclusive, diamanté-encrusted, black and white Op Art gown, yet he also like to use colored leather and silk. He was regarded as a master of cutting technique who helped shape the 1980s and 1990s. He also designed theater and ballet costumes for Béjart and others. Since he was murdered, Versace's sister Donatella has run the house. 60, 76, 83, 95, 103

Vionnet, Madeleine (1876–1975) After serving an apprenticeship at Callot Sœurs and Doucet, in 1912 she established her famous haute couture house, which continued until 1940. Dispensing with preparatory sketches, she worked with the fabric directly on a wooden dummy. She invented the bias cut, which

followed the line of the body, additionally freeing the body from the corset. This resulted in flowing and mysterious dresses with a low waistline as well as robes de style in crepe de Chine. 25, 29, 34, 36, 46, 49

Westwood, Vivienne (b. 1941) Award-winning British "queen of fashion" whose prêt-à-porter designs are impressive for their workmanship and provocative spirit. During the 1970s she and her partner Malcolm McLaren launched the punk look and the Sex Pistols. Thanks to her eclectic genius, the self-taught designer has succeeded in making latex and leather biker and fetish fashions respectable. She has copied Teddy boy suits and rococo gowns, created collections based on Native American and pirate dress, and designed skirts for men as well as eccentric shoes. 7, 9, 54, 60, 66, 72, 81, 108

Wimmer-Wisgrill, Eduard Josef (1882–1961) As an artist, fashion illustrator, and designer, he was a proponent of the rational dress conceived by the Vienna Workshops, whose director he became in 1911. Between 1910 and 1914 he designed a range of pants for women. 13, 32

Worth, Charles Frederick (1826–95) This British designer and astute businessman is widely recognized as the founder of haute couture. He was the first to use real people rather than dummies to model his clothes when he presented his designs to the European aristocrats who comprised his clientele. His inventions included the prototypes of several creations that were milestones of fashion history. 8, 12, 14, 28, 65, 111

Yamamoto, Yohji (b. 1943) The Japanese clothes artist puts fabric and its relation to the body at the forefront of his creativity. Following the presentation of his first collection in Paris in 1981, it was a long time before his manner of creating clothes like architectural constructs became acceptable to the Western press. *Notebook on Cities and Clothes*, Wim Wenders' 1989 movie about Yamamoto, ensured that his creations became the chosen style for many artists and intellectuals. 88

ACKNOWLEDGMENTS

The publishers would like to thank the following fashion houses, photographic archives, and photographers for the use of the images that appear in this book and for their support in its production.

© The Advertising Archives, London 70 b.r., 86, 99, 103

© Angeli/Pandis/Telepress, Paris 49 bottom, 63 r., 83 b., 94, 95, 101 t., 102 b. (Photographs: Frédéric Garcia, Bertrand Rindoff), 104 (Photograph: Brema)

© André Courrèges Archive, Paris 69

© Inge Astor-Kaiser Archive, Munzenberg 52 t.

© Benetton Archive, Munich 97 t.

© Brioni Archive, Rome 79 t.

© Christian Dior Archive, Paris 48 t.

© Archiv für Kunst und Geschichte, Berlin 4 (2. b .3. t), 10 b.l., 13 t/b., 14 b., 25 t., 35 b., 40 t., 50 b., 51, 58 t. (AP), 62 t.l. (Photograph: Paul Almasy), 72, 76 b. (Photograph: Gert Schütz), 84 (AP/Photograph: Herbert Pöpper), 70 t., 100 b. (Photograph: Gert Schütz)

© Givenchy Archive, Paris 11 t., 75 (Photograph: Robert-Jean Chapuis)

© Hennes & Mauritz Archive, Hamburg 102 t.

© Hugo Boss Archive, Metzingen 101 b.r.

© Marie Claire Archive, Paris 23 r. (Photograph: Morange)

© Norma Kamali Archive, New York 5 (2. b.), 87

© Paco Rabanne Archive, Paris 68

© Piaggio Archive, Frankfurt 53 b.

© Pierre Cardin Archive, Paris 5 t., 67 (Photograph: Yoshi Takata)

© Sonia Rykiel Archive, Paris 78

© Vivienne Westwood Archive, London 108 b.l.

© W.&LT. Archive, Künzelsau 110 t.

© Yves Saint Laurent Archive, Paris 5 (2. t.), 62 l.b., 63 r., 74 b.,

© Zandra Rhodes Archive, London 80 (Photograph: Clive Arrowsmith)

© Archivi Alinari/Archivio Team, Florence 76 l.

© Art and Commerce, New York 108 t. (Photograph: Inez van Lambsweerde)

© Baby Jane, Mailand 105

© The Bata Shoe Museum, Toronto 54 l. (Photograph: Roth), 55 t.

© Bildarchiv Preussischer Kulturbesitz, Berlin 32, 48 b. r., 82 b., 100 t.; Kunstbibliothek (Photographs: Dietmar Katz) 20, 21 b., 24, 25 b., 27 b., 28 b., 30 t., 43 b., 45 t/b., 59, 96 t.

© Erwin Blumenfeld/Courtesy Vogue, Paris 33

© Bridgeman Art Library, London 4 t., 9 b.

© Siegfried Büker, Berlin 55 Center

© Charles Jourdan, Romans 54 t.

© CNMHS, Paris 9 (Photograph: Nadar)

© Collezione Missoni, Sumirago 17 t., 91

© Courtesy of the Trustees of the Victoria and Albert Museum, London 55 b.

© Ted Croner, New York 22 b.r.

© Daniel Simon-William Stevens/Gamma, Vauves 88 t.r.

© Descharnes & Descharnes, Paris 39 b.

© dpa, Frankfurt 82 to.

© The Fashion Institute of Technology, New York 4 b., 44 b. (Photograph: Louise Dahl-Wolfe), 66 (Photograph: Irving Solero)

© Helmut Fricke, Frankfurt 23 l., 48 b.l., 77 b.r., 83 t., 88 b.l., 96 b., 110 b., 109 b.

© Galerie Bartsch & Chariau, Munich 61

© Galerie Gmurzynska, Cologne 30 b.

© Gamma/Studio X, Vauves 107

© F. C. Gundlach, Hamburg 64 b., 71 b.

© Hachette Filipacchi Associes/Scoop/Elle, Levallois-Perret Cedex 62 r., 73, 74 t. (Photographs: Peter Knapp), 93 (Photograph: Oliviero Toscani)

© Hulton Getty Picture Library, London 6, 7, 10 t., 12, 15, 17b., 18, 22 b.l., 27 t., 34, 41 b., 42 (Alan Band Photos), 46, 50 t., 52 b., 53 t., 54, 55 t/b., 64 t., 65, 81, 98

© Inter Topics, Hamburg/LIFE-Magazine 49 (Photograph: Loomis Dean)

© Nick Knight, London 89 (Art Director: Marc Ascoli), 101 l. (Art Director: Marc Ascoli), 111 (Art Director: Alexander McQueen)

© The Kobal Collection, London 79 b., 58 b.

© Könemann Verlagsgesellschaft, Cologne (Photographs: Günter Beer) 11 b.r., 70 b.l., 71 t.r./t.l.

© Edland Man, Mailand 106 t.

© Niall McInerney, London 5 b., 77

t./b.l., 92, 108 b.r., 109 t.

© Ministère de la Culture, Paris, France/A.A.J.H.L 21 t. (Photograph L J. H. Lartigue)

© Musée de la Mode et du textile Palais du Louvre, UFAC, Paris 8 t., 16, 29, 38 b., 39 t., 41 t.

© Museo Salvatore Ferragamo, Florence 54 b.

© Pandis/Telepress, Paris 85

© Patrimonie Lanvin, Paris 28 t.

© Rex/Action Press, Hamburg 60, 90 b.

© Roger-Viollet, Paris 8 b., 14 t., 19 t., 40 b.

© Roman Schlemmer, Oggebbio 31

© Stiftung Deutsche Kinemathek, Berlin 35 t., 47,

© Studio Beate Hansen, Düsseldorf 90 t.

© Studio Holle-Suppa, Frankfurt 88 b.r. (Photograph: Martine Sitbon)

© SVT TV/Das Fotoarchiv, Essen 37 b.

© Ullstein Foto, Berlin 19 b.

© Ullstein Foto/Inter Topics, Berlin 11 l.

© VIVA Fernsehen, Cologne 106 b. (Photograph: Frank Peinemann)

© Courtesy Vogue by Condé Nast Publications Inc, New York 22 t.r., 36 (Photograph: Hoyningen-Huené), 38 t. (Photograph: Edward Steichen)

The publishers have made every effort to contact the owners of the copyright of the photographs that appear in this book. Those who have not been contacted are invited to notify the publishers.

Front cover

Left: Mode 1900. © Viollet collection, Paris
Right: Prêt-à-porter fall/winter 1995, Rifat Osbek collection. © Sygma, Paris (Foto: Pierre Vauthey)
Background: white silk drapery. © Tony Stone Bilderwelten, Munich (Photograph: Mark Harwood)

© VG Bild-Kunst, Bonn 1999: Giacomo Balla; Erwin Blumenfeld; Georges Lepape
© Demart pro Arte, Amsterdam: Salvador Dalí
© Andy Warhol Foundation for the Visual Arts/ARS, New York 1999: Andy Warhol